Writing Center Research
Extending the Conversation

Writing Center Research
Extending the Conversation

Edited by

Paula Gillespie
Marquette University

Alice Gillam
University of Wisconsin—Milwaukee

Lady Falls Brown
Texas Tech University

Byron Stay
Mount Saint Mary's College

LEA
2002

LAWRENCE ERLBAUM ASSOCIATES, PUBLISHERS
Mahwah, New Jersey   London

Lawrence Erlbaum Associates, Inc., Publishers
10 Industrial Avenue
Mahwah, NJ 07430

Cover design by Kathryn Houghtaling Lacey

Library of Congress Cataloging-in-Publication Data

Writing center research : extending the conversation /
edited by Paula Gillespie ... [et al.].
    p. cm.
Includes bibliographical references and index.
ISBN 0-8058-3446-x (cloth : alk. paper) —
ISBN 0-8058-3447-8 (pbk. : alk. paper)
1. English language—Rhetoric—Study and teaching. 2.
Report writing—Study and teaching (Higher) 3. Interdisci-
plinary approach in education. 4. Writing centers. I.
Gillespie, Paula.

PE1404.W694454   2001
808'.042'00711—dc21

                                    2001023049
                                         CIP

Printed in the United States of America
10 9 8 7 6 5 4 3 2 1

Contents

About the Authors and Editors

Julie Galvin Bevins teaches composition and interdisciplinary studies courses at Davenport University in Grand Rapids, Michigan. Her studies, presentations, and writings focus on writing portfolios and literacy and social justice issues. She has also published pieces of poetry and is a recipient of the 1998 Dyer-Ives Poetry Award.

Beth Boquet is the Director of the Writing Center and an Associate Professor of English at Fairfield University in Fairfield, Connecticut. Her scholarly interests include studying the history of writing centers and reconceiving theoretical models for writing center work. Her articles have been published in the *Writing Lab Newsletter, Composition Studies,* and her book entitled *Noise from the Writing Center* is currently under contract with Utah State University Press. For the past 7 years, she has been active in both the national and regional writing center associations.

Lady Falls Brown is Director of the University Writing Center at Texas Tech University, Lubbock, Texas, where she is also a member of the Teaching Academy. A past president of the National Writing Centers Association, she has also served as a regional representative and member at large. She received the Outstanding Service Award from the NWCA in 1994 for her work with WCenter (1991–present). Most recently, she has been involved in the TIPS Project, a writing partnership between writing center tutors and K–12 students in rural schools. Her article "OWLS in Theory and Practice: A Director's Perspective" appears in *Taking Flight with OWLS: Examining Writing Center Work.*

Peter Carino is Professor of English and Director of the Writing Center at Indiana State University, where he has taught writing courses, American literature, and criticism. He is a past president and treasurer of the East Central Writing Centers Association, and has published three basic writing textbooks, and articles on writing centers, teaching writing, and literature.

Mary Ann Krajnick Crawford, Assistant Professor of English, is the Director of Basic Writing and the Writing Center at Central Michigan University where she also teaches composition and linguistics. Her research, publications, and conference presentations focus on a variety of discourse, language, and literacy areas, particularly genre issues and the effects of oral, written, and technology mediums on language use, communication, teaching composition, and student learning. She is also Assistant Editor of SHAW: The Annual of Bernard Shaw Studies, and she is working on a biography of Lowell Thomas, the radio and newsreel personality.

Danielle DeVoss worked as the Technology Projects Coordinator—a graduate research assitant post—at the Michigan State University Writing Center. She recently completed her doctoral degree in the Rhetoric and Technical Communication program at Michigan Techological University, and is an assistant professor in the Department of American Thought and Language at Michigan State University. Her work has most recently appeared in the *Writing Center Journal, CyberPsychology and Behavior,* and in *Moving a Mountain: Transforming the Role of Contingent Faculty in Composition Studies and Higher Education.* Her research interests include women's interactions with and resistances to computer technologies, computer-related literacies, and the performance of gender in online realms.

Adelia Falda is a graduate student at Oregon State University, where she is currently finishing her thesis for a Master of Arts degree in Applied Anthropology. Her study focuses on language and cross cultural communications. Ms. Falda has recently been working as a language tutor, helping students increase their English skills. She is a graduate of Seattle University, where she won the Robert Cousineau Award for her translation of the French play "Le Monde Casse'" (The Broken World) by Gabriel Marcel.

Alice Gillam teaches rhetoric and writing at the University of Wisconsin—Milwaukee, where she directed the Writing Center from 1986 to 1993. Her essay "Writing Center Ecology: A Bakhtinian Perspective" won the National Writing Centers Association's Outstanding Scholarship Award in 1992. Her current research interests include rhetoric and the emotions, and feminist rhetorical theories.

Paula Gillespie teaches in the English Department and directs the Ott Memorial Writing Center at Marquette University in Milwaukee. She has recently co-authored a book on the history of the criticism of Joyce's *Ulysses* since 1975, and with Neal Lerner is the co-author of *The Allyn & Bacon Guide to Peer Tutoring.* She is currently working on a biography of Agnes Morrogh-Bernard, a dynamic and innovative Irish Sister of Charity.

Muriel Harris is Professor of English and Director of the Purdue University Writing Lab. She founded and continues to edit the *Writing Lab Newsletter* and founded and continues to coordinate the development of the

Writing Lab's OWL. Her publications—including *Teaching One to One: The Writing Conference* and the *Prentice Hall Reference Guide to Grammar and Usage*—focus on writing center theory, practice, and pedagogy, and advocate the writing center as a uniquely effective setting in which to work collaboratively with writers. She and the OWL staff continue to explore the uses of technology in the writing center as well.

Neal Lerner is Assistant Professor of English, Writing Programs Coordinator, and Coordinator of First-Year Experience at the Massachusetts College of Pharmacy and Health Sciences. He is past chair of the Northeast Writing Centers Association and the current treasurer of the International Writing Centers Association. He co-authored *The Allyn & Bacon Guide to Peer Tutoring* with Paula Gillespie, and his publications have appeared in the *Writing Lab Newsletter, Composition Studies, The Journal of College Reading and Learning,* as well as several book-length collections of writing center scholarship.

Jean Marie Lutes is Assistant Professor of American literature at Manhattan College, where she teaches literature and writing. Her scholarly interests include late 19th- and early 20th-century American literature, women's writing, and feminist pedagogy. Her most recent article analyzes the writer as beauty expert in Anita Loos's 1925 bestseller, *Gentlemen Prefer Blondes.*

Dawn J. Moyer was a graduate student at Oregon State University when "Student-Centered Assessment Research in the Writing Center" was submitted. She completed her M.A. in Applied Anthropology in 1999. She is currently the Health Services Coordinator for Community Outreach, Inc., in Corvallis, Oregon.

Joyce Magnotto Neff is Associate Professor of English and Director of Composition at Old Dominion University, where she teaches in the Professional Writing Program. Her research has been published in *Under Construction; Strengthening Programs in Writing Across the Curriculum; Rhetoric, Cultural Studies and Literacy;* and *Research in the Teaching of English.* She is also co-author of *Professional Writing in Context.* She is currently completing a longitudinal study of writing and distance education, and was recently elected as secretary of the Conference on College Composition and Communication.

Jon Olson, Assistant Professor of Writing at The Pennsylvania State University, directs the Center for Excellence in Writing that includes a Writing Center, a Graduate Communication Enhancement Program (which has its own Graduate Writing Center), and a Writing Across the Curriculum Program. His scholarly interests include composition, rhetoric, writing administration, literacy acquisition, and American slave narratives. He has authored articles appearing in *The Writing Instructor, The Writing Lab Newsletter, Teaching with Writing,* and in the edited collections *The Place of Grammar in Writing Instruction* and *The Writing Center Resource Manual.* He is on the boards of the National Conference on Peer Tutoring in Writing, the

International Writing Centers Association, and the Mid-Atlantic Writing Centers Association.

Judith Rodby is Professor of English at California State University, Chico, where she has coordinated the first-year writing program and the Writing Center. She is interested in constructing alternatives to Basic Writing programs and all forms of tracking. She is currently doing research on youth media and literacy practices outside of school formations. She is author of *Appropriating Literacy* (Heinemann) and articles on Basic Writing and ESL literacy.

Byron Stay is Professor of Rhetoric and Communication at Mount St. Mary's College in Emmitsburg, Maryland, and former Associate Dean of the College. He is a former president of the National Writing Centers Association and currently serves as editor of NWCA Press. His publications include *A Guide to Argumentative Writing* (1995), *Writing Center Perspectives* (co-edited with Christina Murphy and Eric Hobson, 1995), *Censorship* (1997), and *Mass Media* (1999).

Sharon Thomas is currently Associate Chair of the Department of American Thought and Language at Michigan State University, where she has also recently been both Associate Director and Acting Director of the Writing Center. Her chapter resulted from a collaborative project designed to provide professional development for the undergraduate and graduate students employed in the MSU Writing Center.

Nancy Welch is an Assistant Professor in English and Women's Studies at the University of Vermont, where she teaches courses in writing, theory, and literacy studies. She is the author of *Getting Restless: Rethinking Revision in Writing Instruction* (Boynton/Cook 1997). Her articles have appeared in *College Composition and Communication, College English, The Writing Center Journal*, and elsewhere. Her short stories have appeared in such magazines as *Prairie Schooner* and *Threepenny Review*.

Kathleen Blake Yancey is Professor of English at Clemson University. Her scholarly interests include rhetoric and composition, writing assessment, poetics, rhetoric, genre and representation, and reflective practices (e.g., teaching professional communication). With Brian Huot, she founded and edits *Assessing Writing*, and she has edited or co-edited several collections of essays, most recently *Situating Portfolios: Four Perspectives*, with Irwin Weiser. She also has authored *Reflection in the Writing Classroom*, a study that theorizes and makes plain the practice of using reflection to teach writing. In 1995–1996, Yancey co-taught in the WPA Workshop; from 1995–1998, she was on the Executive Board of Writing Program Administration; and in January 1999, she became Vice President of WPA.

Preface

Writing Center Research: Extending the Conversation

This project had its beginnings in 1994, at the first conference of the National Writing Centers Association. In a room filled with windows through which we could see the warm spring sunshine of New Orleans, a group of us attended a session on writing center research, chaired by Nancy Grimm. Presenters gave brief overviews of their research projects, and then the large group split up into smaller discussion clusters. Lady Falls Brown and Paula Gillespie sat in the same group, agreeing that they wanted to know more about research projects. Lady and Paula agreed that they would begin a book project, calling for articles on research. Later in the process, they asked Byron Stay and Alice Gillam to join them as editors.

Lady wanted a book that would explain research methodology used in composition studies. Because her formal training was in literature, she wanted a book to provide a framework of research choices and show methodologies at work. She wanted a book that would help inexperienced writing center staffers know how to begin a research project.

Paula came to this project with a bias about research, one based on her undergraduate major in psychology. Her experiences with rats at the psychology department at the University of Wisconsin—Madison convinced her to add a major in English and change her professional goals, but she retained her interest in the rigors of scientifically based empirical research and the statistical interpretations of data. She wanted to integrate that rigor into the research projects she would take on, although writing centers and its theories had begun to make her more interested in qualitative than in quantitative studies, in case studies rather than rat studies. She wanted to learn more about the research that others had undertaken.

Alice was interested in the theoretical dimensions of research and in our discourse about research. What counts as research in the writing center community? How has this changed over time? What kind of knowledge is produced through various kinds of research? To what ends? What epistemological assumptions underlie various methodological approaches? What ethical questions should we be asking? She wanted to understand these issues better, both for herself and for graduate students who may wish to conduct "centered" research.

Byron wanted a book in which the contributors would define their methodologies. As editor of the NWCA Press, he is interested in accounts of research that can benefit the profession.

All of us wanted our contributors not simply to describe their research projects, but also to point readers to sources where they could find the research methodology explained. Additionally, we wanted contributors to critique their own research as well as their methods, if applicable. And we all hoped that this collection would be the first in a series of discussions of research.

As you will see, *Writing Center Research* is organized into three sections, the first containing four chapters, the second containing six chapters, and the last containing four chapters. Of course, any system of classification is somewhat arbitrary and some of the texts could be placed in more than one category, but we hope the organizational schema makes sense to readers.

Part I: Writing Centers as Sites of Self-Reflective Inquiry—Alice Gillam uses rhetorical analysis in "The Call to Research: Early Representations of Writing Center Research" to examine "unspoken assumptions, contradictions, unresolved, and perhaps unresolvable, dilemmas" that have shaped writing center discourse and research. In "Disciplinary Action: Writing Center Work and the Making of a Researcher," Beth Boquet chronicles her struggles beginning as a peer tutor, progressing to a doctoral student, and continuing as a professional to question what constitutes research in order to reconcile practice and theory. Next, in "Beyond the House of Lore: WCenter as Research Site," Paula Gillespie complicates Steve North's argument that most writing center talk constitutes lore by demonstrating how list members begin with discussions of practice that lead to discussions of theory, theory supported and informed by practice. Finally, in "Insider as Outsider: Participant Observation as Writing Center Research," Neal Lerner employs participant-observer research, a form used in ethnographic studies, to demonstrate how difficult it is for a person to study the behavior of colleagues, although the insight gained can be valuable.

Part II: Writing Centers as Sites of Institutional Critique and Contextual Inquiry—Muriel Harris's "Writing Center Administration: Making Local, Institutional Knowledge in Our Writing Centers" provides a treasure trove of potential research questions for writing center directors, and shows how the kind of information directors collect about their writing centers in their institutions qualifies as legitimate research. In "Reading Our Own Words: Rhetorical Analysis and the Institutional Discourse of Writing Centers," Peter Carino analyzes the language writing center directors use in publicity materials to reveal their insecurities concerning the role they play in their institution. Not only can writing centers benefit by looking closely at themselves, they can also benefit when students employ the ethnographic technique of rapid assessment, as Jon Olson, Dawn J. Moyer, and Adelia Falda demonstrate in "Student-Centered Assessment Research in the Writing Center." in chapter 8, Joyce Magnotto Neff, interested in literacy research, describes grounded theory as a methodology that enables a researcher to collect information from different viewpoints to present as complete a picture as possible of what actually transpires in situations. To study the effectiveness of writing center tutorials at their institution, in chapter 9 Sharon Thomas, Julie Bevins, and Mary Ann Crawford describe a longitudinal study of students' resistance to and acceptance of disciplinary expectations for writing. This section concludes with "Computer Literacies and the Roles of the Writing Center" by Danielle DeVoss, who reports conducting usability testing on materials the center developed by the center staff to assist students as they learn to write for and on the web.

Part III: Writing Centers as Sites of Inquiry Into Practice—This section focuses on tutor training and the roles of tutors within the larger institution. In "Seeing Practice through Their Eyes: Reflection as Teacher," Kathleen Blake Yancey refines the concept of reflection-in-action to constructive reflection for the reader, and then uses selections from tutoring journals and letters to indicate how reflection enables tutors to understand both their tutoring practices and their clients, and how teachers of tutoring courses can also benefit from reflection on their teaching. Nancy Welch employs object relations theory, a facet of psychoanalysis, in "The Return of the Suppressed: Tutoring Stories in a Transitional Space," to look for repressed stories told by tutors in order to help them reveal to themselves otherwise unacknowledged truths about their tutoring and themselves. Next, Judith Rodby bases her analysis of subjects/subjectivities in literacy research. In "The Subject Is Literacy: General Education and the Dialectics of Power and Resistance in the Writing Center," she demonstrates how students and tutors react to the demands made on them by both the role they are called to play by the institution and the assignments with which they must work. This section concludes with Jean Marie Lutes' "Why Feminists Make Better Tutors: Gender and Disciplinary Expertise in a Curriculum-Based Tutoring Program." Using feminist theory, she examines the challenges faced by tutors assigned to courses within and outside their majors, and argues for the need to prepare such tutors to be critical change agents.

ACKNOWLEDGMENTS

First, we want to express our appreciation for the extreme patience our authors have demonstrated as four people located in various parts of the country and at various stages of their lives (mostly marriages of children and in one instance himself) have worked on this project.

We also want to thank the entire staff at Lawrence Erlbaum Associates. Their courtesy, efficiency, and professionalism made editing this volume much easier. Thanks also to the Erlbaum reviewers, Duane Roen, Arizona State University and Carrie S. Leverenz, Florida State University.

We thank our schools for encouragement and support: Marquette University, University of Wisconsin-Milwaukee, Texas Tech (especially Mary Valdez for help during the production stage), and Mount St. Mary's College.

Finally, we thank our many tutors and our colleagues both in and out of writing centers.

Introduction

What research means in a given rhetorical situation depends partly on the type of research in question and partly on the synonyms invoked to stand in for this keyword.

—Tom Kerr (1996, p. 201)

Since the inception of a professional discourse about writing centers, the center has been imagined as a kind of "natural laboratory," a research site that would yield unique insights into students' writing development and the pedagogies that assist such development. In the inaugural issue of *Writing Center Journal* (1980), for example, editors Lil Brannon and Stephen North express high hopes for the "great new discoveries" about the learning and teaching of writing to be discovered through writing center research. Some 20 years later, opinion varies over the current state of writing center research although most agree that this great promise remains as yet unfulfilled and probably unable to be fulfilled in the ebullient terms originally imagined. Such decidedly mixed opinion about the current state and future direction of writing center research suggests a need for more explicit talk about what we mean by research, what should count as research, and how to conduct research. Many of the chapters in this volume address these questions directly or indirectly through their meta-level reflections about research. As a backdrop for these chapters, we begin with a consideration of terminology and the ways in which writing center research has defined itself in relationship to and in distinction from composition research.

COMING TO TERMS

As the excerpt from Tom Kerr's keyword entry on *research* suggests, "what research means" is context-specific and rhetorically strategic. Although the terms *research* and *scholarship* are often used interchangeably, there is some evidence that in composition studies, our "parent" discipline, the term *research* is more closely allied with empirical inquiry, and the term *scholarship* with conceptual inquiry.[1] The distinction between *empirical* and *conceptual inquiry* combines terminology recommended by the American Educational Research Association (AERA) and that recommended by Mary Sue MacNealy in *Strategies for Empirical Research in Writing* (1999). AERA uses the term *conceptual inquiry* for the kind of research carried out by literary scholars, philosophers, and others in the humanities and the term *research* for empirically based investigations most commonly carried out in the social sciences. MacNealy, by contrast, prefers the terms *empirical research*, which she defines as "research that carefully describes and/or measures observable phenomena in a systematic way planned out in advance of the observation," and *library-based research*, which she defines as "research efforts largely carried out in libraries, both personal and institutional" (6). In short, her distinction turns on the object of inquiry: observable phenomena or texts/ideas. We find the term *conceptual inquiry* preferable to *library-based research*, not only because the latter is in need of updating, but also because the former suggests a wider range of intellectual work and thus more precisely captures the broad nature of inquiry that includes theoretical speculations, historical investigations, hermeneutical/critical inquiry, or some combination of these approaches. Similarly, the term *empirical*, once it is detached from assumptions of positivism and scientific objectivity, can be used to refer to a broad category of research that includes case studies, ethnography, and various forms of practitioner inquiry.

Although we acknowledge the limitations of this distinction with its suggestion of a false binary, elision of differences within each category, and failure to account for many hybrid forms of inquiry that do not fit easily into either category, we nevertheless find this distinction a useful point of departure. Specifically, we use the terms *empirical inquiry* and *conceptual inquiry* to discuss the two types of research that have dominated writing center knowledge production: *practitioner inquiry*, arguably a form of empirical research, whose aim is to understand, improve, and/or change practice; and *theoretical* or *conceptual inquiry*, whose aim is to justify, guide, or critique practice. Our concern in this introduction is threefold: to contextualize these two strands of research and scholarship in terms of larger debates about knowledge making; to acknowledge the political

---

[1]The distinction is perhaps most evident in Stephen North's *The Making of Knowledge in Composition* (1987), where he categorizes "scholars" as those who do historical, philosophical, and critical work, and "researchers" as those who do various kinds of empirical work (experimental, clinical, ethnographic, and so on).

dimension of research methods and methodologies, and to raise questions about current and future directions for writing center inquiry.

EARLY DEFINITIONS OF RESEARCH IN COMPOSITION STUDIES

We begin with a brief history of early research paradigms in composition studies because it is to this field that writing center researchers looked as they began to articulate a research agenda for the writing center. As many scholars have suggested, the "modern" period of composition research and the field's bid for disciplinary status began in 1963 with Braddock, Lloyd-Jones, and Schoer's pronouncement about the dismal state of composition research: "Today's research in composition, taken as a whole, may be compared to chemical research as it emerged from the period of alchemy ... the field as a whole is laced with dreams, prejudices, and makeshift operations" (5). In reaction to the suggestion by Braddock et al. that composition research was anecdotal, unsystematic, and, in short, not scientific, early composition research (1963 to mid-1980s), not surprisingly, emphasized systematic, empirical methods, and observable data (95). The term *research*, the more common term for social scientific inquiry, thus became the preferred synonym for early composition inquiry, and distinctions among types of research—experimental versus descriptive, quantitative versus qualitative—were borrowed from the social sciences, which had, in turn, borrowed many of their terms for research from the natural sciences.

Beach and Bridwell (1984), for example, make the distinction between "basic research," that is, research that seeks to explain or understand phenomena like the writing process and writing development, and "applied research," that tests or evaluates particular theories or practices like the use of sentence combining. These terms are not, of course, value-neutral, and just as "basic" (sometimes called "pure") research is more highly valued than "applied" research in the natural sciences, so it came to be more highly valued in the social sciences and arguably in early composition studies. Mosenthal, Tamor, and Walmsley's *Research on Writing* (1983), for example, opens with a chapter by Bereiter and Scardamalia on "Levels of Inquiry in Writing Research," which identifies six levels of inquiry. Despite their insistence that *higher* levels are not "more worthy," the very term "higher" as well as the progression from less formal and subjective modes of inquiry ("reflective inquiry") to highly controlled and objective modes of inquiry ("computer simulations") suggests a hierarchy in which the scientific values of acontextual, objective inquiry is privileged (4). In short, composition's early adoption of the social scientific paradigm influenced *how* research was conducted as well as *what* was valued, and inevitably the epistemological assumptions about how we come to know (through objective methodologies) and what can be known (unmediated understanding of the phenomenal world, discovery of universal truths) were adopted along with the social scientific vocabulary and methods.

Like those in composition studies generally, early writing center researchers believed it was possible to study practice in systematic and objective ways that would reveal universal underlying principles that could, in turn, improve and guide practice. In this goal, they differed from early writing center theorists only in that these would-be empirical researchers began with close observations of practice, hoping to work inductively and by accretion toward a covering or metatheory whereas theorists began with a metatheory, hoping to demonstrate deductively that this theory could explain and guide practice.

PRACTITIONER INQUIRY

Not surprisingly, early calls for writing center investigations of practice reflect the assumptions of the social scientific paradigm, which was only beginning to give way to other inquiry paradigms in the composition community at the time. Stephen North's "Writing Center Research: Testing Our Assumptions" (1984b), an essay discussed at length in chapter 1 of this volume, urges the writing center community to move beyond reflections on experience, speculations, and surveys toward systematic, assumption-testing empirical studies: "Writing center researchers are going to have to ... engage in research that is neither simple nor integrated [into everyday practice] ... . There will be a need, as with case studies, to create a methodology, one borrowed from disciplines like ethnography, social psychology, and cognitive psychology" (29-30). North's specific methodological recommendations for investigating "good" tutoring as a construct entail observing tutors as they confront *high-fidelity simulation problems* (a methodology borrowed from cognitive psychology) and debriefing both tutors and tutees by using *stimulated recall sessions* (another methodology borrowed from cognitive psychology and used in many early studies of the writing process by composition researchers).

Despite North's call for systematic, social-scientific empirical research, the dominant form of writing center research continued to be "unsystematic," descriptive, and practice-based. Not only was such research more familiar to most humanities-trained writing center administrators but it also was more congruent with their everyday work in writing centers. However, without an alternative paradigm for defining research goals and guiding research methodologies, it continued to be difficult to assess the relative value of the amalgam of what North had called reflections on experience, speculations, and surveys.

Even though there was a tolerance for a wide range of approaches and, beginning in 1976, a venue for the publication of various forms of practitioner inquiry in *The Writing Lab Newsletter*, there continued to be deep uncertainty about the value and legitimacy of the practice-centered, applied nature of most writing center research. Consider, for example, the treatment of practitioner inquiry in Stephen North's influential *The Making of Knowledge in Composition* (1987). To be sure, North is referring to practitioner inquiry in composition studies generally, but his ambivalent treatment of this form of research can surely be taken to indicate something of the writing center community's ambivalence about its main form of knowledge production at that time. After all, as co-founder of *The Writing Center Journal* and writer of what is probably still the most influential essay in the field, "The Idea of a Writing Center," North was widely regarded as a leader and spokesperson for writing center work both within and outside the writing center community.

Credit for legitimizing practitioner "lore" as a form of inquiry is often given to Stephen North's seminal chapter on "Practitioner Inquiry" in *The Making of Knowledge in Composition* (1987). Although North acknowledges that "what marks [composition studies'] emergence as a nascent academic field more than anything else is this need to replace practice as the field's dominant mode of inquiry" (15), he nevertheless identifies practitioners as one of three types of "knowledge-makers," the other two being scholars and researchers. Most often recalled and cited for its insistence on the value of practitioner inquiry, North's chapter is less often recalled for its ambivalence about the status of *lore*, the term he coins for the informal knowledge produced and exchanged among practitioners. On the one hand, North tries to legitimize lore as driven by pragmatic logic and verified by experience; on the other hand, he argues that "writing is, by definition, the medium least amenable to representing the results of Practitioner inquiry" (52). He claims that "when Practitioners report on their inquiry in writing, they tend to misrepresent both its nature and authority, moving farther and farther from their pragmatic and experiential power base. And the harder they try, it seems to me, the worse things get. They look more and more like bad Scholars or inadequate Researchers" (54-55). For North, lore is best communicated orally since the lore that gets written down tends to become prescriptive, codified, and acontextual. As an antidote, North sets certain conditions for defining practice as inquiry and recommends systematic approaches to practitioner research. Thus, he arrives at the somewhat contradictory conclusion that practitioners need to be "more methodologically self-conscious" than other researchers and more careful to limit their claims about what he has effectively characterized as elusive and unrepresentable (55).[2]

Ironically, perhaps, legitimation of practitioner inquiry and lore as a form of knowledge production came finally from the turn to more conceptual

---

[2]Bruce Horner offers a similar but more elaborated critique of North's treatment of lore as a mode of inquiry in "Traditions and Professionalization" (378–381).

forms of inquiry and away from social scientific notions of empiricism. Since the 1980s, writes Gary Olson (1995) "Composition has been shifting from a social science-dominated discipline to one that privileges theoretical, speculative, hermeneutical scholarship" (53), what we are calling conceptual inquiry. Precipitated by what is variously called the linguistic, social, and/or postmodern "turn" in English studies and throughout the humanities,[3] this shift entailed a critique of social scientific methods and epistemology and an advocacy of modes of inquiry more congenial to humanities-trained scholars such as theoretical speculation and interpretive accounts of practice influenced by postmodern ethnography.

This paradigm shift, although hardly complete nor uncontested, has resulted not only in a burgeoning of more conceptual forms of inquiry in composition studies but also in the transformation of empirically based practitioner inquiry. Replacing the view of the researcher as a disinterested observer who systematically gathers data and objectively interprets it according to verifiable constructs that mirror external reality is the view of the researcher as an interested observer who selectively gathers data and subjectively interprets it according to various terministic screens. Similarly, the goal of discovering underlying consistent principles to explain and guide practice is abandoned in favor of situated descriptions of practice that lead to critiques or limited recommendations that make no pretense to guaranteeing success when applied in differing contexts.

Understandably, the eroding of the social scientific or positivistic paradigm with its rigid demands for systematicity and statistical knowledge has been a great boon to one of the most prevalent forms of writing center research, practitioner inquiry. The linguistic/social/postmodern turn legitimized practitioner inquiry and lore in a way that positivistic paradigm could not. If the foundational knowledge promised by positivism was not possible, then contingent, local knowledge was all that might be hoped for, and surely practitioner lore is one form of such knowledge. Explaining the value of lore as a form of postmodern knowledge-making, Patricia Harkin writes, "Lore procedurally and pragmatically blurs relations of cause and effect [and therefore] is able to deal more effectively than traditional science with 'overdetermined' [that is, complex phenomena with multiple, overlapping causes] situations [like teaching and tutoring]" (134).[4]

The other form practitioner inquiry has taken in writing center research since the linguistic/social/postmodern turn is the carefully contextualized qualitative study of practice. The latter differs from lore in that the

---

[3]"Where Did Composition Studies Come From?" by Martin Nystrand, Stuart Greene, and Jeffrey Wiemelt (1993), reminds us that developments in composition studies are "part of a broader intellectual history affecting linguistics and literary studies, as well as composition" (267).

[4]According to Bruce Horner (2000), Harkin's defense of lore as a mode of inquiry does not escape the problem articulated by North—that is, in translating lore into the "templates" that count as academic knowledge production, lore is "denaturalized" and thus misrepresented (379).

practitioner/researcher is often, but not always, observing the practice of others; his or her methods of data collecting are more "formal" than those of practitioners informally reporting on their own practices; and the aim is reflective, theoretical, or critical, rather than pragmatic.

With the turn toward the "social," leading composition theorists began to view writing center practice as an ideal site for inquiry into the collaborative nature of writing and learning. In "Writing as a Social Process: A Theoretical Foundation for Writing Centers?" (1989), Lisa Ede argues that writing center practitioners are "uniquely" positioned to contribute to the "intellectual dialogue" in composition studies about the social nature of writing (101). Similarly, Lil Brannon asserted at the 1990 CCCC's roundtable entitled "The Writing Center as Research Center: Issues and Directions" that writing center professionals should eschew the desire to conduct "'Research with a capital R'" and instead recognize in the writing center "fertile ground for the sorts of ethnographic research and contextual knowledge which ought to be our concern" (quoted in Bushman, 1991, 27). A number of writing center researchers responded to this call for contextualized local studies of writing center practice. In particular, case studies and ethnographic studies, free from the pretense of positivistic claims to generalizable truth, have been clearly valued as a form of knowledge making by the writing center research community. By contrast, the status of informal practitioner inquiry and lore as research has been less clear.

The most ardent defense of informal practitioner inquiry and lore as a form of knowledge production is found in two essays by Eric Hobson, "Maintaining Our Balance: Walking the Tightrope of Competing Epistemologies" (1992) and "Writing Center Practice Often Counters Its Theory. So What?" (1994). In the first essay, which in many ways sets the stage for the second, Hobson argues against the quixotic search for a "true epistemological home," a totalizing theory that will explain and guide all writing center practice, calling instead for an "epistemological mix" that is more adequate to the complex, contextual, and elusive nature of writing center practice (74). In the latter essay, Hobson argues more forcefully for the full validation of practitioner lore as postmodern, postdisciplinary knowledge making. According to Hobson, the unrepresentability of practitioner knowledge noted by North explains the impossibility of a seamless coherence between theory and practice, and affirms the value of "patched together," contradictory theories: "The unique circumstances of every instance of application [or practice] require a unique appropriation and implementation of theory into practice" (8). Of necessity, lore is situated, contradictory, and eclectic. Furthermore, lore is not the product of inquiry removed from practice, but rather is produced through the act of reflective, self-critical practice in "the intermediate space where activity and reflection transact" (Phelps quoted in Hobson, 1994, 9).

Despite Hobson's (1994) call to celebrate rather than discount lore as not "methodologically or theoretically sufficient to provide valid knowledge" (8), there is evidence that the writing center community's attitude toward lore remains ambiguous. In their Introduction to *Landmark Essays on Writing Centers* (1995), for example, Murphy and Law offer a narrative of progress for writing center research and scholarship in which "the focus of inquiry is already shifting from practitioner lore to a broader understanding of the social influences upon knowledge production within a culture" (xv). By implication, practitioner lore is represented as parochial and less sophisticated, a kind of research that is giving way to "broader" research questions and agenda.

One of those broader agendas is the political agenda set forth by Nancy Grimm in "Contesting 'The Idea of a Writing Center': The Politics of Writing Center Research" (1992). Although Grimm does not directly mention lore in her essay, clearly the type of scholarship she calls for is beyond the scope of lore with its focus on the immediate concerns with practice. Specifically, Grimm advocates for the study of "how difference is managed in the academy and about how students' subjectivities are constructed by educational discourse," not in order to improve practice in the terms set by the institution but to challenge institutional practices and change the context of teaching and learning (5-6). Significantly, the exemplar she uses to illustrate the political work that might be done through writing center research is Anne DiPardo's "'Whispers of Coming and Going': Lessons from Fannie" (1992), a case study that combines a close reading of a particular tutorial relationship with reflections on the inadequacies of both composition and writing center pedagogy in meeting the needs of student writers with nontraditional literacy backgrounds.

In short, the comments of Murphy and Law and Grimm raise questions about the status of lore and the broader purposes of practitioner inquiry. If the Outstanding Scholarship Awards are any indication of the kinds of practitioner research the writing center community values, then one would have to note that the forms of practitioner inquiry most valued are those that couple qualitative empirical research (mainly case study or quasi-ethnographic studies) with theoretical speculation like Dipardo's, which won this award in 1993. Recognition for what we might call lore usually comes in the form of awards for the accumulated lore found in textbooks, such as Reigstad's and McAndrew's (1984), Clark's (1985), Harris' (1986), and Farrell's (1989).

Perhaps the larger question is what constitutes lore? And depending on how we define it, is all lore equally valued and valuable? What is the place of qualitative empirical studies of practice? What methods and methodologies might guide the work of such researchers? What methods ensure the ethical representation of others? What is the relationship of qualitative empirical research to lore, and what political and cultural work ought each to perform? Is it the case that we have given up on the possibilities of inductively derived generalizations about "best practices"? And if not, then what might be the basis for such generalizations given our understanding of practice as context-specific?

THEORETICAL INQUIRY

Unlike practitioner inquiry, theoretical inquiry has enjoyed a relatively privileged status in the writing center community, despite complaints from time to time about its elitism and disconnection from practice. In the inaugural issue of *The Writing Center Journal* (1980), editors Lil Brannon and Stephen North give first place to "essays that are primarily theoretical" in their solicitation of scholarly articles (2). Explaining the privileged place of theoretical inquiry since the mid-1980s, Peter Carino writes in "Theorizing the Writing Center: An Uneasy Task" (1995b) that "Theory thus … is empowered as academic currency in a way that practice is not, even though the two cannot be cleanly separated … . Because writing center work, historically and presently, is not recognized as a discipline . . .theory beckons as a means of establishing disciplinary and institutional respectability" 23-24). Further confirmation of the privileged status of theoretical inquiry in the writing center community comes from a review of the 18 individual essays that have received Outstanding Scholarship Awards from the National Writing Center Association, the vast majority of which involve primarily theoretical or conceptual inquiry.

If the work of theory is to explain and justify practice, as Carino suggests, then it is not surprising that early writing center theorists sought a covering theory that might serve as a foundation for writing center practice. Furthermore, given the close tie between writing center theory and practice, it is not surprising that pedagogical paradigms—current traditional, expressivist, cognitivist, and social constructionist—have served as the basis for much writing center theorizing. Tilly and John Warnock's "Liberatory Writing Centers: Restoring Authority to Writers" (1984), for example, tried to found writing center practice on theories of Romantic expressivism whereas Kenneth Bruffee's "Peer Tutoring and the 'Conversation of Mankind'" (1984) argued for social constructionism as a metatheory that might explain, guide, and legitimate writing center practice. Social constructionist theory, in particular, seemed to hold out promise not only for providing theoretical justification for writing center practice but also for placing "writing centers at the heart, rather than the periphery, of current theory in composition studies" (Ede, 1989, 101).

However, neither social constructionism nor any other comprehensive, generalized theory has proven to be satisfactory in explaining and guiding writing center practice. As Carino explains (1995B), such metatheories fail to explain the complexities and context-bound exigencies of practice and usually refer to practice only in abstract idealized terms. Carino notes, for example, that while Lisa Ede touts social constructionism as a theory that can found writing center practice, "the workings of a social-constructionist tutorial are never represented" (31). Offering a similar explanation for the limitations of social constructionism as a covering theory, Christina Murphy writes in "The Writing Center and Social Constructionist Theory" (1994) that "social constructionism provides us with a paradigm that explains a number of aspects of writing instruction; however, to argue that it provides all the answers, or even answers sufficient to warrant the devaluing of other theories and philosophies of education—especially Romantic or humanistic—seems unwise" (36). In sum, writes Eric Hobson, "twenty years of trying to produce such a metatheory ... have not brought us any nearer to the consistency which disciplinary thought makes us desire" (1994, 8).

Hence, if theoretical inquiry cannot hope to offer an unified theory, what kind of work can such inquiry perform? The key word in Carino's title, "theorizing," provides an answer, according to Gary Olson, who writes that the goal of postmodern theoretical inquiry is not theory with a capital T, but the act of theorizing: "the act of engaging in critical, philosophical, hermeneutic speculation about a subject .... Theorizing can lead us into lines of inquiry that challenge received notions or entrenched understandings that may no longer be productive; it can create new vocabularies for talking about a subject and thus new ways of perceiving it" (1995, 54). Writing center theorizing has quite clearly moved in this direction, drawing on the vocabularies of educational theory (Murphy, 1991), cultural studies (Cooper, 1994), feminism (Woolbright, 1992), psychoanalytic theory (Welch, 1999), and postmodernism (Grimm, 1996, 1999), to name only a few, in order to create new ways of perceiving writing center work.

Additionally, much theorizing over the past 10 years has taken a decidedly critical turn. Rather than discovery of a comprehensive theory, the aim of much theoretical inquiry has been to offer various forms of critique—of practice, of writing center discourse and self-representation, of received writing center histories, and of literacy education generally. For example, the disjuncture between theory and practice has been a fruitful site for theoretical inquiry (Behm, 1989; Clark, 1988; Trimbur, 1987). Received histories have been revised and challenged by the work of Peter Carino (1996) and Beth Boquet (1999). As well, writing center discourse has been analyzed rhetorically for its underlying assumptions, contradictions, and cultural work—Hemmeter (1990), Runciman (1990), Carino (1992), and Healy (1995).

Accompanying this shift away from self-justification and toward critique has been a shift in audience and scope. Although the writing center community remains the primary audience for much theoretical inquiry, there has been an increasingly broad sense of audience and purpose. If, as Gillam asserts in the first essay in this volume, writing center research initially sought to position itself within the field of composition studies, more recent writing center work has sought to position itself within broader interdisciplinary fields such as educational theory and literacy studies. As

Murphy and Law (1995) and Grimm (1992) argue in the previously mentioned essays, the knowledge about writing produced in the writing center has ramifications far beyond just improving writing center work or informing composition studies. In their conclusion, Murphy and Law noted:

> The idea of a writing center has now become the multidimensional realities of the writing center within the academy and within society as a whole. What the writing center's role will be in future redefinitions of the educational process, how that role will be negotiated and evaluated, and how writing center professionals will shape educational values will constitute the future landmark directions and essays on writing center theory and practice. (1995, xv)

Although it seems clear that the achievements of theoretical inquiry have gone a long way toward establishing the writing center's development as a field, there remain questions about the direction and purpose of future theoretical work. What ought to be the relationship between theoretical and practitioner inquiry in writing center scholarship? How can we avoid reproducing the inequity between the status of theoretical and practitioner inquiry found in the academic community generally? Whose interests ought theoretical inquiry serve? How can theorists formulate ethical positions from which to speak given the postmodern and poststructuralist critique of foundational theories? On what basis might we make judgments of more and less useful theorizing?

METHODOLOGICAL PLURALISM
AND AN ETHICS OF INQUIRY

With the more frequent publication of writing center research in major composition journals like *College Composition and Communication*—Nancy Grimm's "Rearticulating the Work of the Writing Center" (1996), Beth Boquet's "'Our Little Secret': A History of Writing Centers, Pre- to Post-Open Admissions" (1999), Nancy Welch's "Playing with Reality: Writing Centers after the Mirror Stage" (1999)—as well as the publication of single-authored book-length studies of writing center work like Grimm's *Good Intentions: Writing Center Work for Postmodern Times* (1999), the long-sought recognition of the writing center as a research community seems at hand.

Moreover, the move toward methodological pluralism in English studies generally has expanded the possibilities for approaches to inquiry. Hybrid forms of scholarly writing have emerged such as Nancy Welch's blending of autobiography, creative writing, psychoanalytical and feminist theorizing, and descriptive case study in "Collaborating with the Enemy" and "Migrant Rationalities," the writing center-based chapters in her 1997 book *Getting Restless* (which is also notable for its integration of writing center research with classroom-based research). The collapsing of disciplinary boundaries in all fields has opened new subjects of inquiry and resulted in a blurring of "high" and "low" theory. An example of the latter is found in Nancy Grimm's *Good Intentions* (1999), where popular self-help books as well as "high" postmodern theory are used as critical lenses.

Scientific empiricism is even finding new advocates such as Davida Charney (1996) and Cindy Johanek (2000). In "Empiricism Is Not a Four-Letter Word" (1996), for example, Charney reminds readers, on the one hand, that "not all empiricists are positivists" (570), and, on the other hand, that the traditional methods of scientific research methods ought not be dismissed out of hand: "By operating within the constraints of formalized conventions for collecting and interpreting data, researchers create the potential for communal scrutiny and refinement of disciplinary work" (588). In somewhat different terms, Linda Flower also argues for a recuperated and revised approach to empiricism in "Observation-Based Theory Building" (1997). Citing the work of feminist scientists like Sandra Harding and Donna Haraway, Flower claims "it is time to go beyond textual analysis and mere critique and to develop more adequate images of objectivity … . Just because objectivity is not an absolute, we can't dismiss its role in building convincing arguments that justify our claims … . The more difficult alternative [these feminists] propose is a rhetorical one that depends on case building" (166-67). Flower concludes by arguing that

> observation-based theory turns to empirical methods because it is sensitive to its own limitations … . In observation-based theory building, these two attempts to test claims—that is, to test for reliability and for a fit to the data with or without statistics—are powerful not because they are an instrument of proof, but because they are a hedge against our own fallibility (179, 183).

What all of this suggests is a new era of openness and tolerance, along with renewed debates about old epistemological and methodological questions. However, of central concern to researchers and scholars of all persuasions is the matter of ethics and the need for self-reflective inquiry. Recent work that takes up these issues directly includes Paul Anderson's "Simple Gifts: Ethical Issues in the Conduct of Person-Based Composition Research" (1998), Ellen Barton's "More Methodological Matters: Against Negative Argumentation" (2000), and Gesa Kirsch's *Ethical Dilemmas in Feminist Research: The Politics of Location, Interpretation, and Publication* (1999).

Along with Gesa Kirsch, we believe that methodological pluralism can encourage ethical, self-reflective approaches to inquiry. Such pluralism, in other words, does not mean an uncritical acceptance of all forms of research; rather, it demands a rigorous self-critique and an equally rigorous effort to understand the work of others. We conclude by directing Kirsch's challenge to composition researchers to those of us who conduct writing center research: "Only by understanding the nature and assumptions of various research methodologies can scholars [and practitioners in writing centers] make informed decisions about the relevance, validity, and value of research reports. And only through shared, critical reflection on various research practices can [writing center researchers] come to define the emergent [field of writing center studies] for themselves" (Kirsch, 1992, 247–248). It is our hope that this book invites just such understanding and shared critical reflection and, by doing so, extends the conversation about the nature and purposes of writing center inquiry.

—Alice M. Gillam
University of Wisconsin-Milwaukee

REFERENCES

Anderson, P. (1998). Simple gifts: Ethical issues in the conduct of person-based composition research. *College Composition and Communication, 49*(1), 63–89.

Barton, E. (2000). More methodological matters: Against negative argumentation. College *Composition and Communication, 51*(3), 399–416.

Beach, R., & Bridwell, L. S. (1984). *New directions in composition research.* New York: Guilford.

Behm, R. (1989). Ethical issues in peer tutoring. *The Writing Center Journal, 10*(1), 3–12.

Bereiter, C., & Scardamalia, M. (1983). Levels of inquiry in writing research. In P. Mosenthal, L. Tamor, & S. Walmsley (Eds.), *Research on writing : Principles and methods* (pp. 3–25). New York: Longman.

Boquet, E. (1999). "Our little secret": A history of writing centers, pre- to post-open admissions. *College Composition and Communication, 50*(3), 463–82.

Braddock, R., Lloyd-Jones, R., & Schoer, L. (1963). *Research in written composition.* Champaign, IL: NCTE.

Brannon, L., & North, S. (1980). From the editors. *Writing Center Journal, 1*(1), 1–3.

Bruffee, K. (1984). Peer tutoring and the "conversation of mankind." In G. A. Olson (Ed.), *Writing centers: Theory and administration* (pp. 3–15). Urbana, IL: NCTE.

Bushman, D. (1991). Past accomplishments and current trends in writing center research: A bibliographic essay. In R. Wallace & J. Simpson (Eds.), *The writing center: New directions* (pp. 27–38). New York: Garland.

Carino, P. (1992). What do we talk about when we talk about our metaphors: A cultural critique of clinic, lab, and center. *The Writing Center Journal, 13*(1), 31–42.

Carino, P. (1995a). Early writing centers: Toward a history. *The Writing Center Journal, 15*(2), 103–116.

Carino, P. (1995b). Theorizing the writing center: An uneasy task. *Dialogue: A Journal for Writing Specialists, 2*(1), 23–37.

Carino, P. (1996). Open admissions and the construction of writing center history: A tale of three models. *The Writing Center Journal, 17*(1), 30–49.

Charney, D. (1996). Empiricism is not a four-letter word. *College Composition and Communication, 47,* 567–93.

Clark, I. (1985). *Writing in the center: Teaching in a writing center setting.* Dubuque, IA: Kendall Hunt.

Clark, I. (1988). Collaboration and ethics in writing center pedagogy. *The Writing Center Journal, 9*(1), 3–12.

Cooper, M. (1994). Really useful knowledge: A cultural studies agenda for writing centers. *The Writing Center Journal, 14*(2), 97–111.

DiPardo, A. (1992). "Whispers of Coming and Going": Lessons from Fannie. *The Writing Center Journal, 12*(2), 125–44.

Ede, L. (1989). Writing as a social process: A theoretical foundation for writing centers? *The Writing Center Journal, 9*(2), 3–13.

Farrell, P. (1989). *The high school writing center: Establishing and maintaining one.* Urbana, IL: NCTE.

Flower, L. (1997). Observation-based theory building. In G. Olson & T. Taylor (Eds.), *Publishing in rhetoric and composition* (pp. 163–185). Albany: State University of New York Press.

Grimm, N. (1992). Contesting "the idea of a writing center": The politics of writing center research. *The Writing Lab Newsletter, 17*(1), 5–6.

Grimm, N. (1996). Rearticulating the work of the writing center. *College Composition and Communication, 47*(4), 523–548.

Grimm, N. (1999). *Good intentions: Writing center work for postmodern times.* Portsmouth, NH: Boynton/Cook, Heinemann.

Harkin, P. (1991). The postdisciplinary politics of lore. In P. Harkin & J. Schilb (Eds.), *Contending with words: Composition and rhetoric in a postmodern age* (pp. 124–38). New York: Modern Language Association.

Harris, M. (1986). *Teaching one-to-one: The writing conference.* Urbana, IL: NCTE.

Healy, D. (1995). The writing center as church. In B. Stay & C. Murphy (Eds.), *Writing center perspectives* (pp. 12–25). Emmitsburg, MD: NWCA Press.

Hemmeter, T. (1990). The "smack of difference": The language of writing center discourse. *The Writing Center Journal, 11*(1), 35–48.

Hobson, E. (1992). Maintaining our balance: Walking the tightrope of competing epistemologies. *The Writing Center Journal, 13*(1), 65–75.

Hobson, E. (1994). Writing center practice often counters its theory. So what? In J. Mullin & R. Wallace (Eds.), *Intersections: Theory-practice in the writing center* (pp. 1-10). Urbana, IL: NCTE.

Horner, B. (2000). Traditions and professionalization: Reconceiving work in composition. *College Composition and Communication, 51*(3), 366–398.

Johanek, C. (2000). *Composing research: A contextual paradigm for rhetoric and composition.* Logan: Utah State University Press.

Kerr, T. C. (1996). Research. In P. Heilker & P. Vanderberg (Eds.), *Keyword in composition studies* (pp. 201–205). Portsmouth, NH: Boynton/Cook.

Kirsch, G. (1992). Methodological pluralism: Epistemological issues. In G. Kirsch & P. Sullivan (Eds.), *Methods and methodology in composition research* (pp. 247–269). Carbondale: Southern Illinois University Press.

Kirsch, G. (1999). *Ethical dilemmas in feminist research: The politics of location, interpretation, and publication.* Albany: State University of New York Press.

MacNealy, M. S. (1999). *Strategies for empirical research in writing.* Boston: Allyn & Bacon.

Mosenthal, P., Tamor, L., & Walmsley, S. (1983). *Research on writing: Principles and methods.* New York: Longman.

Murphy, C. (1991). Writing centers in context: Responding to current educational theory. In R. Wallace & J. Simpson (Eds.), *The Writing Center: New Directions* (pp. 276–88). New York: Garland.

Murphy, C. (1994). The writing center and social constructionist theory. In J. Mullin & R. Wallace (Eds.), *Intersections: Theory-practice in the writing center* (pp. 25-38). Urbana, IL: NCTE.

Murphy, C., & Law, J. (1995). Introduction. In C. Murphy & J. Law (Eds.), *Landmark essays on writing centers* (pp. xi-xv). Davis, CA: Hermagoras.

North, S. M. (1984a). The idea of a writing center. *College English, 46*(5), 433–46.

North, S. M. (1984b). Writing center research: Testing our assumptions. In G.A. Olson (Ed.), *Writing centers: Theory and administration* (pp. 24-35). Urbana, IL: NCTE.

North, S. M. (1987). *The making of knowledge in composition: Portrait of an emerging field.* Upper Monclair, NJ: Boynton/Cook.

Nystrand, M., Greene, S., & Wiemelt, J. (1993). Where did composition studies come from? *Written Communication, 10*(3), 267–333.

Olson, G. (1995). Theory and the rhetoric of assertion. *Composition Forum, 6*(2), 53–61.

Reigstad, T. & McAndrew, D. (1984). *Training tutors for writing conferences.* Urbana, IL: ERIC and NCTE.

Runciman, L. (1990). Defining ourselves: Do we really want to use the word *tutor*? *The Writing Center Journal, 11*(1), 27–34.

Trimbur, J. (1987). Peer tutoring: A contradiction in terms? *The Writing Center Journal, 7*(2), 21–29.

Warnock, T., & Warnock, J. (1984). Liberatory writing centers: Restoring authority to writers. In G.A. Olson (Ed.), *Writing centers: Theory and administration* (pp. 16–23). Urbana, IL: NCTE.

Welch, N. (1997). *Getting restless: Rethinking revision in writing instruction.* Portsmouth, NH: Boynton/Cook, Heinemann.

Welch, N. (1999). Playing with reality: Writing centers after the mirror stage. *College Composition and Communication, 51*(1), 51.

Woolbright, M. (1992). The politics of tutoring: Feminism within the patriarchy. *The Writing Center Journal, 13*(1), 16–30.

I

*Writing Centers as Sites
of Self-Reflective Inquiry*

Chapter 1

The Call to Research:
Early Representations
of Writing Center Research

Alice Gillam
University of Wisconsin–Milwaukee

In his introduction to *Writing Centers: Theory and Administration*, arguably the first collection of essays devoted to writing center research and scholarship, Thom Hawkins (1984) predicts a bright future for writing center research, given its "superb position to make discoveries about language development and composition," and its "fertile ground for study" (xiv). Approximately 13 years later, Christina Murphy (1997), one of the leading writing center scholars during the intervening years, pronounced this promise unfulfilled and lamented the "absolute bankruptcy of writing center scholarship at the moment" in her remarks at the Third Annual Conference of the National Writing Center Association. Whether one disagrees or agrees with Murphy's assessment, one must admit she raised unsettling and important questions for the writing center community. How do we account for her and others' disillusionment with the state of writing center scholarship? What counts as "good" or worthwhile research and by what criteria do we make such judgments? What role has research played in defining our professional identity? Whose interests are served? Although it is beyond the scope of this chapter to address all of these questions, I aim to begin a much-needed conversation about writing center research by investigating writing center talk about research for what it reveals about our conceptualizations of research. Specifically, I analyze early essays that focus on the subject of writing center research to determine their ways of representing the writing center as a site for research, the exigencies and agendas for writing center research, the activity of research itself, and writing center professionals as researchers.

Surprisingly, since this handful of early essays, there have been few essays devoted to writing center research qua research, and I believe there are several possible reasons for this scarcity of explicit talk about research. For one thing, the oppositional topoi of great promise/failed promise suggested by Hawkins' and Murphy's comments have dominated our talk about research, discouraging close analysis of the possibilities and limitations of writing center research. For another, we have depended on the larger field of composition studies for our research paradigms, epistemology, and hierarchy of values although this dependence is often unacknowledged and rarely considered critically. By and large, writing center research has defined its primary objects of study—its site and its practice[1]—as well as its research methods—empirical, ethnographic, theoretical, and practitioner inquiry—alternately in terms of its congruence with or difference from the primary objects of study and methods in composition studies. Finally, and perhaps most importantly, the material circumstances of many writing center directors and the diverse disciplinary backgrounds we bring to writing center work have militated against a sustained conversation about epistemology, methodology, and hermeneutics, although, to be sure, there has been extended debate about theory versus practice in terms of the nature of knowledge most important to the writing center community. What has been missing, however, are discussion and assessment of various methodologies for their appropriateness as well as debate about standards for judging the quality or value of various kinds of writing center research. Critiques like Murphy's suggest that this situation may be changing, but so far such critiques have done little to invite conversation and debate about what research and scholarship might and ought to be. I do not mean to suggest that community agreement is possible or even desirable; I do mean to suggest that we would all benefit from discussion, debate, and constructive criticism. Issues would be open for discussion; options for research and the advantages and disadvantages of various forms of research would be available to novice researchers. Clearly, such discussion and debate is necessary for the growth and health of the writing center as a research community, and this book is a step in that direction.

Whatever the cause for the paucity of published talk about writing center research, the literature that does exist tends to fall into three categories: the

---

[1] Beth Boquet (1999) in "'Our Little Secret'" points out that writing center identity has often been represented in terms of its unique method and unique site (465). Thus, it is not surprising that calls for writing center research have also focused on these aspects of writing center work.

call to research, the survey or overview of research, and the critique, that is, in its own way, a call to research differently. In this chapter, I focus on early calls for research, arguing that these groundbreaking essays offer a useful perspective for interpreting recent critiques. By analyzing these essays rhetorically and symptomatically, I hope to illuminate unspoken assumptions, contradictions, and unresolved (and perhaps unresolvable) dilemmas that continue to influence writing center inquiry in acknowledged and unacknowledged ways.

In a book that foregrounds reflective research, I would be remiss not to identify my own research method.[2] I classify my primary interpretive method as rhetorical criticism, a not uncommon mode of scholarship in writing center studies, although it is not often labeled as such. Peter Carino's (1992) "What Do We Talk About When We Talk About Our Metaphors," and indeed, his essay in this collection, as well as Thomas Hemmeter's (1990) "The 'Smack' of Difference," are examples that come readily to mind. Critical methods, originally associated for most of us with literary criticism, are simply ways of reading, theoretical frameworks or lenses for interpreting texts or phenomena. Rhetorical criticism, although variously defined, is analysis and interpretation of how symbolic acts, usually discursive acts, work rhetorically, that is, work to influence or construct realities for audiences (Foss, 1989). Although rhetorical criticism takes many forms, it often focuses on figures and tropes, style, commonplaces, argumentative strategies, and/or cultural and rhetorical contexts. In my reading of early essays about research, for example, I discuss clusters of metaphors—spatial, human growth, and scientific—that are used to represent writing center research[3] as well as the relationship between style and purpose, and claims and warrants.

I also describe my method as symptomatic in that I interpret these texts for what is not said as well as what is. As Kathleen McCormick, Gary Waller, and Linda Flower (1987) explain, symptomatic reading involves looking "for 'symptoms' of underlying ideology in the text" (47), "tensions or contradictions in the social formation within which the text was produced and which are then reproduced, often unconsciously within the text" (McCormick, 1994, 54). In reading these texts symptomatically, I do not mean to suggest that the authors of the texts under scrutiny should have known what they could not possibly have known at the time or that they should have been in more complete control of their text's potential meanings

---

[2]In *Feminism and Methodology*, Sandra Harding (1987) points out that the term *method* is often used to refer to three separate but interconnected aspects of research, that she delineated as method, methodology, and epistemology. *Method*, she goes on to explain, "is a technique for (or way of proceeding in) gathering evidence"; *methodology*, "a theory and analysis of how research does or should proceed"; and *epistemology*, "a theory of knowledge" (2–3).

[3]Lakoff and Johnson (1980) discuss the ways in which "[o]ur ordinary conceptual system, in terms of that we both think and act, is fundamentally metaphorical in nature" (3).

and ideological implications. Indeed, the theoretical frameworks that engendered symptomatic reading—poststructuralism, psychoanalytical theory, and postmodernism—deny the possibility of such authorial control and view the meanings of all texts as multiple, contradictory, ideological, and finally indeterminate. Additionally, I see in these texts many of the tropes, commonplaces, and assumptions I have used in my own work on writing centers—the spatial metaphors, the optimism about the writing center as a location for research, and the desire for generalizable truths. As interpretive acts, both rhetorical and symptomatic readings are shaped, and inevitably limited, by the interpreter's perspective, knowledge, ideological biases, and experience, and thus are always open to dispute and competing interpretations.

Most early essays about writing center research are overt or covert "calls to research" that exhort writing center practitioners to engage in research for one of three reasons: to legitimate writing center work through the production of scholarship and research, to understand and improve writing center practice, and to prove the writing center's value to local institutions. Although all three exigencies receive mention and are represented as essential to writing center growth and survival, there is a clear hierarchy of values in that, not surprisingly, the first exigence is viewed as most compelling. The strongest calls in rhetorical terms are those that urge writing center professionals to conduct research that will prove the intellectual worth of writing center work in the eyes of others. In short, these early calls send the sometimes subtle, sometimes not so subtle, message that the research that counts most in our developing field is either that which contributes to larger domains of inquiry, specifically to composition studies, or that which resembles the scholarship in this field enough to garner respect.

THE WRITING CENTER AS FRONTIER
AND AS ADOLESCENT

In their preface to the inaugural issue of the *Writing Center Journal*, Lil Brannon and Steve North (1980) invoke both spatial and human growth metaphors, specifically the tropes of *frontier* and *adolescence,* to justify yet "another journal in the teaching of writing" (1). This journal, they argue, will act as an "outward sign of a growing professional legitimacy" (1), specifically by establishing scholarly legitimacy in the eyes of the larger field of composition and political legitimacy in the eyes of the academic establishment. Declaring the writing center "the absolute frontier of our discipline," Brannon and North base their claim for scholarly legitimacy on the writing center's potential as a site for "great new discoveries" about the two "seminal ideas" that define composition as a discipline: "the student-centered curriculum" and "concern for composing as a process" (1). What makes the writing center a frontier, in other words, is the practice native to this environment and the opportunity this practice offers to observe writers' processes more fully and naturalistically. Importantly, this frontier status is geographically determined by the writing center's relationship to the larger field (another spatial metaphor) of composition. On the one hand, this relationship is represented in terms of similarity: Student- and process-centered instruction are central to both writing center and composition studies. Furthermore, writing center professionals are assumed to be members of the composition community: "As scholars, as teachers, and researchers *in composition*," we recognize how writing center teaching contributes to *"our discipline* [my emphases]" (1). On the other hand, the relationship is represented in terms of difference: These seminal ideas "operate most freely" in the writing center which can provide "opportunities for teaching and research that classrooms simply cannot" (1).

As Nedra Reynolds (1998) reminds us in her essay "Composition's Imagined Geographies," writing center scholars are hardly the first to use the frontier metaphor. Indeed, this metaphor is commonplace in composition discourse and has often served as a way of establishing disciplinary status: "The frontier metaphor endures because composition's professional development was dependent on sounding 'new,' bold, untamed, and exciting" (24). In other words, to the extent a new field makes a bid for disciplinary status, it must do so in terms of the "new" knowledge it offers, resulting in what Laura Micciche (1999) labels the "politics of difference." Brannon and North deploy the frontier metaphor not to establish separate disciplinary status but instead to stake a territorial claim within the larger field of composition studies. The writing center is figured as "bright with promise" if explored and mined for the new knowledge it can contribute to the larger domain of composition, but its future is "full of deadly threats" if left unexplored and unannexed. Thus, the frontier metaphor simultaneously connects writing center research with composition's "pioneering" efforts to investigate writing processes and pedagogies while at the same time differentiating writing center research as located in a distinct, further frontier.

The second type of metaphor deployed by Brannon and North is that of human growth: "Writing centers are at crucial junctures in both their political and scholarly growth. Perhaps it would be most apt metaphorically to say that in both contexts writing centers are adolescent .... If writing centers do not mature ... , they will surely, deservedly, wither away" (1–2). The figure of the writing center as adolescent entails two tropes: metonymy in that the term *writing center* stands for the whole—place, practice, writing center workers, and clients; and personification, in that the writing center is an adolescent who needs to grow up. To demonstrate its maturity, the personified writing center must produce research and scholarship that is recognized and valued by the "parent" discipline of composition without whose approval the writing center cannot hope to become a part of the academic establishment "since administrations generally follow the profession's lead" (Brannon & North, 1980, 1–2).

Whereas the role of writing center professionals is presumably to carry out this research, the figure of the writing center as agent obscures the difficulties actual human agents face in taking up this task. Furthermore, this discussion of political exigence situates writing center professionals differently in relation to the larger composition community. The "we" no longer refers to the profession at large but rather to the separate and distinct community of writing center professionals who are marginalized and misunderstood by the larger community, who are represented as disapproving "parents": "As clearly as *we* see the potential of writing centers, our profession as a whole—that slow, conservative creature—lays our past and their sins heavily on us. In their eyes, writing centers are still correction places ... the last bastions of bonehead English" (Brannon & North, 1980, 1). To correct this misunderstanding, Brannon and North call for three kinds of publication submissions, the first two directed toward the goal of scholarly and professional legitimacy, the latter toward the production of local, insider knowledge: 1) research that is "primarily theoretical, that explore[s] or explain[s] the *whys* of writing center instruction"; 2) "articles that connect theory with practice, that take the findings of research (in composition and related fields) and put it to work in writing centers"; and 3) "essays that draw on experience in writing center teaching and administration to offer insights and advice" to writing center insiders (2–3). Without the first two kinds of scholarship, there will be no parental approval, and without parental approval, there will be no future or, at least, not any future worth having. Not surprisingly, there is a hint of adolescent rebellion in a parenthetical aside. Although "we" who are defined as adolescents may have no choice in doing whatever is necessary to become a part of the academic establishment, we may, perhaps, "maintain [our] anti-establishment posture" (2).

Here, again, Reynolds' (1998) analysis of composition's use of spatial metaphors is instructive in considering the implications of the combined tropes of *frontier* and *adolescent*. Spatial metaphors, Reynolds explains, obscure "how spaces and places are socially produced through discourse" and how these constructed spaces connect to material reality (13). In particular, this early figuration of the writing center as a new frontier for composition research acknowledges only through a parenthetical aside the politics of defining research in terms set by the academic establishment. Similarly, the figuration of the writing center as an adolescent in need of the composition parent's approval constrains both the writing center's research agenda and menu of possible methodologies because both what and how inquiries are carried out will determine whether or not they count as legitimate. Furthermore, optimistic calls to explore the writing center frontier ignore the material constraints that prevented many early writing center professionals from engaging in research.

In their brief essay, Brannon and North introduce two types of metaphors that appear and reappear in discussions of writing center research—spatial metaphors that figure the writing center as an ideal location or site for research, and human growth metaphors that figure the writing center at some stage of human development in terms of its identity as a research community. Only with the production of a certain kind of knowledge, argue Brannon and North, will the writing center community attain "adult" professional status. Additionally, this essay's tone as well as its message conveys a sense of urgency. Research is necessary not only to establish the academic credibility of writing center work, but also to ensure its survival. This urgent tone is communicated through use of the superlative in characterizing writing center work—"writing center teaching is the *absolute* frontier of our discipline"—and hyperbolic, melodramatic claims—"while the future is *bright with promise,* it is full of *deadly threats* as well [my emphases]" (Brannon & North, 1980, 1–2). Perhaps most importantly, this early essay raises questions that remain subjects of debate within the writing center community. How does research figure into the writing center professional's work and identity? Do writing center professionals identify primarily as members of the larger discipline of composition, or as members of the "subdisciplinary" community of the writing center? What is (or ought to be) the relationship of writing center research and composition research? To what extent can or does scholarly research establish writing centers as part of the academic establishment? What are the costs to the students we serve, to the center's mission, and/or to individual careers of becoming a part of the academic establishment?

Both spatial and human growth metaphors also appear in Aviva Freedman's (1981) "Research and the Writing Center" in *New Directions for College Learning Assistance*, albeit in somewhat different form than is found in Brannon and North's (1980) work. Like Brannon and North, Freedman defines writing center research in terms of its relationship to composition research: "The emergence of writing centers is particularly congruent with the new thrust in research and theory [in the discipline of composition], for the structure of writing centers encourages intervention in the writing process, especially at those stages inaccessible to traditional composition teaching" (83). As the title suggests, the article's purpose is to bring composition research to the writing center. Research is represented as occurring outside writing centers; it is something that needs to be "added" to the writing center, which is represented as an ideal site for testing the insights discovered by composition researchers and investigating questions set by composition's research agenda. Perhaps for this reason, Freedman's tone and style is decidedly less urgent and more matter of fact. In the last paragraph, writing center professionals are "encouraged" to take advantage of the opportunities their work provides for research on composing, but not implored as they are in Brannon and North (1980) nor threatened with dire consequences should they not take up these opportunities.

Not surprisingly, Freedman regards writing center practitioners primarily as consumers of research who "have much to gain from the new knowledge offered by scholars and researchers concerning the nature of the composing process" (83). For Freedman, the writing center's role in research is as an "ideal locatio[n]" for carrying out composition's research agenda, which is the investigation of writers' processes (83). Research conducted in writing centers can assist composition in "mapping the terrain [of writers' processes]," specifically those areas of the terrain that are "inaccessible" to composition researchers studying writers' processes in classroom sites. Acting in a distaff role, writing center researchers can help composition mature from its "infancy" as a research community and put together the "fragmented" pieces of research to date into a comprehensive whole (83–84). Both Freedman's tropes for composition research and for the role of writing centers in that "search" are telling. The metaphor of growth, for example, suggests that the current state of incomplete knowledge is a natural and temporary stage in the inevitable organic development toward "mature" knowledge. The metaphors of "mapping" and "terrain" suggest that the knowledge composition research seeks about the learning and teaching of writing exists as a fixed, bounded reality "out there," waiting to be fully discovered and charted. Similarly, the metaphor of "fragments" eventually being put together as a whole like pieces of a jigsaw puzzle suggests that research can eventually create a complete "picture," a stable, preexisting and knowable "whole" truth.

Such conceptualizations of composition research lead Freedman to imagine the writing center in geographical or spatial terms as a newly discovered, yet-to-be-explored region or part of the terrain, a newly found piece of the puzzle. Furthermore, by figuring the writing center's research role as one of "location" or "site," Freedman reiterates the metonymy employed by Brannon and North, subsuming all writing center activities and actors into a single object or territory to be investigated, eliding the potential role of writing center professionals as agents of knowledge production. Although she mentions in conclusion some recent promising research by writing center practitioners, her last sentence reinscribes writing center practitioners in a passive role: "We must work more closely with our colleagues in research, who offer us, perhaps, only hints and suggestions now, but who will one day be able *to provide us* [my emphasis] with the comprehensive understanding essential to a sound pedagogy" (91).

Several similarities and differences between the call to research by Brannon and North and the call to research by Freedman are worth mentioning. Whereas both essays use spatial metaphors to foreground the writing center's promise as a research site, Brannon and North use the frontier metaphor for hortatory purposes, to entice writing center professionals into research and publication. By contrast, Freedman uses spatial metaphors to suggest a positivistic epistemology in that new knowledge, like geographic territory, is out there waiting to be discovered. For Freedman, it is only a matter of time until the territory is mapped, the puzzle solved; thus, the trajectory of research is imagined as a process of natural development toward definitive knowledge. Yet another difference between the two essays is their deployment of the human growth metaphor. Brannon and North represent composition as the parent in relation to the adolescent writing center, whereas Freedman represents composition as still in its "infancy" and in need of maturation. The latter figuration more clearly subordinates the writing center's research agenda and writing center researchers to composition's research agenda and researchers than does that suggested by Brannon and North.

One other early essay that makes use of the human growth metaphor and passing use of a geographical metaphor—the writing center as "fertile ground" (xiv)—is Thom Hawkins' (1984) aforementioned introduction to Olson's *Writing Centers: Theory and Administration*. Picking up on Olson's suggestion in the preface that "the writing center's period of chaotic adolescence is nearly over," Hawkins attributes these "growing pains" to larger forces, to "a general state of flux and tension in the humanities, a condition caused by dropping enrollments and a changing student body" (xi). In a sense, these forces are represented as having given birth to the "new" writing center: "Writing centers are coming of age ... because they make room, provide space and time, for students to talk about ideas, to explore meaning, and to freely engage in the trial and error of putting their thoughts into writing" (xi). In other words, writing centers are figured less as the offspring of composition studies and more as a product of larger movements—"the search for new vitality in the humanities" (xi). Consequently, the metonymized and personified writing center is represented more as partner, a status equal within the larger communities of composition, the humanities, and the academy generally:

> As researchers and scholars are redefining what it means to write, so too are writing centers helping to redefine what it means to teach writing.... In tandem with the new theories of composition that emphasize process, the teaching practices of writing centers are influencing the way writing is taught in the classroom.... Writing centers are one of the chief agents of this movement toward individualization and collaborative learning, there has been no extensive documentation of their impact. (Hawkins, 1984, xii)

In Hawkins' view, the writing center is a key player, beholden to no one, and he calls for research and theoretical inquiry in order to "enlarge [the writing center's] sphere of influence" and to control better the direction of its own growth. However, this sense of equality is accompanied by a sense of suspicion, a wariness about identifying with the academic establishment: "[T]his liberatory function of writing centers may best be carried out if they remain on the sidelines and avoid being swallowed up by the larger academic units" (xiv). Later, Hawkins refers to the "double-bind" faced by writing center professionals in trying to conduct research while at the same time serving students, but the more paralyzing double-bind is the one just suggested: How can the writing center enlarge its sphere of influence and achieve power in the academy and yet "remain on the sidelines," unbesmirched by the politics involved in becoming a player within the academic scene?

Another problem with this albeit more empowered and independent representation of the writing center is the oddly disembodied emphasis on the writing center as distinctive site and practice. It is as though this is a naturally occurring environment and practice, something that took root and grew without the intentional, fully conscious agency of the native inhabitants, that is, writing center professionals. As Hawkins (1984) puts it, "Writing center professionals themselves suffer from a knowledge gap ... often their practice outstrips their theoretical grasp" (xii). Represented as naive but intuitively wise, writing center locals, according to Hawkins, are "daily discover[ing] new elements in students' writing processes ... [but] they often cannot see the forest for the trees" (xiii). The call, then, to writing center professionals is to replace their primitive ways of knowing through "conjecture and experimentation" and work toward more "solid understanding": "If they are to reach a productive and long-lasting maturity, they must do more than patch together fragments of successful practices" (xiii). Belatedly, that is, in the last paragraph, Hawkins acknowledges "the double-bind" of writing center professionals who wish to contribute "beyond their local realm" through research and scholarship but whose obligations to students and lack of institutional support make this difficult. Although Hawkins urges harried writing center professionals to fight for the released time to write and publish, he also suggests that faculty from other departments could be profitably lured to the writing center's "fertile ground for study" (xiv).

Hawkins' call is offered in an enthusiastic though modulated tone, which is sometimes laced with light humor. Although writing center professionals are encouraged to take advantage of their unique opportunities for investigating "this movement [in higher education] toward individualization and collaborative learning," they are represented as "one of the chief agents," but not as the *only* agents of such pedagogical innovations, thus making the call to research compelling but not a singular responsibility nor one on which the continued existence of the writing center depends (xii). Furthermore, the failure of compositionists to understand and appreciate "the way writing centers have shaped classroom teaching" is characterized not in strident terms but through a humorous, somewhat oxymoronic understatement as an "abundance of ignorance" (xii). Similarly, rather than castigating writing center professionals for their "knowledge gap," Hawkins self-consciously recasts Steve North's (1984b) "scathing" suggestion that *"we don't know what we are doing"* (Hawkins' emphasis) into "less incriminating" terms: "Much more is going on in writing centers than meets the eye" (xii). In short, Hawkins exhorts by encouraging and cajoling, by representing research possibilities as "tantalizing invitation[s] to further speculation" (xiii).

Finally, two related points about the nature of the knowledge to be discovered in the writing center deserve note. On the one hand, Hawkins suggests that the knowledge to be discovered is theoretical principles, that lie "behind" writing center work (xii). Because the writing centers' chief practices, individualized and collaborative learning, seem to work, there must be discoverable principles that can explain why they work. On the other hand, Hawkins declares writing centers to be outside of traditional disciplines and thus to have no "canon of knowledge" (xiii). Although Hawkins sees this adisciplinary/transdisciplinary/postdisciplinary status to be an advantage that encourages resourcefulness, it obviously also perpetuates the very problem he identifies earlier, that is, a focus on discrete, concrete practices. Without the methodologies for pursuing the questions "that cry for further investigation" nor theoretical frameworks for interpreting and explaining practical experience that disciplinary discourse communities provide, it is difficult to see the forest for the trees.

THE WRITING CENTER
AS LABORATORY OR TESTING GROUND

A different type of spatial metaphor, coupled with scientific metaphors, appears in two other early essays about research, Harvey Kail and Kay Allen's (1982) "Conducting Research in the Writing Lab," that appeared in *Tutoring Writing: A Sourcebook for Writing Labs*, and Stephen North's (1984b) "Writing Center Research: Testing Our Assumptions," that appeared in *Writing Centers: Theory and Administration*. These essays, like those that deploy the frontier metaphor, see the writing center as a site for a heretofore-unexamined practice, the one-to-one writing tutorial, which merits investigation. However, here the act of research is figured as scientific "testing" rather than as mapping "virgin" territory.[4] Thus, these two articles prefer "scientific" to geographic metaphors in their representations of research aims and methods.

On first glance, Kail and Allen's tempered call for research appears to conceptualize writing center research in entirely different terms than do the calls of authors who represent the writing center as frontier and adolescent, and to be sure Kail and Allen's conceptualizations do differ from the preceding ones in important ways. For one thing, Kail and Allen regard writing center professionals as potential initiators of research as

---

[4]North (1984b) does make one reference to the frontier metaphor when he refers to early "reflections on experience" as the work of "pioneers" (26).

signaled by their title, use of direct address, and pragmatic, "how-to" recommendations. At the same time, Kail and Allen understand writing center professionals to be practitioners first, making research difficult given the multiple and competing demands on their time. The purpose of Kail and Allen's article, then, is to persuade center colleagues to conduct research and to advise them in how to do so in ways that conflict minimally with their primary commitments to practice. Indeed, Kail and Allen represent research as closely related to and growing out of practice: "First of all, a research project can improve your teaching.... By carefully and objectively putting your teaching techniques to the test, you will learn a great deal, not only about those particular techniques, but about the assumptions underlying your pedagogical approach" (233).

Kail and Allen go on to assure readers that research can be conducted without interfering with or compromising practice if one keeps in mind "integration" and "simplicity," if one chooses "a research method that will fit in with what you already do, a research design that will tie in with normal teaching procedures" (234). Advised toward "simple," "exploratory" methodologies like case study and survey and against projects calling for "sophisticated statistical analy[ses]," writing center practitioners are, with no condescension intended, regarded as neophyte, part-time researchers best suited to simple, manageable projects—"lite" (my term) research (234). Appropriately, the tone is reassuring, matter of fact, and low key; after all, Kail and Allen's purpose is to persuade writing center professionals that research is within their grasp and not impossibly time-consuming nor intimidatingly complicated.

A further point worth mentioning about Kail and Allen's discussion of writer center professionals as potential researchers is their expectation that writing center researchers be personally disinterested, motivated only by the benefits such work will bring to the center and not by the desire for individual professional credit or recognition. Indeed, to ensure such "pure" motives, Kail and Allen recommend that all research be collaborative: "All staff members can and should participate; the research project must belong to the lab, not to certain individuals working there" (234). In short, Kail and Allen, although representing writing center professionals as researchers, also send conflicting messages about the status of writing center researchers and set up an ideal of the "selfless" researcher, an ideal that will be a source of controversy as the increasing professional status of writing center faculty pressures them to produce research that they, rather than the writing center, can "own."

Another notable difference between Kail and Allen's discussion of writing center research and the preceding discussions is Kail and Allen's notion of the purpose and agenda for writing center research. For Kail and Allen, the exigence for writing center research arises not out of a need for outside professional legitimacy, but instead out of needs in the center to test and improve its own teaching practices, to conduct ongoing staff development, and to educate university administrators. In regard to the latter purpose, Kail and Allen mention administrator demands to produce quantitative evidence of writing center effectiveness with little editorial comment: "Like it or not, administrators need numbers" (233). In later talk about writing center research, this externally imposed exigence for research is often regarded as sinister, as requiring us to engage in what I've come to call "alienated" research, which offers the appearance of results in terms administrators understand and value, all the time masking the reality that "real" results cannot be represented in those terms. Here, however, Kail and Allen present this requirement as benign and as one that can easily be appropriated by writing center practitioners as an occasion to enlighten "unaware" administrators (233).

Yet despite the differences among the essays mentioned so far, there are certain shared themes. All four articles, for example, assume that research will uncover the truth regarding writers' processes and better tutorial practices. Furthermore, all of these authors make a distinction between systematic and intentional inquiry and informal reflections on practice, what Stephen North later called practitioner "lore." Finally, although these authors cite differing exigencies for writing center research, they all assume that the ultimate goal of writing center research is to enable better or more effective intervention in writers' processes, that, of course, is the goal that has dominated composition research.

Stephen North's (1984b) "Writing Center Research: Testing Our Assumptions" provides a fitting culmination to this series of early calls in that it alternates between pragmatic advice found in some of the early calls and the urgent hortatory tone found in other early calls. Furthermore, North positions his essay in relation to two of the previously mentioned essays (Freedman, 1981; Kail and Allen, 1982), thus suggesting that he sees his call as part of an emerging dialogue on writing center research and as a step toward the formation of a writing center research community. As the title suggests, North conceives of legitimate and legitimizing research in scientific terms: It is "formal" and "systematic" (25); its "basic" assumptions are empirically "testable" (30); its aim is discovery of "unified theory" (29).

Divided into five subsections—"Current Research," "Identifying Basic Assumptions," "Research on the Tutorial Relationship," "Research on the Composing Process," and "Further Assumptions and the Aims of Research"— North frames his practical, highly specific advice about what and how to research with opening and closing sections that reiterate the idea that the chief exigence for research is recognition and respect from the larger academic community, both of which he sees as imperative to writing center survival. Thus, the "scientific" stance constructed in the body of the essay is framed by an hortatory stance in which North again issues the call to research in urgent, even apocalyptic terms—research or die. The call is compelling; the time for action is limited. North begins by quoting from

Lee Odell's Braddock-award-winning essay, "Teachers of Composition and Needed Research in Discourse Theory," in which Odell, a leader in the field of composition studies, claims that writing teachers have a dual obligation to both teach well and investigate the discourse theory that guides their teaching (24). Extending this challenge to writing center professionals, North ups the ante: "The burden of responsibility on writing center people is perhaps even greater" not only to test our theories about discourse but also to test our practice, "*how* we teach writing" (24). North goes on to state bluntly the warrant for this greater burden: "We are considered by our contemporaries to be at best unconventional and at worst 'ad hoc' and essentially futile" (24). Although we may have been excused for our failure heretofore to "test" our practices and assumptions, given our rapid and "chaotic" growth, the time has come, North asserts, to prove our legitimacy or face probable elimination: "By 1995 we will either have some answers [to questions about our practice and assumptions]— or we won't be around to need them" (33). From this perspective in 1984, North had no way of knowing that authoritative answers based on positivistic research would be eschewed by 1995 and that writing center practice and scholarship would be flourishing despite his dire predictions.

Save for an occasional exclamatory phrase emphasized through italics—"*there is not a single published study of what happens in writing center tutorials*" (28)— North's tone in the body of the essay reflects the qualities he calls for in research: "formal" and "systematic" (25). Current forms of research—"reflections on experience," "speculation," and "surveys"— are systematically categorized, assessed, and found lacking in rigor. "Important and fruitful," perhaps, in their time, these forms of research are characterized as outmoded and no longer strategically useful. The "reflections on experience" may have been "uplifting" and encouraging to newcomers but are "no longer necessary"; the "bare-bones" surveys may have offered "pioneering" writing center folks a "sense of group identity" and administrators quantified evidence of the writing center's services, but these questionnaires that "count" and "enumerate" are no longer required to "conjure up images of what writing centers are"; even theoretical speculations such as those by Kenneth Bruffee, although still necessary for the "new intellectual blood" they bring to our work, are deemed of secondary importance in the new research paradigm that North calls for in this essay (1984b, 25–27).

If the informal and unsystematic methods used in forms of research previously described are inadequate to the challenge of the day, so too have been the prior calls to research, like those of Freedman and Kail and Allen, that fail to identify the issues in need of inquiry and to lay the "groundwork for what might be called a research paradigm" (North, 1984b, 27). Although North attempts to soft-pedal his criticism of Kail and Allen, he refers to their essay rather condescendingly as a "levelheaded, realistic primer (in the best sense of the word) for research neophytes" (27).

Although their "bywords" for research are "simple" and "integrated," North insists that the research most needed is "neither simple" nor easily "integrated" into other daily tasks.

Specifically, North calls for research that tests "basic" assumptions. Both the terms *test* and *basic* suggest a social scientific research paradigm in that "tests" are objective, systematic, and replicable and the research grows out of "basic" questions that investigate and attempt to discover "first principles." North is explicit in his insistence that academic credibility requires identification of unifying principles that, in turn, will give the field a kind of identity that is lacking given the current hodgepodge of practices: "Facilities enlisted under the writing center-writing lab banner now include places as theoretically and functionally diverse as programmed materials-and-tapes labs; peer tutoring drop-in centers; wholesale sentence-combining labs ... and so on" (27). Dismissals of writing center work as "ad hoc" result from "the failure of writing center professionals to define clearly what they do, to offer a united theory and pedagogy they have tested themselves" (28). To remedy the situation, North goes on to provide such a definition: "All writing centers ... rest on this single theoretical foundation: that *the ideal situation* [my emphasis] for teaching and learning writing is the tutorial, the one-on-one, face-to-face interaction between a writer and a trained, experienced tutor; and that the object of this interaction is to intervene in and ultimately alter the composing process of the writer" (28). North then proceeds in the next two sections to illustrate in very specific terms two hypothetical research projects that would meet the standards he is calling for in this new research paradigm. For example, the first sample study investigates what goes on in tutorial sessions, specifically the practices of "good" tutors, by using a collection of tried-and-true methodologies drawn from such social scientific disciplines as cognitive psychology: selection of two categories of subjects (operationally defined as "good" and "not-so-good" tutors) for comparative purposes, the creation of "high-fidelity simulation problems" (or tutoring situations) for these subjects to "solve," and so on (30).

Throughout the essay, the old and new research paradigms are distinguished by a series of oppositions: The old agenda is "parochial" and local whereas the new agenda is dictated by "basic" questions that can lead toward an "united theory"; the old methods are anecdotal and informal whereas the new are formal and systematic; projects in the old paradigm are "simple" and can be integrated into the day-to-day work of writing center professionals whereas projects in the new paradigm are "complex" and "disruptive." North's faith in social scientific modes of research and his positivistic assumptions about the possibility of uncovering "universal" basic principles to guide practice are not surprising given the dominance of the social scientific paradigm in composition studies at the time. And, as North makes clear from the outset, the task or primary exigence for research is to establish the intellectual legitimacy of writing center work in the eyes of this community.[5]

FROM CALL TO CRITIQUE

Following these early calls to research, metaphoric references to the writing center as a "rich" research site became commonplace in writing center discourse, topoi, which required no explanation nor validation. Research of various sorts continued to be produced; indeed, yearly awards for outstanding scholarship began to be awarded in 1985, and anthologies of writing center essays that included what could arguably be called research increased in publication. However, there emerged no sustained scholarly conversation about research, no consensus about the writing center's research agenda, no burgeoning of the formal and systematic research called for by North. For one thing, the research paradigm in composition studies shifted in the mid-1980s from one that favored social scientific research to one that favored critical, theoretical scholarship. For another, the material conditions identified by these early calls persisted—that is, there continued to be little time, money, and institutional support for writing center research. Additionally, however, I argue that the discourse about research in these early calls has also worked against the development of a sustained conversation about research and set the stage for the critiques that emerged in the mid-1990s.

The inflated claims of difference—the writing center as the "absolute frontier" and "the ideal situation" for writing instruction—set up unrealistic expectations for what might be discovered about writers and writing instruction through writing center research. The contrary exigencies of, on the one hand, declaring independence from the composition community through research that would prove the distinctiveness of our work and, on the other hand, claiming full membership through research that the composition community would recognize as worthy, sent a mixed message about the aims and audience for writing center research. In either case, the question of whose interests are served by research was left unasked in these early calls, raising questions for many writing center professionals about the potential conflict between their goals as student-centered practitioners and their goals as institutionally recognized researchers. Finally, the optimism and energy that fueled early calls grew out of a foundational epistemology that has since been lost. And with this loss, it has been difficult not only to

---

[5]In "The Idea of a Writing Center," published in the same year, North (1984a) more emphatically and concisely defines the idea of writing center work as "to produce better writers, not better writing" (76) through "talk about writing with the writer" (80). He reissues the call to investigate this unique "idea" in forceful terms: "If the writing center is ever to prove its worth … it will have to do so by describing this talk: what characterizes it, what effects it has, how it can be enhanced" (82–83).

articulate a compelling mission for research but also to come to any consensus about what ought to count as meaningful research. If only local knowledge is possible, then of what use is this knowledge to others? If general principles that might guide practice do not exist, then how can research change or improve practice?

Critiques of writing center research that began to appear in the mid-1990s take a variety of stances in relation to the previously mentioned issues. For some, the call is to research differently; for others, the call is to cease and desist from research. Recalling the topos of selfless service invoked by Kail and Allen, Terrance Riley (1994) in the "The Unpromising Future of Writing Centers" laments the increased professional recognition that has been achieved through research and publication, and warns against continued bids for success in the academy's terms. For Riley, the very "books and dissertations on writing pedagogy" that are the sign of our academic credibility also work against our "capacity for providing an alternative to mass education" (20). "[A]s we professionalize," he argues, "less and less are we able to assert that our philosophy is liberatory and contrarian" (29). In what might be described as a prophetic call to "repent for the end is near," Riley strikes an urgent tone reminiscent of earlier essays: "We may be approaching the last time we are able to make a choice about the sort of future we want to inhabit" (20). Using imperatives, he dramatically petitions writing center professionals to forego the traditional academic reward system and instead dedicate themselves to a higher calling: "Stake your reputation on service rather than on publication" (31).

More often, however, critiques are calls to research differently. In Christina Murphy's (1997) remarks at the Third National Writing Center Conference about the "bankruptcy" of writing center research, we hear echoes of earlier themes, specifically, the complaint about writing center professionals' "parochial" perspective and dependence on the composition community for approval. What Murphy calls the "politics of justification" has led to publications in "broader" journals, publications that she believes have not served the writing center community well. More importantly, she implies that writing center researchers have aimed low in their research projects and continue to recycle old topics and questions rather than contribute to "larger intellectual conversations," a direction she clearly advocates for writing center research. Similarly, Nancy Grimm (1992) in "Contesting 'The Idea of a Writing Center': The Politics of Writing Center Research" calls for a radical rethinking of the nature and purpose of writing center research. Like Murphy, Grimm criticizes the narrow scope of current research and called for a broader, more politically defined research agenda. "Thinking of writing centers as linguistic contact zones," argues Grimm, "would politicize our research" and enable us to "open a dialogue with English departments and with the institution as a whole, to rethink the way we practice literacy, to renegotiate a relationship with teachers of writing" (6).

Such critiques offer a starting point for renewed talk about writing center research and scholarship, talk that moves discursively beyond the oppositional topoi of great promise/failed promise. Two examples are worth mention as models for this new sort of talk about research and scholarship. Rather than lambast earlier researchers for their naive belief in the possibility of a comprehensive theory that would define and explain writing center work, Peter Carino (1995) in "Theorizing in the Writing Center" carefully evaluates the contributions of the first generation of writing center researchers while at the same time pointing out the difficulties with research grounded in totalizing theories. Additionally, Carino acknowledges the many tensions entailed in this early research, with its contrary pulls to explain practice through a covering theory and at the same time use theory politically to establish writing center credibility. Carino concludes by recommending research that is more "modest" in scope, research that acknowledges its limitations and context (33).

Similarly, Lisa Ede (1996) in "Writing Centers and the Politics of Location" models talk about research and scholarship, that is circumspect and self-reflexive. In this essay, Ede responds to the theoretical speculations of the previously discussed Terrance Riley essay and Stephen North's "Revisiting 'The Idea of a Writing Center'." But what interests me is not so much what she says about Riley and North's essays but instead how she says it. Drawing on feminist theory, Ede converses with these two essays in a way that is unusual not only in writing center discourse but in scholarly discourse generally. She identifies her own biases and takes care to discuss points of agreement as well as points of disagreement with Riley and North. In short, she self-consciously works "against the grain of scholarly practices" that pretend to objectivity while creating new binaries to forward one position over another (25). Although acknowledging the need to "develop categories . . ., to argue, to take stands in scholarly discourse," she urges "more attentiveness to the rhetoric of our own [scholarly writing] practices than in the past" (25).

This book aims to take up the questions mentioned at the outset, not with the expectation of offering answers so much as with the expectation of reinvigorating and extending the conversation. Moreover, we aim to do so in ways that are attentive to our own rhetoric, and invite others to conduct and reflect on their own research and that of others.

REFERENCES

Boquet, E. (1999). "Our little secret": A history of writing centers, pre- to post-open admissions. *College Composition and Communication, 50*(3), 463–482.

Brannon, L., & North, S. (1980). From the editors. *Writing Center Journal, 1*(1), 1–3.

Carino, P. (1992). What do we talk about when we talk about our metaphors: A cultural critique of clinic, lab, and center. *The Writing Center Journal, 13*(1), 31–42.

Carino, P. (1995). Theorizing the writing center: An uneasy task. *Dialogue: A Journal for Writing Specialists, 2*(1), 23–37.

Ede, L. (1996). Writing centers and the politics of location: A response to Terrance Riley and Stephen M. North. *The Writing Center Journal, 16*(2), 111–130.

Foss, S. K. (1989). *Rhetorical criticism: Exploration and practice.* Prospect Heights, IL: Waveland.

Freedman, A. (1981). Research and the writing center. In T. Hawkins & P. Brooks (Eds.), *New directions for college learning assistance: Improving writing skills* (pp. 83–93). San Francisco: Jossey-Bass.

Grimm, N. (1992). Contesting "the idea of a writing center": The politics of writing center research. *The Writing Lab Newsletter, 17*(1), 5–6.

Harding, S. (1987). Introduction: Is there a feminist method? In S. Harding (Ed.), *Feminism and methodology* (pp. 1–14). Bloomington: Indiana University Press.

Hawkins, T. (1984). Introduction. In G.A. Olson (Ed.), *Writing centers: Theory and administration* (pp. xi–xiv). Urbana, IL: NCTE.

Hemmeter, T. (1990). The "smack of difference": The language of writing center discourse. *The Writing Center Journal, 11*(1), 35–48.

Kail, H., & Allen, K. (1982). Conducting research in the writing lab. In M. Harris (Ed.), *Tutoring writing* (pp. 233–245). Glenview, IL: Scott, Foresman.

Lakoff, G., & Johnson, M. (1980). *Metaphors we live by.* Chicago: University of Chicago Press.

McCormick, K. (1994). *The culture of reading and the teaching of English.* Manchester, England: Manchester University Press.

McCormick, K., & Waller, G. (with Flower, L.). (1987). *Reading texts: Reading, responding, and writing.* Lexington, MA: D.C. Heath.

Micciche, L. (1999). *Composition studies and the politics of difference.* Unpublished doctoral dissertation, University of Wisconsin, Milwaukee.

Murphy, C. (1997, September). Response to "Are writing centers ethical?" Unpublished remarks presented at the Third Annual Conference of the National Writing Center Association, Park City, UT.

North, S. M. (1984a). The idea of a writing center. Reprinted in S. Murphy & J. Law (Eds.). (1995). *Landmark essays on writing centers* (pp. 71–85). Davis, CA: Hermagoras.

North, S. M. (1984b). Writing center research: Testing our assumptions. In G.A. Olson (Ed)., *Writing centers: Theory and administration* (pp. 24–35). Urbana, IL: NCTE.

Reynolds, N. (1998). Composition's imagined geographies: The politics of space in the frontier, city, and cyberspace. *College Composition and Communication, 50*(1), 12–35.

Riley, T. (1994). The unpromising future of writing centers. *The Writing Center Journal, 15*(1), 20–34.

Chapter 2

Disciplinary Action: Writing Center Work and the Making of a Researcher

Elizabeth Boquet
Fairfield University

Even after 10 years—the amount of time I've spent in classrooms and writing centers—my work in one site never fails to shed light on my work in the other. This has proven true once again as I put this chapter through its final revision and, in so doing, try to address the last of the editors' concerns, a concern that asks me to establish a more explicit link between the narrative of my work with Todd (which I will recount shortly) and my subsequent decision to choose writing centers as my area of intellectual and academic inquiry.

As I have been considering this question, I have also been teaching the second half of our first-year sequence at Fairfield University, a course that, among its other tasks, is designed to introduce students to the conventions of academic research. The bulk of our research time has been spent not in the library, or with style manuals, or even with primary texts. It has been spent discussing, generating, and refining research questions. These activities have involved an inordinate number of discussions about what a research question is and what it might mean to stumble onto one or, even better, to create opportunities that make a person more likely to find one.

I had not thought very hard about why the research question was the key issue for me until I began working concurrently on these two projects—the class and this chapter. It was then that I realized that my work with Todd afforded me my first genuine research questions, questions that were not just academic calisthenics but were instead grounded in real and seemingly (even still) intractable problems. No one ever talked to me about this problem of the research question in terms that prepared me for a student like Todd—not, that is, until the students in my EN 12 class in the spring of 1999.

I met Todd in the fall of 1986. At the time, I was an undergraduate peer tutor at an open-admissions university in the South. He was a student attempting, on this his third try, to pass the first course of the university's three-tiered basic writing sequence. Three days a week we met, for a whole semester—first eagerly, sure that a semester's work in the center would leave him a much better writer, and finally dejectedly, our heads in our hands, just trying to wade through another frustrating day.

I do not offer this story because I think it is unique, but rather because I think it is common, too common. Our story, Todd's and mine, is not a success story. I spent an entire semester with him, following the dictates of the "skills" center, not working on his actual papers but instead conjugating the verb "to do" in the present tense and checking pronoun-antecedent agreement exercises and quizzing him on subordinating and coordinating conjunctions.

Todd failed the class, and I wanted to place the blame on him. I had been taught to do that, to believe that somehow he wasn't working hard enough or just wasn't "college material" or any of the other things that I, a successful student, needed to think about a student like Todd. But deep down I knew this wasn't the case. I knew how hard Todd worked. I knew how intelligently he could talk about the things he did know. And I knew that he kept coming back and coming back and coming back for more, long after I would have stopped, long after I wanted to stop for him.

It is only in retrospect that I am able to appreciate the degree to which Todd was dis/figured by institutional failure and the extent to which Todd's problems were located in him, a move which left him dis/located with respect to the university that he had hoped would position him (eventually) in some elusive "privileged" class.

Todd asked questions of me that I couldn't answer—that no one I knew could answer—about why he had so much trouble, really, learning to write, about how he might need to be taught differently, and about the ways that I had learned what I knew. Todd made me want to find out the answers to his questions, and now, still, when I write, I am largely trying to answer him. Todd made me feel, in postcolonial terms, no longer at home in my home (Adorno, quoted in Giroux, 1992, 20).

Working on my manuscript over the last 3 years has often left me feeling dis/located as well, although never (I am certain) quite as Todd experienced it. The process of reading and writing, of talking and thinking, of succeeding and failing has left me with questions of my own, questions not only about the "hows" of writing center research but also about the "whys." If you're reading this volume, you've probably already considered these questions. Maybe you already have your answers. But as leading scholars in our field have pointed out, these issues give many people pause, with good reason. The investment—financial , professional, emotional—is great; the rewards, often few.

I see this chapter as addressing several separate, but related, issues: (1) the ways that typical dissertation and manuscript problems are complicated by the status of writing center research in the field of composition studies; (2) the question of what gets defined as "theory" in writing center research; and (3) the connection of those theories to issues of practice.

THE DISSERTATION

As I draft this chapter, in the summer of 1997, my project—a book-length manuscript—is well into its fourth year. The project began in earnest in March of 1993, after I encountered tremendous difficulty compiling a comprehensive exam list focusing on writing center theory and practice. At that time, the few collections focusing specifically on writing centers were dated, and the journals geared toward writing program administrators and writing center professionals tended not to have widespread distribution. So I decided to focus my dissertation on writing centers, using Anne Ruggles Gere's (1987) *Writing Groups: History, Theory, and Implications* as a model, with the hope of condensing and disseminating the scholarship on writing center history and theory while also speculating on current trends in the field.

The cautions raised by members of my committee were numerous, and many of them were well-founded, although in retrospect I'm glad I didn't listen to them. I was warned, for example, that I would limit myself by concentrating on writing centers—that a general compositionist might well be hired to run a writing center but a writing center specialist may be passed over for general composition jobs. I was reminded that jobs in writing centers tend to be the worst of all composition jobs: temporary, underpaid, overworked, vulnerable. I was advised that my work would have limited appeal to a general audience and would therefore be difficult to publish. And, finally, I was cautioned that I would have no colleagues on my campus who really, truly understood why I do the work that I do. From what I now know firsthand about the state of the field, I would say that, for many people, these concerns were warranted.

With that said, I must now say that the appeal of doing research on writing centers is great—at least it is for me. It should be for anyone interested in the scene of literacy instruction at our universities—past, present, and future—as Nancy Grimm (1996) has pointed out in a recent issue of *College Composition and Communication* (523). The frustration that spawned my own interest—my failure to work effectively with Todd—is a common refrain in writing center literature. In my case, my search for answers led me to my doctoral program, where I discovered the work of Mike Rose, Patricia Bizzell, Shirley Brice Heath, and all the other names we've come to expect. But the "Ah-Ha!"

moment came, again while preparing for comprehensive exams, when I read Marilyn Cooper's (1991) "'We Don't Belong Here, Do We?' A Response to *Lives on the Boundary and The Violence of Literacy*." In the introduction to the article, Cooper writes: "Writing centers are, as cultural studies scholars say, a site of struggle within the institution of the university, perhaps the primary site, given the important role we have given to literacy in our society" (48). In my copy of that article, this passage is underlined, "site of struggle" is circled, and "Wow! Now there's a dissertation!!" is scrawled in the margins in my own unmistakable late-night penmanship. And there it was, an invitation for me to bring all of my research interests together—my interest in writing centers, cultural studies theory, and critical educational pedagogies and politics.

As I prepared to write my dissertation, I encountered many obstacles, some of which I have already outlined. One difficulty that I did not anticipate, however, was the level of resistance I found toward my methods of research. I discovered fairly rapidly, for example, a concern among the faculty, members both on and off my committee, about the sheer breadth of my topic. This, I recognized, was a valid consideration, but the advice I received to remedy this problem failed to satisfy me: I was not interested in studying a particular site; I was not going to construct and analyze survey responses; I did not want to do a quantitative or qualitative study of student-tutor talk or tutor-tutor talk or student-student talk. Instead, I wanted to read as much and as widely as I could on all the topics that interested me; and I wanted to think long and hard about how and where those readings complicated my lived experience in the writing center.

This makes for a huge project, I know, and perhaps I was rightfully dissuaded from taking on such a task. I believe, however, that I was discouraged from undertaking such a large project for all the wrong reasons—first because people still maintain that writing centers are institutionally specific (as are all university programs, to one extent or another) despite their long history on the national scene of literacy education and the professional organizations that exist on the local, state, regional, and national levels to support them; and next because people maintain that writing center professionals should be more concerned with the practical than the theoretical aspects of their work.

In addition to their cautions, the members of my committee also offered a great deal of support, both about the process of writing a dissertation and about the means of gathering data on my particular topic. So, in the summer of 1993, I began my research project by reading everything I could get my hands on related to writing centers. This included all the back issues of *The Writing Center Journal* and *The Writing Lab Newsletter* as well as specific pieces printed in other journals closely affiliated with writing centers, such as *Writing Program Administration, Focuses*, and *Composition Studies*. For the historical background, I hand-searched issues of *English Journal, College English*, and *College Composition and Communication* dating back to 1900, looking for any references to supplementary instruction in writing. When I would stumble on other references in the bibliographies of those works, I would try to track them down. This process was clearly not scientific. I missed some pieces, I know. But, after about 5 months of research, I had pretty much completed that leg of the work, adding in only obvious pieces related to my work—new edited collections, for example, and the continuing issues of the journals.

I remember sitting on the floor of my living room, soon after the weather started to turn cold, with piles and piles of journal articles, books, and notes all around me, wondering where I was in all of that writing. So little of what I read in the writing center literature would have allowed me to talk back to Todd, to offer him another version of what we had experienced. Returning to this place, to Todd's questions, helped me to focus time and time again on the interdependence of theory and practice in my work, on my absolute inability to separate the two.

As frustrating as that time was, I do now miss the intensity of it, and I found this period to be satisfying and edifying in countless ways. One early reader of this draft commented, "The dissertation is a scholarly apprenticeship which is necessary to go through in order to develop scholary [sic] authority, judgment, in-depth knowledge of the subject, etc." This same reader then asked me "to consider how much of [my] writing difficulty with the diss. [sic] was similar to what any dissertator faces and how much to the fact that [I was] doing research on writing centers." This has proven to be a useful, although unanswerable, frame for considering the early part of this narrative. These experiences, particularly the struggles with authority and the nature of "original" research, are familiar to most people writing dissertations in any discipline on any topic. What seems specific to our discipline is the lack of established research paradigms in a field as young and as beset with skepticism as ours is. Writers of dissertations in composition studies (including those composing dissertations on writing centers) are searching for authority in and through a field still struggling for authority and identity in its own discipline (if we assume that composition studies desires to be situated in the more general arena of English studies).

My committee, for example, was theory-cautious; therefore, problems with the definition of my study arose early on in the process. This project was clearly not quantitative, but it wasn't really qualitative either. After all, I wasn't doing a case study or an ethnography or a protocol analysis. In the end, I billed my dissertation as a qualitative study of the writing center literature. This meant, as far as I could tell, that I would look for patterns in the literature and organize my dissertation around the categories that I found. Since the work of the dissertation was largely historical, the methodology followed along the lines set out by North (1987) in his chapter on composition's historians. North's taxonomy, however—particularly his distinctions between the work of the historians, the philosophers, and the critics—was never clear to me, and I remain unsure how the methodology agreed on by my committee was different from what I originally proposed. Perhaps rather than being different, the methodology was simply more explicit.

In the end, there was far less of me in my dissertation than I would have liked. Very little but the words of others spilling onto my pages. In an early draft of the ethics chapter, for example, I made a point about the situational nature of ethics in the writing center. My director inked back, "Where is your evidence for this?" Although I considered this statement to be self-evident, he sent me back to the literature in search of support. I found that support in one of Pemberton's (1994) "Writing Center Ethics" columns: "Ethics in the writing center are complex, often relative, and always situational" (7). My point exactly. Dissertations are expected to do a certain kind of institutional work, and the role of the author in them is an odd one, an impossible one. I needed to find space for me and for my voice in and around the voices of others.

Because I couldn't locate that space in the dissertation itself, I started looking in other places. Through *The Writing Lab Newsletter*, I found WCenter (the electronic bulletin board for writing center professionals), a ready-made group of people willing to offer advice, response, or simply support on issues related to writing centers, teaching writing, and beyond. Not long after that, while I was still writing my dissertation, I accepted a full-time, tenure-track position, so I left graduate school and set out for the East Coast. These things lent authority to my writing, I believe, allowing me to argue successfully and from a position of relative strength in my dissertation for the relevance of theoretical work on writing centers. This is a battle I still find myself fighting.

THE MANUSCRIPT

The battle has since shifted venues, and I am now struggling to figure out the protocols of academic publishing, a process that began shortly after I defended my dissertation, when I minimally revised my dissertation and sent it to an appropriate press. The responses I received, even the positive ones, were discouraging. All five of the reviewers, either implicitly or explicitly, admitted to having no expertise and little knowledge of the current state of writing center scholarship. For example, one reviewer who recommended revision and resubmission offered this:

> I have to attach one important caveat to this recommendation, however: I do not know very much about the status of writing center research and theory—so I cannot adequately evaluate the author's representation of works in that field, nor can I say whether the author's treatment engages current issues and discussions. My intuitive sense is that the author does have a current and comprehensive sense of the field, and that this book would be immensely helpful and significant to the field—but I am not the best judge of that.

Another reviewer began his recommendation with the following statement:

> My one reservation about this manuscript has to do with the fact that I don't read the literature on writing centers. I am not in a position to determine whether or not this is "old hat" for anyone up on the field. With that caveat, I can say that this was informative for me as a relative outsider to this part of the composition/rhetoric/literacy field....

Both of these reviewers, despite their lack of knowledge in the area, at least went on to offer helpful suggestions for revision, comments that have proven useful as I've reconceived the manuscript. The same cannot be said for reviewer #1, who, after reading the manuscript, commented: "I'm not convinced that the topic warrants exclusive treatment in a monograph.... While the author does bring together in a single volume some important research on writing centers. . ., it's difficult to see how her interests and ideas speak to the larger issues in the composition field." I am left to wonder, of course, what such "larger issues" might be. The history of writing instruction in our colleges? No, that was covered. The ethics and the politics of literacy education? No, couldn't be that. The use of computers in writing instruction? Funding sources? Collaboration? Assessment? No. No. No. No.

Lest this critique be passed off as the rantings of a woman scorned, let me add that ultimately the reviewers did recommend that I revise and resubmit my manuscript. The series editor offered congratulations, but I wasn't so sure about that. I eventually pulled the manuscript from consideration. Looking back at these comments nearly 2 years later, I am still struck by the unapologetic manner in that the reviewers' ignorance somehow became my problem, by the way in that a "well-informed, comprehensive, thoughtful, thorough" manuscript on writing centers still isn't seen as speaking to the "larger issues" in our field. We have to do a better job than that.

At any rate, coming from one of the top presses in our field, these comments offered me little hope. Maybe I was just tired—I don't know—but after sending letters of inquiry to several other presses, none of whom were interested in even seeing a draft, I put the work aside and began to focus on other things.

For 6 months, I didn't touch that manuscript. In fact, I rarely thought about it. I read books and articles because I wanted to, not because I felt they might shed some light on my topic. I went to conference sessions simply because they looked interesting.

Eventually, I found my way back into my work, but I wasn't the same person, and I didn't do it alone. In fact, I don't think I would have done it alone. If it had been up to me, I might never have returned to that writing. During that 6 month period, other people kept my work alive—people like Paula Gillespie, Mickey Harris, Christina Murphy, Al DeCiccio, Meg Carroll, and Dave Healy—who were continually referring questions about the history and politics of writing centers to me, who approached me about writing with them, about reviewing books, about giving conference presentations or serving on committees. And it was because of Neal Lerner, who wanted a copy of my dissertation, that I dusted it off and brought it to CCCC in Milwaukee, where, through a stroke of good fortune (and a common table at the hotel bar), I was able to share my work with Ira Shor. Ira went through that draft in a painstaking manner, and his questions are ultimately the ones that sent me back to try to write again.

Such a roll call in a chapter like this one may seem out of place, and I considered not putting it in at all. To leave it out by design, however, excludes what was for me an important part of coming to see this as a project other than the dissertation, as a work that spoke to other people rather than simply to my own curiosity or only to the members of my dissertation committee. I certainly had hoped that my dissertation would serve such a function, but in the end I don't think it did.

The interest that people have taken in this research project, and by extension in my professional development, is in no way a small thing to me. In general, academics don't do a very good job of talking about the process of publication in the same painstaking detail that we seem able to talk about the content of that publication. It seems important, therefore, to counteract what I consider to be the prevailing wisdom that research projects proceed relatively uninterrupted and to spend some time acknowledging the extent to which I needed that time and those people to turn my project into something other than the thing that it already was. And I want to underscore to those of us in the profession the absolute necessity of taking an interest in work other than our own, for purposes other than our own.

On my return from CCCC '96, I began to think about writing again, wondering how and where to begin. My colleague Geoff Sanborn happened to be finishing a revision of his dissertation-turned-manuscript just as I was beginning mine, so I asked him how he did it—how in the world he set about revising such a thing. He replied, in his self-effacing manner, "I basically just started over."

"You started over?!" I responded, incredulously.

"Basically," and he laughed.

Oh my God.

So I started over.

I did not, however, begin again unadvisedly. I made one frustrating attempt after another to revise the existing manuscript until I felt I had exhausted all of my options. Geoff's advice, I had to admit, echoed the comments of several publishers and reviewers. One series editor, who offered to take a look at the work, did so with this caveat:

> You should know. . .that we seldom take dissertations ... Most dissertations are written to a specific committee rather than an audience of fellow compositionists. Most engage in a lot of summary and citation and often do

not further the author's arguments in important and compelling ways. Because you have revised the dissertation, I think it is worth a serious look, but it is never easy to move from one mode of writing to the other.

Two reviewers from another series spoke more specifically about this issue as it related to my manuscript. The first one wrote, "The author has done a good job of reviewing previous research, but unfortunately that is the problem with this manuscript. It is mostly a literature review. The author relies too heavily on the work of others throughout." Another reviewer agreed and began to cite specific passages where I was doing this before giving up and claiming that "the problem is so fundamental that it will require a rethinking of the entire ms [sic] and reworking of most of the prose."

So it was back to the drawing board for me.

To do this, I took seriously the reviewers' comments about the lack of a consistent voice and the shifts in points of view. One reviewer in particular helped me to remember the concessions that I made for the dissertation. This reviewer wrote:

> I find the use of "theoretical" rather unhelpful—what is a "theoretical examination"? why [sic] not just an examination that includes history, theoretical perspectives, and implications? I am also not sure what it means, from an historians [sic] perspective, to "rely on the words of professionals" (4) if at the same time this is going to be anything like a critical assessment, or how if one is drawing on cultural studies, one can assert that this will be a "fair and accurate portrayal of life" in writing centers—as if one's historiography were empirically naive. Such a phrase, while having common sense meaning suggests a certain naivete about the historical/theoretical project. One might say that this manuscript operates more as a defense of writing centers—nothing wrong with such a purpose—but it is not therefore simply a snapshot of life in the Writing Center.

Reading these comments, I feel transparent, as if the reviewer saw right through what happened as I composed this work. My original intention, in many ways, was for this piece to serve as a defense of writing centers. I was encouraged, however, through the composition of the dissertation, to tone down the overt political agenda forwarded by cultural studies theorists and to keep the work more in line with the categorizations favored by more empirical researchers. The "theoretical examination" explanation emerged from discussions to that I have already alluded, conversations that raised questions about what kind of study exactly I was proposing. So the theoretical examination was not so much an answer to what the work was as a response to what it was not—not an ethnography, not a case study, not a quantitative analysis.

I tried to see the reviewers as issuing me an invitation to write the book that I had wanted to write all along. I thought about my original immersion in writing center scholarship, the reading that took up the bulk of my time with the dissertation, and realized that I would need to do the same type of work with theory and histories. I started concentrating not only on what the work said but also on how it was structured, paying particular attention to compositionists who had done similar kinds of projects, most notably Berlin, Shor, and North. I began by rereading some of the composition work that I had already read, things like *Pedagogy of the Oppressed* (Freire, 1992) and *Contending with Words* (Harkin & Schilb, 1991). I moved on to composition theory that I had not yet read but should have—Fragments of Rationality(Faigley, 1992), for example, and *Composition in the 21st Century* (Bloom, Daiker, &White, 1996). And I've been wading through (and am still wading through) the primary texts for much of the theoretical work in composition—Bakhtin's *Dialogic Imagination* (1981) and Foucault's *Discipline and Punish*—as well as theoretical work less often referenced, specifically the work of Haraway, Laclau, and Mouffe.

The resulting manuscript is, in my mind, more directed. It advocates more clearly for thinking about the writing center in very specific ways. It is written from a particular perspective. Some will no doubt argue that it is less balanced, that it has an "agenda." I prefer to think, and the reviewers I'm sure would back me up, that it is less confused.

Now, reading the manuscript, I hesitate at times to even call it the same project as my dissertation. At other times, I wonder what is really different, if demarcations between projects are ever clear, if interests don't always bleed into each other. What marks it as the same project, in my mind, is the scope of the work, particularly its dedication to examining the institutional placement of writing centers from a sociocultural perspective. What marks it as different, I think, is the integration of the theoretical foundations, which in the dissertation had been relegated primarily to the final chapter. This is a fundamental shift in the direction of the project and it marks a resolution, in my mind at least, of the issues of authority, which had proven so problematic in my dissertation.

THEORY MATTERS

I am not naive enough, however, to think that my authority to speak for and about writing center professionals is no longer under scrutiny. One of the most difficult aspects of composing this work has been my fear that many of my friends and colleagues, people whose work I respect, people who have served as my mentors and compadres, will hate my book. These suspicions were confirmed most recently by responses posted to WCenter referring to Nancy Grimm's latest work. One participant, for example, chose to respond to the following sentence in Grimm's (1996) article: "To enact a different relationship with their institutions, writing centers need a theoretically grounded understanding of their practice" (539). The response read as follows:

> This call for theory is far more complex than the single sentence quoted here, and I apologize for reducing Grimm's arguments to that. But for the sake of discussion here, let me reduce it to an oversimplified form: hey, if we have a theory, we can be like the other kids on the block. That. . .doesn't ring true for a number of reasons. No administrative or institutional pressure on writing centers is staved off by sending them reprints of articles on theories of writing centers. Nor are the faculty who want us to clean up their students' writings. I seriously doubt that I'd manage to get some food sciences faculty member to stop harassing his students so about surface error by sending him reprints or by talking wc [sic] theory with him. Misunderstanding is misunderstanding is misunderstanding, and some talk and some friendly interaction will do more than pulling out theories to hand him.

This response was praised by several members of the discussion group, including one participant who wrote, "I appreciate your strong, pragmatic voice for getting the job done. Sometimes I feel so overwhelmed by theory—that is, by the demand to ground my work theoretically. I think it is grounded in theory, but that theoretical base is sometimes more jelly-like than granite, and I just don't have the time to reflect and analyze it."

I was, and continue to be, perplexed by what people considered to be a negative portrayal of writing centers in the Grimm article. Frankly, I thought Grimm's picture was anything but that. Here I excerpt my own response to these messages, in fairness to the other participants who wrote online as we all write on-line—in the heat of the moment, with phones ringing and students coming in and out and messages piling up:

> I fear that we are too cautious about painting a "happy" face on writing centers, too willing to capitulate to institutional pressures regarding statistics, FTEs, and whatever else our "administrators" [sic] say they want. And I continually fail to see how people can so readily separate this thing called "theory" from this thing called "practice" and how the call to see writing centers as sites of literacy research becomes connected with directors and tenure and institutional demands. We do "research," we do "theory"—directors, tutors, students—every time we ask a question about an assignment, about someone's confusion, about methods, about approaches—the list goes on and on. I've said it before and I'll say it again: we ignore this at our own peril.
>
> And I am called, time and time again, to talk about the "theories" that inform my practice—again, with students, with tutors, with administrators, with other faculty. I have fought long, long battles in my department, with my dean, about the institutional place of literacy, about how what we do speaks to our underlying assumptions about students, knowledge dissemination, etc. Almost without fail, I bring up what I know about the history of composition studies, about the history of writing centers, about how we've gotten to the place we are now and what my predictions would be for where we will end up if we pursue a particular course of action. We have to do this. And if we don't do this, if we just say, OK, we'll keep this statistic or that statistic, we'll be this or that if that's what you want, without thinking about the implications of such involvement (that would be the theory component), then we are guilty of relegating our work to the servile category to that Grimm alludes.

The responses to this thread were, as they tend to be on WCenter, heartfelt and straightforward. Most of them, including the ones quoted here, refer to age-old issues in writing center work: finding the time to keep up with the field, talking to colleagues in ways that inform without compromising the integrity of our work, and defining and maintaining our priorities in the face of institutional pressures and conflicts. I daresay these issues will never be resolved, and they deserve to be revisited.

Binaries (like the theory/practice dichotomy) are frequently useful, as Haraway (1991) points out, but only if we allow a binary pair to participate as part of an "open, branching discourse with a high likelihood of reflexivity about its own interpretive and productive technology" (112). The danger of such taxonomy lies in its potential to become the thing itself, rather than simply a representation of an activity. Practice is not a thing; it is an action. Theory too should imply movement, should be considered a generative category rather than static one. Coming to theory and to practice has involved, for me, loosening up on those terms, digging them out from their sedimented positions so that they can become productive again. Deleuze speaks against the totalizing positions of most theory-practice arguments, highlighting instead the "partial and fragmentary" relationship between theory and practice (quoted in Bouchard, 1977, 204). Later, Deleuze wrote:

> From the moment a theory moves into its proper domain, it begins to encounter obstacles, walls, and blockages that require its relay by another type of discourse.... Practice is a set of relays from one theoretical point to another, and theory is a relay from one practice to another. No theory can develop without eventually encountering a wall, and practice is necessary for piercing this wall. (quoted in Bouchard, 1977, 206)

Deleuze's explanation here seems oversimplified, possibly in part because of the forum in which it was captured (a conversation rather than a critical essay), leaving me with the impression that he means to think of theory and practice as always operating in separate domains, one following after the other; his explanation, however, seems most useful when we consider how theories might help us to push past the limitations of our practices or, conversely, how practices might delineate the limitations of our theories. This concept requires us to stop asking how theory "translates" into practice, or it at least asks us to stop thinking of translation as easy or obvious. Translation is, in fact, often about subtleties, with good translations relying less on one-to-one correspondences and more on capturing the sense, conveying the essence, of ideas.

The essays in this volume demonstrate the variety of approaches that writing center professionals employ to shed light on our work. All of these approaches house theories, stem from them, create and perpetuate them. Writing center professionals' theory, perhaps even simply the word *theory*, is suspect. We seem to have difficulty calling what we do "theoretical" or acknowledging the extent to which it is necessary and beneficial to operate in the realm of theory. My work is theoretical, in the purest (or impurest, depending on your perspective) sense of the term—unapologetically so. There are few specific students, even fewer particular tutors. There is most often only the literature and my reading—informed by cultural studies theory, by postmodern theory, by critical educational theory, by social democratic theory, by feminist theory—of what that literature says about the writing centers it claims to represent. I offer it as one possible, hopefully useful perspective—and only one—on the work that we do.

Work like mine is coming under increasing scrutiny in our profession. Berlin's work, for example, has been critiqued for its macrohistorical perspective (Spellmeyer, 1996; Varnum, 1996). Works that rely on microhistorical analyses, like Varnum's (1996) *Fencing with Words*, are becoming the studies du jour—and with good reason. Varnum's work tells us a great deal that we would never have learned from Berlin, that we couldn't have learned given the purpose of his books. Varnum's work affords readers the kind of detail they will not get in my work. But even she admits that her work would not have been possible, or at the very least would have been much more difficult, without Berlin's.

In a recent *College English* article, Kurt Spellmeyer (1996) describes our profession as being "trapped in theory" (893), arguing that theory, at this moment in our discipline, serves an alienating and gate-keeping function, rather than the liberating function we might like to imagine. At the conclusion of the article, Spellmeyer calls for scholars to "reimagin[e] knowledge as attunement with the world" (905), claiming that "signification cannot occur without an experiential anchoring" (907). Discussing this article with Peter Gray, my colleague in the Writing Center, I voiced my skepticism about many of Spellmeyer's points. In the course of the conversation, I posed the question, "Who didn't come to theory by bumping up against the limitations of their practice?" In other words, who didn't find it after an encounter with a Todd (in my case) or the New Jersey Basic Skills Council (in Spellmeyer's case)? Pete replied, "I think whole hosts of graduate students haven't encountered theory that way. A whole generation met theory in a graduate school classroom." When he phrased it that way, I knew he was right.

In her essay "Situated Knowledges: The Science Question in Feminism and the Privilege of Partial Perspective," Haraway (1991) writes, "We seek not the knowledges ruled by phallogocentrism (nostalgia for the presence of the one true Word) and disembodied vision, but those ruled by partial sight and limited voice. We do not seek partiality for its own sake, but for the sake of the connections and unexpected openings situated knowledges make possible"(196). Haraway's chapter suggests that we are asking the wrong questions of theory if we expect it to provide a grand narrative generally applicable to each of our particular situations. We are asking the right questions of theory if we allow it to surprise us, to raise more questions than it answers, as all good research does. It is in this spirit that I hope readers will experience my work, with the understanding that it presents only a partial (in both senses of that term) perspective of our work in writing centers and our institutions.

CODA

Recently I returned to the small Southern town where I grew up—not for good, not ever again, I imagine, to stay. Just for a visit. On a humid Sunday morning in May, I made the familiar trek from my parents' home to the commuter university where I did my undergraduate work. But this home of my parents is not the home where I spent my childhood; that home has been sold, the result of a depressed economy, shattered dreams, and scattered families. Instead, the walk is familiar to me because the place my parents now call home is the apartment once shared by my three best friends in college, a walk I made not to go to classes but to mingle at football games and block parties, a journey I made usually with much laughter and with many friends.

This time I made the trip alone, and I ended up past the stadium, past the quadrangle, staring at the original campus building, the one that housed the old writing center. I wound my way up the darkened stairwell to the room where I first met Todd, and I stood on my tiptoes, peering into the lower-left pane of glass, just where his face used to appear every Tuesday, Wednesday, and Thursday morning at 10:00 A.M. I gazed up at the righthand corner of the door, where I had once asked Todd to try to imagine how things would look from that perspective. What would be different? Could he write about it? He didn't look up at the door, at that particular pane of glass. Instead, he cast his eyes down at his blank sheet of paper and gripped his pencil so hard his knuckles turned white. He always looked like that when he tried to write, like he was sweatin' buckshot, as he would have described it. He couldn't write about it, and I moved on pretty quickly to some equally brilliant idea, although I don't remember what it was.

Now I realize that I had asked him the wrong question. Why ask him to answer some hypothetical question about a perspective he had never had? And I wonder if he could have answered the one that I would like to pose to him now: What do you see when you look through that pane of glass on the lower-lefthand side of the door, the one you press your nose against nearly every day, at that moment when you're both here and not here, home and not home?

I can't ask that question of Todd now, but I can ask it of myself. And I can remind myself that I have to look someplace else, maybe even simply look up, to see things a little differently, to spring a little change in the world.

REFERENCES

Bakhtin, M. (1981). *The dialogic imagination*. (C. Emerson & M. Holquist, Trans.). Austin: University of Texas Press.

Bloom, Z., Daiker D. A., & White, E. M. (Eds.). (1996). *Composition in the twenty-first century: Crisis and change*. Carbondale: Southern Illinois Press.

Bouchard, D. F. (Ed.). (1977). *Language, counter-memory, and practice: Selected chapters and interviews by Michel Foucault* (D. F. Bouchard & S. Simon, Trans.). Ithaca, NY: Cornell University Press.

Cooper, M. (1991). "We don't belong here, do we?": A response to *Lives on the boundary and the violence of literacy*. *The Writing Center Journal, 12*, 48–62.

Faigley, L. (1992). *Fragments of rationality: Postmodernity and the subject of composition*. Pittsburgh: University of Pittsburgh Press.

Foucault, M. (1977). *Discipline and punish: The birth of the prison*. (2nd ed. Alan Sheridan, Trans.). New York: Vintage, 1995.

Freire, P. (1992). *Pedagogy of the oppressed* (Myra Bergman Ramos, Trans.). New York: Continuum.

Gere, A. R. (1987). *Writing groups: History, theory, and implications*. Carbondale: Southern Illinois University Press.

Giroux, H. A. (1992). Paulo Freire and the politics of postcolonialism. *Journal of Advanced Composition, 12*, 15–26.

Grimm, N. M. (1996). Rearticulating the work of the writing center. *College Composition and Communication, 47*, 523–548.

Haraway, D. J. (1991). *Simians, cyborgs, and women: The reinvention of nature*. New York: Routledge.

Harkin, P. & Schilb, J. (Eds.). (1991). *Contending with words: Composition and rhetoric in a postmodern age*. New York: MLA.

North, S. M. (1987). *The making of knowledge in composition: Portrait of an emerging field*. Portsmouth, NH: Boynton/Cook—Heinemann.

Pemberton, M. (1994). Writing center ethics: "Confronting controversy and practicing politics" *The Writing Lab Newsletter, 18*, 6–7.

Spellmeyer, K. (1996). After theory: From textuality to attunement with the world. *College English, 58*, 893–913.

Varnum, R. (1996). *Fencing with words: A history of writing instruction at Amherst College during the era of Theodore Baird, 1938–1966*. Urbana, IL: National Council of Teachers of English.

Chapter 3

Beyond the House of Lore: WCenter as Research Site

Paula Gillespie
Marquette University

Many of us who sign on to and faithfully read WCenter do so because we are alone on our campuses, the only writing center professionals. While our friends in literature can go for coffee and discuss issues of their scholarship and teaching, we have no one with whom to discuss our latest budget crisis or a recent article in *The Writing Center Journal*. Many of us take our coffee breaks in the office with our colleagues on WCenter. Many of these colleagues become our friends.

When I first signed on in the spring of 1993, WCenter had been in operation for almost 2 years.[1] Not realizing this, I did a naive thing: After lurking for a few days, I raised an issue that *of course* had been discussed before: "How do the rest of you make good use of your staff meetings?" I'd had some comments from my tutors that our meetings were a little boring and that we needed to spice them up, so I asked the online experts. Someone tactfully told me that this had just recently been a topic, but in spite of that, folks chimed in and I got lots of advice, some of which I put immediately into practice, and all of which was useful. "This is what we do," I heard. I was in the House of Lore.[2] And, although I had been subscribed

---

[1]In a private correspondence, Lady Falls Brown said, "I announced the establishment of WCENTER at the CCCC held in Boston, March 20–23rd, 1991, and an announcement appears in the May 1991 *Writing Lab Newsletter*, 7. I modeled WCENTER after MBU-L which Fred Kemp had established for people interested in computers and writing."

[2]This term comes from Steve North's *The Making of Knowledge in Composition* (1987).

39

for barely a week, I had used WCenter for some informal research. As Muriel Harris points out in this collection, I was not simply adopting that lore: I considered our context, our needs, and the makeup of our staff, and I used those strategies that fit our local mission and goals. I had become part of a community that has given itself to questions not only about how to do what we do, but also about why we do things the way we do. The community is also given to looking at the theories that underlie our practices as well as at our audiences. That is to say, WCenter is, among other things, a research site, a community of researchers. And we, as writing center workers, need the knowledge that is made on WCenter.

From large institutions to small private and state colleges, writing centers are increasingly being directed by trained composition and rhetoric graduates with MAs, EdDs, or PhDs. These directors are well grounded in composition research and may have written a dissertation based on their own original research. These directors and staff members are comfortable in the field and knowledgeable about composition theory, but even they may be new to writing center work. However, the majority of centers are directed—and will continue to be directed—by people like me, people who have degrees in literature.

Writing centers, in spite of their gains in the last 20 years, still suffer from small budgets, and department chairs or other people in charge of the writing center still hire non-tenure track people as directors. They often draw from their very talented pool of part-timers or adjuncts, people who are successful in the classroom and who work well with others. These directors may never have worked as tutors, yet they are asked to train tutors and educate themselves. They are also called on to communicate knowledgeably with administrators, manage a budget, and smooth the ruffled feathers of irate faculty members and of writers who expect drop-off proofreading services. In addition, they are expected to run a facility that enhances retention efforts and makes users happy. These directors' jobs are often defined as administrative. I can think of no other field where on-the-job training is so prevalent and so isolated. If colleagues who are experienced in writing center practice or who are conversant with theories of collaborative learning exist at all, it is rarely part of *their* job description to train or mentor the fledgling writing center director. So our training and ongoing education is largely our own enterprise.

If we think of research as "the making of knowledge," then we must ask the question: What kinds of knowledge are we making, and for whom? Recently a thread on WCenter had the subject line "If only I had known." A new writing center director asked for the most useful piece of advice the WCenter community could volunteer. For her, this request was necessary, vital research. She was asking for stories, for lore, for theories, for anything that would help her feel more thoroughly prepared to take on a job that can seem daunting. The editors of our journal and our newsletter have always considered these new directors and have published helpful articles that can be put to immediate use. I remember my own frenzied reading in old newsletters and journals, my own attempts to map out strategies when I was new. The immediate need is for lore; the immediate question is "What works?" Questions of causality, questions of theory follow.

This is often the pattern on WCenter. The discussion often begins with lore and moves towards theory. Like a writing center session, however, this discussion is interactive, polyvocal—a polylogue, the sort of discourse that Gesa Kirsch, among others, calls for in *Ethical Dilemmas in Feminist Research* (1999). The discussion on WCenter is not a one-way article, complete with references, nor is it a forum where the writer has all the authority and agency; rather, those who need more information can ask for it, and those who disagree can take issue or offer alternatives. If we want to read more about a topic, contributors often suggest published articles and give full citations. This situation sounds like the best that research can offer: information we need and access to the writer. It can sound like a conference session with a good give and take, but it has two unique qualities: Those who need to know can determine the shape the discussion will take, because there is no need to mask insecurity behind a show of professionalism. We can say, "We are just starting out and need help." Imagine saying that at a CCCC session. The WCenter session can be more attuned to audience and purpose than a conference session, because the audience will speak up and make its needs known.

As I look over the earliest logs of WCenter in the archives, I'm struck by the clowning, the fellowship, the good-natured community established there, and indeed these qualities are the reasons that many busy administrators do *not* subscribe: it's too much for some people, and they tell us so as they unsubscribe. But in that clowning, there is a sense of community-building that makes it easy to contribute, easy to ask and sometimes answer questions. But if the discussion itself proves too time consuming, we can consult the archives at one of two sites. For postings dated June 1994 to February 2, 2000, people can to go to http://ttacs61.ttu.edu/wcenter/ For postings dated February 2, 2000, to the present, people can to log on to WCenter at http://lyris.acs.ttu.edu/cgi-bin/lyris.pl?enter=wcenter&text_mode=0&lang =english.

When I first logged on to WCenter, I realized almost immediately that many subscribers were using it as a research source, gathering data to use for all sorts of formal and informal purposes. Some of the earliest posts I remember seeing were questionnaires: How large is your center, how many tutors, what is your space like, how many computers, and how do you use them? Some subscribers specified that they needed information to present to administrators, to keep themselves running, to make changes, or to get money. Much of the advice people asked for was the practical sort, but our profession is changing, becoming more interested in theory and more professionally sophisticated, partly as a result of the way we educate and bring one another along on the listserv. We have as members of the listserv subscribers who make research a part of their job, and some who have written dissertations based on writing center research. Subscribers like these bring research questions and results into the dialogue, preventing WCenter from being simply a sprawling lore warehouse with an uncatalogueable inventory.

WCenter allows for a unique continuum or range of research. In "Keywords," Tom Kerr (1996) wrote, "What research means in a given rhetorical situation depends partly on the type of research in question and partly on the synonyms [and tropes] invoked to stand in for this keyword" (201). My synonym for the research we do on WCenter would not usually be considered scholarship or empirical research (especially in the light of the way the respondents self-select and skew the data); rather, my term would be *inquiry*, a form of research more likely to *lead to* scholarship or empirical research or to serve as an invention heuristic for such study. If, however, what we need is local knowledge gathered by others—if reporting on results from other writing centers is sufficient for our audiences—then we often do not need to replicate studies done by others, and we can take reports directly from WCenter to our administrators. This kind of research, however, still seems like inquiry, although it contains elements of both scholarship (study and reading) and empirical research.

Because of the fluid interaction on WCenter, knowledge does not become frozen or static. One interaction last February began with a simple question that asked for research sources but that led initially to lore-type responses and then branched out:

Vainis Aleksa (vainis@uic.edu), Thu, 5 Feb 1998 16:08:58 -0600 (CST)
At our center, it is common practice to take the time to ask students to read essays aloud to our tutors. When students do not want to read the essay, we offer to read it aloud for them. When we do this for ESL students, I'm wondering if it wouldn't be better to make some corrections as we read aloud, so that students could get more exposure to English. I would be glad to know if anyone has had experience with this, or knows of any research on the matter.

Thanks,
Vainis Aleksa

Vainis was asking for more than lore; he was also asking for research sources on reading aloud. A number of speedy replies appeared, including this one the next day:

anne mullin (MULLANNE@isu.edu), Fri, 06 Feb 1998 09:42:34 -0800
Our tutors, also, read aloud students' work for ESOL students—our ESOL specialist tells us how valuable it is to hear the English words spoken by native speakers at every opportunity. When a correction needs to be made, she says it helps if the tutor slows down—gives the students a chance to "hear" the error

(usually they do) and offer their own correction. The tutor can then repeat it correctly —the point is to reinforce the correct sound and shape on the page.

Anne told Vainis not only what they did, but their reason for doing it, and she spelled out the results they'd come to expect; that is, she posited both causality and effect. There were a number of other replies to the list, some of which gave reasons either why no one should read aloud or reasons why the tutor should read. Then this post appeared:

Neal Lerner (*nlerner@mcp.edu*), Fri, 06 Feb 1998 15:57:30 -0500
  Maybe because it's Friday and the sun is finally out, but I just have to be slightly contrary on the reading-aloud thread. Isn't reading a student's paper aloud the verbal equivalent of the tutor "holding the pen" (to introduce another WC shibboleth) or writing all over a student's paper and thereby usurping ownership in some way? After all, what are students doing while we read their papers aloud? We'd like to think they're carefully listening to our articulation of each syllable and our stumbles over confusing bits, but do we know that for sure? At least, when we have students read their own papers aloud, we can be reasonably sure they're focused on the task at hand.

I usually try to have ESL students read their papers aloud, because they're the ones who need the practice with pronouncing English (well, I don't need as much practice, anyway). We can always do some of our own reading of the text as we go back over it with them.

Here Neal was invoking another oft-debated topic of how we show who has ownership of the paper ("holding the pen" has become a sort of red flag on WCenter, one that always provokes a healthy debate). But Neal questions the assumptions we make about what the student is doing while we read. This is the sort of question we need to ask about our easy claims of who is doing what; he is asking here about principles of tutoring we all need to examine. Neal's question raises the possibility of inquiring into the question we take for granted in our lore: what *are* writers doing when we read their texts for them?

Beth Boquet (*eboquet@FAIR1.FAIRFIELD.EDU*), Fri, 06 Feb 1998 17:44:51 +0000

Neal—
  I thought the tutor-holding-pen controversy was settled and that we could hold the pen now. Oh no! Or maybe we can only hold the pen when we want to critique pen-holdership in a post-Freudian disciplinary move.

Beth begins with some good-natured joking, made more enjoyable for those of us who know that both Beth and Neal wrote dissertations on writing centers. Beth goes on:

> At any rate, I could disagree with you—and I will in a minute. But before that, I would like to get at a point you make that I'm afraid might get lost—because I think it is the important point in your text: How do we know what they're focusing on? That seems to me to be the thing to check. So the heart of my disagreement is that I think we can't _assume_ that they're paying attention just cuz they're reading aloud. In fact, it might preclude their paying attention to the kinds of things we might want them to pay attention to—the very same way that less skilled typists often have more difficulty composing at the computer when compared to composing the "old-fashioned" way.

Beth's comment "That seems to me to be the thing to check" suggests a research topic for others and perhaps for herself. If not that, it suggests that we find informal ways to check on writers' attention for our own benefit. But once again, she, like Neal, is questioning the assumptions of our store of lore. She goes on:

> I worked with a guy in grad school whose professors had a problem with his use of BEV. What we discovered, over the course of several sessions, was that when he read his paper aloud, he could not hear his own "errors." When I read it aloud, however, they were almost always apparent to him. It was amazing, really. He would chuckle when things came out of my mouth that didn't "sound right" to him, coming from me.
>
> This brings up another, related issue for me that I think about with my tutors: We very rarely have repeat visits here, where students work with the same tutor over the course of several sessions. Yet, when I think about the really important discoveries I made as I learned to tutor, they very rarely happened the first time I worked with someone. More often, they happened the third or the fourth or the fifth time I worked with them. When I made exceptions to the "rules" (holding the pen, reading aloud, whatever), it was because I had a sense, after working with someone time and again, that the rule wasn't serving its purpose.
>
> You know?

In this section of Beth's post, she calls our hard and fast rules into question, using an example of her experience, and also raising an issue about working with students only once. With this, Beth brings in an additional topic for us to consider: How can we manage to work with students more than once so we give them the best help we can?

Meg replies, encouraged, perhaps by Beth's willingness to admit to breaking with our traditions when the circumstances call for it:

Meg Larson (mgl@svsu.edu), Sat, 7 Feb 1998 09:08:08 -0500
I'm joining the conversation a bit late here, but here's my two-cents: I prefer to read a student's paper to them. This may have been mentioned, but when I read the student's paper, I'm reading with [objectivity] and unfamiliarity, like the paper's reader will do. I don't know about seeing the text, but the student knows the paper, knows what's supposed to be there, and tends to supply missing words automatically; when I read what is on paper, word for word, to them, it sort of forces them to pay attention to their text. I read it through

once, comment on the strong points, and then we go back over the trouble spots. Often the feedback I get is that it helps the student to hear it in another voice, helps the student understand what "reader-based" prose is all about. And a lot of students, at least in [my] experience, don't read their draft when they finish it—they know what they wrote so they don't need to read it.

Meg is addressing issues of audience here, and of increasing the writer's awareness of what the reader will encounter in a text. She is speaking in the beginning about her practice, but she moves from there to her hypothesis about reading the writer's paper.

Neal Lerner (9 Feb 1998) comes back to and enlarges on his earlier question:
... I've begun to wonder a few things about the question of who does the reading aloud in a tutoring session. Mainly, I'm wondering what forms the bases for our feelings on how best to proceed in a conference. And how do those bases relate to some of the more dominant theories that govern writing conferences?

Let me try to explain what I mean. Most of us would follow Stephen North and agree that conferences should result in improvement in students' writing processes, not necessarily their written products. So how does the resolution of who reads aloud fit into this "theory"? How would students' underlying writing processes be revealed depending on whether they or I am reading their texts aloud? Does it matter at all?

Many of what people have offered seems to have come out of a conviction that it "works," while acknowledging some tentativeness. What else are these practices based on?

Neal Lerner
Mass. College of Pharmacy

Sara Glennon then joins in, and her posts are always illuminating. She tutors at Landmark College, a school for students with learning disabilities. Her insights help those of us who occasionally work with LD writers, but they often have applicability to many of our other writers as well.

Sara Glennon (SGLENNON@landmarkcollege.org), Mon, 9 Feb 1998 10:15:59 EST
I have no reservations about reading a student's paper aloud to them, in part because of my experience with students who have significant difficulty decoding text, even their own writing. Many students have written vocabularies that are much more developed and sophisticated than their vocabulary of words they can pronounce easily or automatically. For some, reading aloud takes so much energy and concentration on the basic skills of decoding that they don't have anything left to listen to the words they're saying.

Surely Sara's point applies to the larger population of writers who do not have learning disabilities. Cliff Barnett then makes an interesting connection to linguistic study.

Cliff Barnett (9 Feb 1998)

You raise an interesting issue, one that I think touches on Neal's questions when he asks "How would students' underlying writing processes be revealed depending on whether they or I am reading their texts aloud? Does it matter at all?"

Hmmm ... Let me murder to dissect here for a moment. Reading is to writing as listening is speaking (to put it simply); and in both cases performance always lags competence. That is, just as my reading comprehension will always outstrip my written production, so too will my listening comprehension outpace my spoken production. I understand way more than I will ever be able to speak or write. But what Neal asks and what you bring up is how or even whether performance affects (perhaps even effects) comprehension, and how can we as tutors know such things—what assumptions are we making about language acquisition (writing in particular) and production (again, writing in particular)?

So is Neal asking what the hell does orality have to do with literacy—spoken word with written word? I suppose reading a paper is actually secondary orality inasmuch as what is being vocalized has already been scripted. And if I accept the existence of secondary orality, I suppose I'm tacitly admitting a direct relationship between the written and spoken word. And, well, oh hell, now I've gone and done what James did, just confused myself more.

Better go now and let someone help me focus.

Cliff Barnett
PSU Writing Center

So far the talk has centered on what writers get out of the reading aloud. I answer Neal, speaking of what my tutors gain from this process and the way the session progresses.

Paula Gillespie (*gillespiep@vms.csd.mu.edu*), Mon, 9 Feb 1998

Neal, we find that the reading-aloud period (when the writer reads) allows my tutors to take notes, to hold off comments until the end, but to outline the paper, to jot down notes about questions they might have, to think about large concerns first. If the tutor is reading the paper aloud, he or she can't do this, and might end up focusing on sentence-level concerns first.

We do offer to read for ESL students who are not fluent readers, though.

Meg Carroll went on:

Meg Carroll (*mcarroll@grog.ric.edu*) 9 Feb 1998

... Reading conference papers to a tutor is incredibly beneficial both for the reasons Paula outlined, but also for some other very practical ones. Spoken language, if it's to be effective, must be different from the written. How many times have we sat through presentations which were difficult to follow because the presenter was reading a potential journal article? Reading to a tutor or tutors makes us think of how to present difficult concepts in a user-friendly way. We notice if our listeners are being put to sleep. We can try out a variety of rhetorical devices. If we're really on top of things, what better way to try out the interactive stuff we like to see in our presentations?

At this point, I'm about to try out our own presentation on some guinea pigs (angelic ones)—it's a little theoretical and we're worried about getting everyone involved.

Neal's post then received a reply:

Lauren Fitzgerald (fitzger@ymail.yu.edu), Mon, 9 Feb 1998 17:39:43 -0500 (EST)
Neal & all other readers—
I'm really intrigued by your suggestion that where we place ourselves on the reading aloud issue might say something about our theoretical perspectives. After reading the different—and often strongly argued—points of view, I was reminded of an article by David Bartholomae, "The Study of Error,"—already almost 20 years old—in which, among other things, he calls into question the assumed virtue of getting students, particularly basic writers, to read out loud.
So maybe my initial response to this discussion—that the _student_ should be the one reading out loud, _of course_—says more about my own deeply-rooted expressivism than any well-thought-out notions about this activity. And maybe this discussion is yet another version of the expressivist/social constructivist argument? Just wondering...

Lauren Fitzgerald
Yeshiva College Writing Center

I take a shot at an answer to Neal's question:

Paula Gillespie (Gillespie@vms.csd.mu.edu), Mon, 9 Feb 1998 1601 -0600 (CST)
Neal, we ask students to read aloud, and we do so without tentativeness. We try to avoid making them feel squirmy by explaining what kinds of notes we're going to take, and we explain that we're going to be listening first for the first (or higher) order concerns. We don't worry if students aren't reading precisely what's on the page, because they're probably going to revise it, and that comes later.
Reading gives them a new, different context for knowing what they've written. I'd argue that reading it aloud when they are alone is different, because there is no audience for it.
One of our favorite questions after the writer has read aloud is, "Now that you've heard your paper, what revisions do you want to make in it," or "What did you notice this time that you hadn't noticed before?" Often, then, the writer gets to kick off the conference (and take more control) than if we begin by firing questions at them.
Usually when we take notes, we try to outline, so we can help the write see the structure and so we can see the way the paper is laid out, get a sense of it.
If all's well, then we do a second read-through, with the tutor reading this time, and we do an error analysis, asking the writer to stop us when she spots an error. But this is assuming that there isn't going to be a major overhaul of the entire thing.

We find that this works really well, once we get used to the system, and it takes some training to listen well and take notes well and to stay silent till the writer finishes the whole draft.

But we like the idea of giving the control to the student; in reading, in emphasizing, the writer gets to choose what gets emphasis, what gets stressed, what's important. The writer gets to interpret the paper for us.

The issues, then, for us, are student control and first things first.

My answer draws on North, but it also draws in a good amount of lore: "Here's what we do and here's how it works for us." But my underlying warrant is that the tutor's grasp of the writer's paper matters a great deal to the tutorial, as does the writer's control of it. We find that our question after the student's reading really opens the session, and also that the notes the tutor takes during the reading are of enormous help in the tutorial that follows. My theory is that the more mastery the tutor has over the material, the more he or she can relinguish control and let the writer take an active role in the session.

Dennis Paoli joins in the discussion:
Dennis Paoli (dpaoli@shiva.hunter.cuny.edu), Mon, 9 Feb 1998 18:48:31 -0500 (EST)

I have just removed my alpha from my omega and checked in on the reading aloud thread. It is where the student steps into the manhole—or the "beance" as some Frenchified critics would have put it a few years ago—when they read their own prose, and the slippage between what they thought they wrote and what they think they hear themselves writing that leads to a case of the Uncannies, which changes their minds, literally, about their relationship to their prose. And that will always be hit-or-miss to some degree, because the near random relationship of hit and miss makes the perspective shift a "discovery," lending it the disturbance and authority of discovery, seeming to authenticate expressivism and social construction at once. "Oh, that's what I said." Oh, that's what other people think I said." "Oh, that's what I thought I said."

I think.

Dennis Paoli

Then finally Jon Olson delivers something of a Coda to this discussion.

Jon Olson (jeo3@psu.edu). Thu, 12 Feb 1998 04:17:49 -0500

Reading aloud anecdote: I went to an administration of justice class, 140 students, to hype the benefits of the Writing Center experience yesterday (none of the peer tutors picked up the class-visit opportunity). Four students testified … about what a waste of time it was to take a paper to the Writing Center. The chief complaint had to do with reading aloud. :)

Jon informed me in a private correspondence about his post that he is a firm believer in reading aloud and meant his comment ironically.

These excerpts represent only a fraction of the responses to Vainis' questions; there were flippant replies, repetitive ones, serious ones. Recently, Moira Sennett, a student of mine, was working on a theory/practice paper for the peer tutoring class (Sennet, 1999). She was writing, coincidentally, on the topic of reading aloud, so I was able to give her not only the URL of the WCenter archives, but the specific date of Vainis' inquiry. She was surprised to find so many various responses to the question, responses so well reasoned. The rest of the class wanted to research their topics on the archives as well, after Moira reported back to the class on the dialogues she found there. Interestingly enough, she concluded in her study that those who argued for reading aloud were concerned with higher-order concerns, while those who wanted to skip that step were more concerned with later-order concerns.

Although very valuable, and arguably even vital to some of us, WCenter has its critics, and for good reason. Eric Hobson (1999) critiques the use of WCenter for quick-fix research in his NWCA News Column in the *Writing Lab Newsletter*. He wonders if, in this computer-mediated age, anyone bothers to research their questions before they ask them online. He objects to our "growing (co-) dependence on responses in twenty minutes, or fewer" (12), and he reminds readers that "most of the material/advice … is decidedly first draft" and is "decidedly anecdotal and context specific" (12). Experienced users of WCenter know that this is so. Yet many of us, for our purposes and for our intended audiences, would rather get a shoot-from-the-hip response from Muriel Harris or Neal Lerner or Beth Boquet than comb the periodicals, hoping for an answer that fits our complex or context-specific question.

Still, we all recognize and accept for what it is the rough draft approach in WCenter dialogue. The well-meant reference to David Bartholomae's "Study of Error," mentioned earlier, misrepresents Bartholomae's claim as well as his purpose. Still, anyone who wanted to cite Bartholomae in a more scholarly forum would surely look at the article itself. What he does actually say about reading aloud and about basic writing is very interesting and relevant to this discussion, so the reference to him is helpful.

Even if WCenter were only a lore storehouse, it would be valuable. Patricia Harkin (1991) sums up Steve North's observations that

> … lore should (sometimes) count as "inquiry" in the fully valorized sense of that term. He writes that when a practitioner [as opposed to an empirical researcher] identifies a problem, searches for and disseminates that information (36), that practitioner may be said to have conducted an inquiry, even if his or her procedures vary from disciplinary and professional criteria. (126)

Harkin goes on to argue that disciplinary knowledge can only be replicated under certain specific circumstances; but that "lore adapts" (132). She critiques the "institutional blindness that prevents us from seeing how lore produces knowledge. Disciplines look at what they recognize, or, more precisely see only what they recognize no matter where they look" (130). Lore, she argues, is postdisciplinary:

> "As lore procedurally and pragmatically blurs relations of cause and effect, it is able to deal more effectively than traditional science with "overdetermined" situations. Unlike the linear, cause-and-effect relations that are represented by disciplinary techniques, lore arranges its data serially, spatially, paratactically, like a rhizome ... "(134).

The processes of writing and of tutoring are so complexly overdetermined (that is, they have multiple, interlocking causes and countless variables), that when I begin to picture an empirical researcher making up, let's say, a four-way grid to account for the dependent and independent variables, I picture a grid so huge that it begins to look like pixels in a JPEG we can never really describe. Bobbie Silk gave a fascinating paper at the 1997 NWCA conference in which she described heat-sensitive brain scans of a person writing. As opposed to other activities during which one or another area of the brain heated up, the brain, during writing, looked like a lightning field viewed from the air, with one area after another lit up and flashing. And this mental activity is only one element in the complicated process that makes up our experiences with writing, our anxieties, our relations with the instructor, the wording of our assignment, our learning styles, our auras, our astrological signs; the complexity of it all makes me feel awe that we make any progress by tutoring at all.

Practitioners, Harkin argues, can cope with overdetermination because of their "eclectic foraging among theories ... ." They are also "antiessentialist as they deal with situations in which single causes cannot be discriminated from effects" (134). Harkin almost describes WCenter when she says, "I envision a series of conferences that ask us to work up from the practice of lore, not down from a theory of writing, conferences in which experienced, gifted teachers address a problem delineated for the occasion...."(136).

WCenter goes well beyond lore and tries to look at cause-effect relationships and theories that underlie our various and/or canonical practices. WCenter allows knowledge to be made by a community in a collaborative way. A simple question often takes on a life of its own, moving from lore to theory (if by theory we mean a search for causality or of generalizable principles) to research questions and back to lore again. Lady Falls Brown noted to me in a personal communication that she was struck by the way we "practice, question our practice, try to find answers to our questions, and then perhaps arrive at some kind of theory." But she commented then on the way discussions on WCenter "frequently question what has become theory." The knowledge that is made here is accessible not only to our own community, which needs it—sometimes for its own survival—but also to the larger community of learning, to the community of rhetoric and composition as well as to the community of learning centers.

Around the country, writing centers are getting the funding they need, getting the equipment and spaces, getting the staffing, getting the tutor training, generally getting what they need—largely because someone asked a question on WCenter or consulted the archives. North's House of Lore is a rambling structure, a place that reminds me of my den, where nothing is ever thrown away, and where the things I need are often hard to find. But in the WCenter archives, a word search can turn up a simple-to-follow thread, aptly named for its metaphorical weaving-through, but also aptly named for its ability to pucker and reshape the fabric that makes it up.

REFERENCES

Harkin, (1991). The postdisciplinary politics of lore. In P. Harkin & J. Schilib (Eds.), *Contending with words: Composition and rhetoric in a postmodern age* (pp. 124–138). New York: Modern Language Association Press.

Hobson, E. (1999). NWCA news from Eric Hobson, President. *Writing Lab Newsletter, 24*(3), 12.

Kerr, T. (1996). Keywords. In Heiker & P Vandenberg (Eds.), *Keywords in composition studies*. Portsmouth, NH: Boynton/Cook.

Kirsch, G. (1999). *Ethical dilemmas in feminist research: The politics of location, interpretation, and publication*. Albany: State University of New York Press.

North, S. M. (1987). *The making of knowledge in composition: Portrait of an emerging field*. Portsmouth, NH: Boynton/Cook.

Sennett, M. (1999). *Reading the written word: The politics of possession*. Unpublished paper. Marquette University, Milwaukee, WI.

Silk, B. (1997, September). *The power of naming: A writing-centered reconsideration of process*. Unpublished paper presented at National Writing Centers Association conference, Park City, Utah.

Chapter 4

Insider as Outsider: Participant Observation as Writing Center Research

Neal Lerner
Massachusetts College of Pharmacy & Health Sciences

Writing center research has entered an important new era. The surveys and questionnaires that have dominated our inquiry have played a significant role. However, as in the language arts (Athanases & Heath, 1995) and in composition studies (Bishop, 1992), those studying writing centers are choosing qualitative methods—interviews, audio recordings, field notes, among other sources—to describe what happens in writing center sessions. From these descriptions, researchers are proposing theories to explain the phenomena they observe, and are building a base on which our knowledge can be constructed and our practice refined.

Qualitative methodologies, however, are not without challenges. In particular, for those studying sites with which they are familiar—directors studying their own writing centers and undergraduate or graduate students investigating the settings in which they tutor—the narrative of negotiating dilemmas can seem as compelling as the findings of the study itself. Our "insider" status in the writing center often challenges the relationship between researcher and participants as our roles shift from colleague and friend to observer and evaluator. These shifting roles can limit the methods we choose to collect data and threaten the veracity of our accounts. Furthermore, we bring a set of assumptions or an ideological framework that can overwhelm our attempts to understand what we observe. As best we can, we must articulate these assumptions—both to us and to the readers of our research narratives—in order to allow our observations an existence of their own, apart from (or alongside) our powerful biases and preconceived notions.

In what follows, I offer the narrative of my negotiation of the dilemmas I encountered as I studied the writing center where I worked. I discuss four questions that were intertwined with my role as participant—observer:

1. What kind of research was I actually doing: Ethnographic? Qualitative? Interpretive?
2. What methods of data collection did I need to ensure that my findings were valid and that I was answering the preliminary questions I brought to my study?
3. How could I maintain good relationships with the colleagues whom I was studying and balance my role as both an insider and an outsider?
4. How could I account for and mitigate the influence of my ideological and practical notions of tutoring when I tried to make sense of what I was observing?

Following my narrative, I turn to the small body of qualitative research on writing centers to show how other authors have dealt with participant-observation dilemmas. Finally, I discuss the field of teacher research in K–12 settings and how these studies offer us a way of emphasizing the strengths of our insider positions in our writing centers and lead us to the kind of knowledge making that is vital to our field.

For those who investigate writing centers—whether that inquiry is as formal as a dissertation or as informal as reflection on practice—I hope this chapter illuminates the challenges we might encounter. Elliot Eisner (1991) writes that our investigations require a certain "consciousness," and "with such consciousness we are in a better position to exercise sensibility, taste, and that most precious human capacity, rational judgment" (226). My consciousness includes reflecting on why I made the choices I made, how others who have studied writing centers made those choices, and what promise research in familiar settings holds for those who tutor in and direct writing centers.

BLAME IT ON STEPHEN NORTH

Like many in the writing center field, the first article handed to me once I was hired at my university's writing center was Stephen North's (1994a) "The Idea of a Writing Center." It was included in an orientation packet filled with our policy on proofreading ("We are not a proofreading service!") and copies of forms we needed to fill out after every session. This incident occurred during my second year in a doctorate in education program, and my decision to tutor in the Writing Center was primarily based on the need for a job that would allow me to make a respectable salary (in university terms) but did not require the time commitment of classroom teaching. Writing center tutoring seemed like an obvious choice. At the same time, I was in search of a dissertation topic. It only took a few weeks for me to realize that the search was over—once I read North, that is.

Perhaps there is some sort of subliminal message in that text, in North's declaration that "in a writing center the object is to make sure that writers, and not necessarily their texts, are what get changed by instruction. In axiom form it goes like this: Our job is to produce better writers, not better writing" (438). Perhaps a certain subtext in North's article reaches out to like-minded individuals and pushes them off intended paths. "Follow me," the message says, "Join us." I wanted to be about writers and not merely writing; I wanted to revel in the margins and reveal the marginalized; I, too, was misunderstood by an academic community that saw knowledge as a transmittable commodity, passive students' heads filling with pages of lecture notes. My gadfly-ish, Mina Shaughnessy-ish, Paolo Freire-ish sensibilities ceased to operate merely as an undercurrent. No, this North was on to something. Not only my teaching niche but also my research niche in the academy was revealed. I would study the Writing Center, I decided, and began the process of collecting data from tutors and students via interviews, audiotapes of tutoring sessions, and Writing Center session records and evaluation forms. Making sense of these data and presenting that interpretation to a reader were all influenced by my pre-conceived notions of "effective tutoring," by the relationships I would need to establish with my colleagues, and by my reading of writing center literature. When I started, however, I was only slightly aware of the extent of those influences.

RESEARCH METHODS
AND ETHNOGRAPHIC INTENT

Once I had decided to study the Writing Center and obtained the permission of the Center's director, the task seemed somehow familiar to me. Qualitative research, with its goal of "rich description of people, places, and conversations" (Bogdan & Biklen, 1992, 2), appealed to the writer and reader within me. When the professor of a quantitative methods course dismissed qualitative work with "Oh, that's just story telling," the appeal only increased. After all, what better way to learn about life in classrooms or writing centers than simply to ask people what they thought was occurring, to listen to their stories about the motivations for their actions, and to record those responses in "thick description" (Geertz, 1983) much like the "saturation reports" or detailed-filled descriptions of a place I had been assigning my composition students for several years?

In composition studies, there is certainly precedent to my choice of this methodology. Ethnographic studies have become a fixture in the study of "teaching and learning of English language arts in classrooms and other naturalistic settings" (Athanases & Heath, 1995, 263). These studies can range in intensity from Shirley Brice Heath's (1983) 10-year immersion in the life of three communities in the Piedmont Carolinas captured in *Ways with Words*, to Melanie Sperling's (1990) 6-week study of teacher-student conferencing in a ninth-grade English classroom. Several doctoral students have also made writing centers the subject of ethnographic dissertations, including James Bell (1989), Joyce Magnotto (1991), and Barbara Roswell (1992). The use of ethnographic methods has also been the subject in collections of writing center scholarship. These include Neuleib and Scharton's (1994) "Writing Others, Writing Ourselves: Ethnography and the Writing Center" and Werder and Buck's (1995) "Assessing Writing Conference Talk: An Ethnographic Method."

Ultimately, my choice of qualitative or ethnographic methods to study the Writing Center was in accord with what Beverly Moss (1992) describes in her account of examining literacy behaviors in the African-American church:

> This was the only research method I had been introduced to that allowed a researcher to tell a story about a community—a story told jointly by the researcher and the members of the community.... Ultimately, ethnography allowed me to be part of the research project in more than some abstract researcher way. It allowed me to take a picture of the community (through fieldwork) and be in the picture at the same time, something that other research methods frown on. (154)

However, the more I studied qualitative methods and, more specifically, ethnography, the more complex my task became. My first problem came with the concept of ethnography itself. Harry Wolcott (1987) defines the purpose of ethnographic research as "to describe and interpret cultural behavior" (43). The notion of "culture" presented problems. The Writing Center that I would be studying was staffed entirely by graduate students from various disciplines—theology, English, applied linguistics, American studies, sociology and education. Each worked alone for a 3- or 4-hour shift, and our most frequent contact came via e-mail messages and twice monthly meetings. Although we had undergone some degree of social bonding as we shared stories of recalcitrant students and nightmare assignments or griped about a new work rule that limited our access to email during tutoring hours, it was difficult for me to justify that we were a microculture or cohesive group.

Additionally, it was not necessarily the tacit rules, roles, and relationships of group life that I wished to study. My initial purpose was simply to investigate what my colleagues did when they tutored, what motivated those actions, and what students would perceive to be their own roles in tutoring sessions. I wanted to make "the obvious obvious," as Wolcott (1987) writes. This desire was simply an extension of reflection on my own tutoring. Why did I act the way I did in a tutoring session? How did I expect students to act and why? What were students expecting from me? How would these questions be answered in regard to my colleagues' tutoring sessions?

In this phase of my dilemma—simply figuring out a label for what I was getting myself into—I found solace in Frederick Erickson's (1986) use of interpretive research "to refer to the whole family of approaches to participant observational research" (119). What I would be reporting, in essence, was how my tutor colleagues and the students with whom we worked interpreted the "events and experiences" (Mishler, 1990, 427) that made up their activities in the Writing Center. An important aspect of my methodology, however, was not to rely merely on interviews—not to ask simply what tutors and students did during tutoring sessions and why. As Mishler (1990) describes, "The account produced during the interview is a reconstruction of the past, shaped by the particular context of its telling" (427). Instead, I also needed to examine actual tutoring sessions. This was for two reasons:

First, I could interview tutors and students, examine records of conferences, and study students' texts and even observe and take notes during tutoring sessions, but without a complete transcript of tutoring sessions available for systematic analysis I could make few claims about the ways participants use language during tutorials to achieve their goals. Without these data, my study would move little beyond the nearly ubiquitous surveys of student, tutor, and faculty attitudes that have dominated much of writing center research over the last 25 years—bringing Stephen North to declare in 1984 that "there is not a single published study of what happens in writing center tutorials" (1984b, 28). Studying language in use is the only real way to examine the potential learning that might occur in these contexts, according to Athanases and Heath (1995):

> Examining language uses in their social contexts enables ethnographers to cast cognitive processes in active form, accounting for language and activities that give evidence of remembering, thinking, and perceiving rather than as objects such as memories, perceptions, and cognitions in the heads of the writers and readers. (266)

Second, I needed data that would test the veracity of the accounts my participants offered in interviews. This process, known as "triangulation" (Delamont, 1992, 159), is essential to interpretive research and was a constant source of concern as I designed and carried out my study. How would I know that the representations that participants offered me in interviews reflected any sort of actual practice? How were the interviews themselves affected by my participants' notions of the "right" answer to an interview question (for instance, one of my participants would say after responding to a question, "Is that what you were looking for?")? Miles and Hubeman (1984) describe triangulation as a "state of mind": "If you self-consciously set out to collect and double-check findings, using multiple sources and modes of evidence, the verification process will largely be built into the data-gathering process, and little more need be done than to report on one's procedures" (235).

Nevertheless, the state of my mind was not altogether at peace. This unrest was largely due to the extent of my involvement in this Writing Center. I was not merely studying a site where I worked, where I had "insider" status, because by the time my first year had passed and I was ready to begin collecting data for my dissertation, I had partial responsibility for hiring and training most of my colleagues. I was both participant and observer, and, at times, the overlapping nature of those roles seemed a source of anxiety and confusion rather than a means of completing a successful study.

DR. OBSERVER AND MR. PARTICIPANT

Choosing to study a site where I was a "member" or "insider" seemed at the time to be the single riskiest aspect of my research. Would my status as a senior tutor, with responsibility for hiring and training my tutor colleagues, threaten not only to alter the accounts those colleagues offered in interviews, but also limit my access to any true picture of their tutoring? From the beginning of my study, I stressed to the other tutors that what I was doing was not evaluative—I was not checking up on my six colleagues to find out whether or not they were "good" tutors. I assured them that they had all been hired because they were good tutors. My research was more descriptive in nature, a means of taking a sociolinguistic view of how tutors and students use language in tutorials to achieve their goals. That was what I said.

With these assurances, I seemed to have complete compliance from my colleagues. All expressed eagerness to be interviewed about their tutoring practices, to tape record tutoring sessions, to complete reflective notes and content records on each tutoring session, and to engage in e-mail conversations about tutoring issues. However, by early October in my first semester of data collection I began to get worried, as I recorded in my notes:

> October 3: Non-compliance is a primary concern—none of my fellow tutors has recorded any of their sessions. I need to find out why since that in and of itself is important to the study. Confidentiality? Unease with what they do or how they do it? Afraid of tainting their sessions somehow? Perhaps I need to play a more direct role in recruiting students [to consent to have their sessions taped]; I'm not quite sure how to do that. The other angle I need to pursue is to tape some of my own sessions, starting today. Perhaps I can then play that back at my next interview—if we can't deconstruct their sessions, we can at least deconstruct mine.

My position in this study, the participant-observer role, is a common one in qualitative research in educational settings. As Moss (1992) writes, "Because participant observation is the major data gathering technique in ethnography, the ethnographer's role in the community influences the level of participant observation in the field" (158). Spradley (1980) defines the role of the participant-observer along continuums of low to high involvement and complete participation to nonparticipation. Certainly, my high involvement and complete participation in the daily life of the Writing Center were aspects that influenced my study.

This level of involvement, however, does not necessarily constitute a problem. Michael Burawoy (1991a) writes that participant observation is the most appropriate method for discovering meaning in day-to-day behavior: "The pursuit of non-discursive knowledge, that is, knowledge that is assumed rather than unconscious—both the observer's as well as the participant's—calls for participation but not immersion, observation but not marginality. This privileges participant observation" (5).

Because I was examining the teaching and learning practices of tutors and students, I needed to make explicit my own knowledge of those acts, as Burawoy (1991a) describes, as well as my participants' knowledge. One means of doing the latter was to conduct a "stimulated recall" of tutoring sessions during interviews: playing audiotapes of sessions and having the participants comment on what they heard and try to recollect what they were thinking at the time. This method was vital to my study in that I wanted to uncover the often-unexpressed goals that tutor and student bring to their interaction. What is behind a student's request for a tutor to check "if my paper flows"? What preconceived notions of learning in one-to-one settings are revealed by a tutor asking the students to read their texts aloud? Answering these questions depended on my having taped sessions. Two months into my study, I had none.

This tension between the researcher and participants is inevitable, according to Burawoy (1991b). In sharing the advice he gave to his own graduate-student researchers, Burawoy writes: "'The roles of participant and observer are inherently in conflict, and tension and anxiety are an intrinsic part of field work', I reassured them. 'Other things being equal', I advised, 'the greater the tension the better the product'" (293).

Early in my collection of data, this tension was causing me considerable anxiety; it seemed I would not have any product at all and would have to spend a depressing period ruminating over a new dissertation topic. My relationship with my tutor colleagues was relatively young, however. Five of the six tutors other than myself were new to the Writing Center that semester. Our interaction had been limited to a presemester workshop on tutoring issues, several twice-weekly meetings, and my first round of interviews, conducted in the first 2 weeks of the semester. We had had little chance to establish the social bonds that mark many researcher-participant relationships. As

Deyhle, Hess, and LeCompte (1992) point out, this relationship can be akin to friendship with all the complexity that entails:

> Like most friendships, relationships with fieldwork participants are far more complex than those with survey or questionnaire respondents or experimental subjects.... Like most friendships, which they frequently become, traditional fieldwork relationships are of long duration; they mandate patterns of nurturing, caring, and reciprocity; and they permit and necessitate deeper personal disclosure on the part of both researcher and researched than is the case in other forms of research. The risks and rewards are great. (619)

The risks, I was finding, were that my study would be a bust because I had no data of actual tutoring sessions. Perhaps I needed to take Cassell's (1980) advice: "Fieldwork, like friendship, requires a number of social lies to keep interaction flowing smoothly" (35). Although my pledge not to be evaluative was a "social lie" of sorts in that notions of effective tutoring could not help but be present in my analysis, perhaps my initial round of interviews had made my colleagues too self-conscious about their work. Had I simply blown it by asking questions about my colleagues' backgrounds as students and tutors and by eliciting their initial models for the responsibilities that tutor and student should assume in a session?

In a field note following a tutor meeting, I wrote, "Still no taped sessions, a real compliance problem. I do next round of interviews in two weeks. To address: why haven't they taped? What are [the] reasons and how can they be overcome? Why haven't they been filling out the blue [evaluation] forms?" By the end of that note, I was contemplating moving my research to another site the following semester, trying to focus in on the essential difficulty: "If my own writing center tutors won't tape their sessions, why would another set of writing center tutors tape? Yet my role (perceived) as an evaluator might not be present at another site."

My noncompliance problem was eventually resolved during a tutor meeting in the middle of that semester when we reached a milestone of sorts: I was able to bring up the question of why my colleagues had not been taping their sessions, and we openly discussed the performance anxiety several felt. Also, one tutor who had taped several of his sessions the previous weekend reported how easy and unobtrusive it was to do (and taping included the tutors having the student read and sign an informed-consent form prior to the session). Still, one colleague reported that she was afraid of "saying something wrong" on tape, a clear indication that despite my assurances, the evaluative qualities of my study were clearly on some minds. However, by that point it seemed that my colleagues and I had established a relationship and could trust each other enough to admit that as tutors we succumbed to "guided proofreading" at the end of eight consecutive sessions over 4 hours or sometimes did not have a clue as to how to help some challenging students. These disclosures created a level of comfort in which my colleagues could consider subjecting their tutoring to my scrutiny.

By the end of the fall semester, four of my six colleagues had taped several of their tutoring sessions. Although I continued to interview all six, I eventually realized that it would only be the four who had taped sessions who would be included in the report of my findings. This did not present a serious problem, however; I had stacks of data, much more than I could reasonably handle. It would take another year of sorting through it all until I could declare my study finished. Along the way, I had experienced what Stephen Ball (1990) describes: "Ethnography not only implies engagement of the researcher in the world under study; it also implies a commitment to a search for meaning, a suspension of preconceptions, and an orientation to discovery. In other words, ethnography involves risk, uncertainty, and discomfort" (157).

My role as an "insider" to my research site, combined with a need to be an "outsider" in order to study the Writing Center, caused me a great deal of "uncertainty and discomfort," inevitable perhaps. However, an additional dilemma was the need to clarify my theoretical framework that I was bringing to the study. This was not simply a matter of driving down to the local "Theories R Us" and pulling either "ethnomethodology" or "symbolic interaction" off the shelf. Instead, as in dealing with my participant-observer role, this process required deliberate introspection, occasional confusion, and some measure of compromise.

THEORETICAL FRAME-UPS

Zaharlick and Green (1991) describe ethnography as "more than a set of field methods, data collection techniques (tools), analysis procedures, or narrative description. It is a theoretically driven, systematic approach to the study of everyday life of a social group" (205). Most problematic for me in this definition was the need to clarify the theoretical perspective I brought to my research. This perspective was informed primarily by two components: 1) my reading of what the writing center literature offers for theoretical analysis of tutor-student interaction; and 2) the expectations, "folk theories" (Gee, Michaels, & O'Connor, 1992), and biases—either conscious or hidden—that I held.

In the writing center literature, I was particularly struck by the historical struggle of writing centers to escape the stigma of remediation. Writing centers have aligned themselves with the attention to the processes of invention, drafting, and revision, and to the development of students' knowledge and control of these processes. However, the result of this alignment is often an identity defined by what a writing center is not—not about being a "fix-it shop" (North, 1984a, 435), not about "handing out skills and strategies" (Lunsford, 1991, 4), and not about being places that "simply reproduce the interpersonal relationships of conventional schooling" (King, 1993, 17). These identities position writing centers as an alternative to perceived classroom approaches (Hemmeter, 1990) but are not shaped by a body of systematic primary research on what happens when students and tutors meet.

In immersing myself in this literature, I wanted to contribute toward a "reconstruction of existing theory," as Michael Burawoy (1991a) describes. My intention was to find what was problematic with dictums for tutors to be "minimalist" (Brooks, 1991) and to let students' expressed needs guide the conference at the same time that a student's primary goal might be simply to emerge from a session with a corrected text. My approach was what Burawoy (1991a) labels the "extended case method," in which "we search for theories that highlight some aspect of the situation under study as being anomalous and then proceed to rebuild (rather than reject) that theory by reference to the wider forces at work, be they the state, the economy, or even the world system" (6).

Reconstructing writing center theory was a goal of my research from the beginning. Rather than posit theory based on readings of other theorists, I intended to provide a research-based analysis of the phenomenon central to writing center work—the interaction of tutors and students.

My perspective was also shaped by the experiences and expectations I brought to tutoring and studying tutorials. Atanases and Heath (1995) write that "ethnographic reporting is the construction of a reality, made possible by the researchers essential instrument, the self" (278). In Wendy Bishop's (1992) terms,

> Data are collected and transformed into texts, and texts are authored, that is, constructed. In author-saturated texts, those that acknowledge their constructedness and invoke authority through overtly rhetorical and persuasive techniques, there is a better chance for engaging a reader in our sometimes confusing and always modest cultural journal. (152)

My study was "author saturated" in every move of data collection, analysis and reporting, from choosing whom to study and how, to conducting interviews, to identifying patterns and themes in the data, to choosing representative quotes to present to my readers. Bogden and Biklen (1992) write that "qualitative researchers try to acknowledge and take into account their own biases as a method of dealing with them" (47). Nevertheless, I could not help but feel my biases—particularly my notions of "effective" tutoring based on my experiences as a tutor—would shape my study.

Tutoring writing was coming full circle for me, a return to how I started teaching when I worked in a writing center while pursing my MA. Tutoring gave me a powerful vantage point from which to view what it meant for students to write in college. As a tutor, I could see first-hand the impact of tasks (particularly poorly conceived ones), the often overlooked power of an instructor's expectations and criteria (sometimes poorly communicated to students), and the value of tutoring in supporting learning to write in college. I embraced—and still do—the notion, as North (1984a) describes, that "the ideal situation for teaching and learning is the tutorial, the one-on-one, face-to-face interaction between a writer and a trained, experienced tutor" (28). Would this stance limit my ability to question the practices I observed or to seek data that might contradict my long-held beliefs? This question, while never fully resolved, shaped my study by its mere presence. Athanases and Heath (1995) lay out an ambitious agenda for working to resolve this problem, an agenda I attempted to follow as closely as I could:

> The author of a well-researched and well-reported ethnography has the responsibility to reveal how theoretical assumptions and philosophical and political biases, as well as practical considerations, have shaped methodological choices and research moves. One challenge for the ethnographer is to re-articulate these assumptions, biases, and considerations, and then to explicate how these have informed decisions at all stages of the research process, from choice of research method, to selection of research sites, and on through data collection and analytic procedures. (278)

Effectively dealing with one's own biases as a researcher is no easy matter. In fact, Michael Burawoy (1991a) suggests that altering one's biases might also be a product of research: "The purpose of fieldwork is not to strip ourselves of biases, for that is an illusory goal, nor to celebrate those biases as the authorial voice of the ethnographer, but rather to discover and perhaps change our biases through interaction with others" (4).

However, what is often missing in accounts of qualitative research in education, are the "metanarratives," as Wendy Bishop (1992) labels "the discussions of how ethnographic research actually gets completed" (153). These include the influences the author brings to bear on the study, the attempts to make those influences visible, and the ways the research itself might have changed the author's orientation. For me, studying the tutoring of my colleagues was one way to reconcile my notions of student-centered tutoring and long-term development with the powerful daily pressures for students to emerge from sessions with corrected texts. As a result of my research, my bias toward the infallibility of writing center tutoring was revealed. I learned to consider the at-times competing goals that are present in writing center sessions. The college or university, the writing center itself, the tutor, the student, and the student's classroom instructor all influence that moment when the tutor asks, "What can I help you with?" and the student replies, "Can you tell me if this flows?"

Although qualitative or interpretive research requires that researchers "come clean" to their readers, the appropriate place for this cleansing is certainly problematic. In my dissertation, it was acceptable form to add a section to my methods chapter titled "Theoretical and Experiential Framework of the Researcher." Throughout the text, I could remind the reader of my presence, whether simply through the use of the first-person pronoun or through descriptions that included clues that it was my point of view that I was detailing. Nevertheless, the space for articulation of biases, assumptions, and preconceived notions is not always readily obvious or available in our field's publications and remains unresolved. Perhaps what is most important is that researchers conduct their studies with self-knowledge of potential cognitive and affective filters and foreground these to their readers as much their texts allow.

Keeping in mind the signature of the researcher on the conduct and presentation of a study, I now put my research dilemmas aside and turn to several published accounts of writing center research. By examining how those researchers reported on the ways they dealt with dilemmas of being a participant–observer, we can see where writing center research has been and what it must move toward in order for our field to establish a respected research base.

WRITING CENTER RESEARCH AND THE INVISIBLE INVESTIGATOR

Most published qualitative studies of writing center conferencing often have an authorial quality that Wendy Bishop (1992) labels the "cool" style of the "outside knower," characterized by a lack of first-person pronouns and a researcher operating invisibly. The relationship between participants and researcher, if noted at all, often comes in a footnote, as if that relationship is an aside to the "real" work of analyzing tutorial discourse. For example, several researchers negotiate the dilemma of the participant–observer by limiting themselves to analysis of transcripts, audiotapes, or videotapes of tutoring sessions (e.g., Cook-Gumperz, 1993; Davis, Hayward, Hunter & Wallace, 1988; Severino, 1992), As Carol Severino (1992) notes in her study, "Studying these two particular sessions and other videotaped tutoring sessions and their written transcripts has helped me inductively identify key features of situations and interpersonal dynamics that affect the nature of collaboration" (54).

Severino's readers are not told why she chose those particular sessions or those particular tutors, nor do we find out what she brought to her analysis in terms of expectations and assumptions nor her relationship to those she studied. The power of a researcher's preconceived notions can overwhelm the data collected, as Stephen Jay Gould (1981) has amply demonstrated in his accounts of the influence of bias in early studies of brain size and intelligence in *The Mismeasure of Man*. Even an act as seemingly benign as choosing sessions to analyze and present is encumbered with ideology, partial theories, and unstated agendas.

Similarly, Davis et al. (1988) and Cook-Gumperz (1993) give little indication as to the motivations behind their methodological choices. Davis et al., tell their readers that both tutors and students were chosen "at random" and that each gave consent to have tutoring sessions recorded. In terms of making expectations clear, we are told that the authors analyzed tutoring sessions using categories derived from another study of teaching, one involving talk in ESL classrooms. The authors note that "although writing centers differ from ESL classrooms, we feel the principles in question are the same: Is *real conversation* going on, or are tutors engaging in forms of *teacher talk*" [my emphasis]" (47). In this question are the hints of bias—is "teacher talk" necessarily a strong-armed, close-minded, just-do-what-I-say command? Is real conversation necessarily superior? Many people engage in conversations daily without opportunities to insert their points of view or are simply bored to tears. While Davis et al. do not make an official statement of preconceived beliefs, those beliefs strongly shape their study.

Willa Wolcott (1998), in her "qualitative study of writing center conferencing," is much more forthcoming in revealing her relationship to her participants: "One limitation of my study is my involvement in the center; as I have coordinated the writing program there for a number years, my viewpoint is not completely objective. However, the tutors, who knew I was there for research purposes and not for evaluative reasons, did not appear to mind" (17). Aside from the question of whether any "viewpoint" can ever be objective, Wolcott's surety in the non-invasiveness of her relationship to those she studied is not investigated, nor is it part of her text. Giving her reader that knowledge, however, is an important element in allowing us to judge the merits of her findings, an element missing from studies that assume access to participants and negotiating relationships are clean and problem free,

James Bell (1990), Joyce Magnotto (1992), and Barbara Roswell (1993) are the authors of three qualitative dissertations that attempt to account for their authors' biases. Bell negotiates his relationship with those he studied by choosing a writing center "because it was located in the city to which I moved and because the director and acting director of the center agreed to my conducting this research" (42). On Spradley's (1980) continuua, Bell has a low degree of involvement and is a nonparticipant in the activities he is studying. Nevertheless, Bell makes substantial use of his participants' reactions to his findings in his dissertation, allowing each a space to comment on his conclusions. This inclusion of participants' "voices" works to fulfill what Linda Brodkey (1987) describes as a central element of ethnography: "Ethnography proceeds from the possibility of understanding others on their own terms" (41).

Both Magnotto (1992) and Roswell (1993) include in their dissertations accounts of their relationships to the settings they investigated and explicitly describe the methods they used to collect data using multiple sources and methods (and both came out of the same doctoral program). Barbara Roswell also gives her reader an inkling of the dilemmas she faced as a participant–observer, one who was the previous director of the writing center she studied and had taught the undergraduate peer tutor methods class:

> The fact that I had previously taught and directed many of the tutors also left residual role expectations, however, and I often struggled to distance myself from the role of evaluator and to focus on the research questions I had established for the study rather than the host of practical and pedagogical issues that had been my major concern as Writing Center Director. (63)

Although the relatively ample space of a dissertation can allow more disclosure of expectations and relationships than can a journal article, the precedent set by Bell, Magnotto, and Roswell is an important one. Awareness of these issues is vital for those undertaking inquiry into the writing centers where they tutor or direct, as is conscious means to minimize the effects of these influences. This terrain, however, is not uncharted. The work of "teacher research" or qualitative inquiry by classroom teachers into their own settings can provide a guide for writing center research.

TEACHER RESEARCH AND THE (NOT SO) GREAT UNKNOWN

In writing center settings, the rapid turnover of personnel (particularly undergraduate peer tutors), fiscal and time constraints, and contested institutional identity often rule out the idea of systematic research. Some even see the "theorizing" done in the pages of our journals and collections as somehow removed from the realities of day-to-day practice as Albert DeCiccio, Michael Rossi, and Kathleen Shine Cain (1995) have recently written: "While writing center theorists debate with one another, a parallel conversation among tutors and tutees is constructing real theory" (26).

Teacher research attempts to bridge the perceived gaps between theory and practice in K–12 schooling and offers an opportunity for those involved with writing center teaching to formalize, in a sense, the acts that many of us do already—investigate our questions regarding learning to write in college and the one-to-one teaching of writing that arise in every tutorial. Teacher-research advocates propose that the classroom teacher (or writing center tutor or director) is best qualified to offer the insider's perspective on day-to-day work (Cochran-Smith & Lytle, 1993). As Cathy Fleischer (1995) writes, "Teachers who are intimately involved in the complex context of the classroom are best able to see into the dynamics in it" (14).

Marilyn Cochran-Smith and Susan Lytle (1993) offer a qualitative methodology of teacher-research that contains features of many tutor-training programs: 1) journal accounts of "classroom life over time"; 2) "oral inquiries" or "collaborative analyses and interpretations" among teachers; 3) systematic explorations of practice based on "observation, interview and document collection"; and 4) essays in which teachers offer "interpretations of the assumptions and characteristics of classroom and school life and/or research itself" (27). Each of these components can be easily adapted by tutors or directors studying their practice (see Werder & Buck [1995] for an account of ethnographic methodology as applied to writing center tutor evaluation).

Local qualitative research offers the opportunity to create disciplinary knowledge that is "self-serving" in the best sense. Ruth Ray (1992) describes teacher research as "an emancipation proclamation that results in new ownership—teachers own research into their own problems that results in modification of their own behaviors and theories" (174). Teacher research thus acknowledges that we all carry out our teaching with theoretical assumptions, whether those assumptions are "folk theories" (Gee, Michaels, & O'Connor, 1992) or untested expectations based largely on personal experience or are largely unexamined models delivered in the pages of our journals. Ann Berthoff (1987) sees teacher research as essentially examining what practitioners already bring to their work:

> Research, like REcognition, is a REflexive act. It means looking—and looking again. The new kind of REsearch would not mean going out after new data, but rather REconsidering what is at hand. REsearch would come to mean looking and looking at what happens in the English classroom. We do not need new information: we need to think about the information we have. (30)

As I have described, my study of the writing center where I tutored started with such reflexive questions: Why do I act the way I do in tutoring sessions? What goals and expectations do I bring? How can I interpret students' language to understand more fully the goals and expectations that they bring? While I pledged non-evaluation to my colleagues, I was starting with an evaluation of my own practice or at least a desire to improve that practice. I was a teacher/tutor-researcher, albeit with the more formal trappings of a dissertation committee, human subjects review board, and a sometimes elusive degree as a motivation. I was invested in improving our field's knowledge of practice.

REACHING CONCLUSIONS

The results of my study showed me that four graduate student writing tutors, operating without formal supervision and with minimal training, had defined, sometimes rigid expectations for the ways students should act in tutorials. All expressed a desire to focus on the "writer" and not necessarily the "writing," but each felt frustrated by the powerful influences that students bring to a session, particularly the goal to have their texts corrected (often dictated by the students' classroom instructors). This goal conflict was not present when a certain match could take place—tutor and student shared academic disciplines or simply some history of working together. However, in this Writing Center, most students visited only once or twice per semester, a powerful constraint on tutors in achieving their long-term goals. The writing tutors' most consistent contribution to students who struggle to write in college was perhaps to give them some assurance, some indication that they were not struggling alone, and that the tutor was there for a supportive word, a look at the text, and a confirmation that students were on the right path. This contribution is not a trivial accomplishment but might have little impact on students' long-term writing development.

In reaching these conclusions, my role as participant–observer caused no small measure of anxiety; nevertheless, I am quite convinced that this role (and perhaps the anxiety) and qualitative methods were best suited to examine my questions. Marilyn Cochran-Smith and Susan Lytle (1993) describe a similar match for teachers examining their classrooms, a description I have slightly modified for writing center settings:

> [Writing center] research is concerned with the questions that arise from the lived experiences of [tutors] and the everyday life of [tutoring] expressed in a language that emanates from practice. [Tutors] are concerned about the consequences of their actions, and [writing center] research is often prompted by [our] desires to know more about the dynamic interplay of [tutor–student] events. Hence, [writing center] research is well positioned to produce precisely the kind of knowledge currently needed in the field. (59)

The prospect of the many "insiders" in writing centers conducting qualitative inquiry—and publishing that inquiry in books, journals and conference talks—is an exciting one. While my experience as an insider with an outsider's research agenda was filled with dilemmas, exploring those dilemmas—examining and countering my biases, making clear my expectations and their origins, establishing working relationships with my participants—was at times as valuable as any answers I might have discovered. Perhaps I should blame my dilemmas on Stephen North (1984a) again, for it was he who wrote, "Writing centers are simply one manifestation—polished and highly visible—of a dialogue about writing that is central to higher education" (440). Our research on *our* writing centers continues this dialogue, interrogates and expands it. We are all participant–observers, and we all have much to discuss.

REFERENCES

Athanases, S. Z. & Heath, S. B. (1995). Ethnography in the study of the teaching and learning of English. *Research in the Teaching of English, 29*, 263–287.

Ball, S. J. (1990). Self-doubt and soft data: Social and technical trajectories in ethnographic fieldwork. *Qualitative Studies in Education, 3*, 157–171.

Bell, J. H. (1989). Tutoring in a writing center (Doctoral dissertation, University of Texas at Austin, 1989). *Dissertation Abstracts International, 50*, 2763.

Berthoff, A. E. (1987). The teacher as REsearcher. In D. Goswami & R. Stillman (Eds.), *Reclaiming the classroom: Teacher research as an agency for change* (pp. 28–39). Portsmouth, NH: Heinemann.

Bishop, W. (1992). I-Witnessing in composition: Turning ethnographic data into narratives. *Rhetoric Review, 11*, 147–158.

Bogdan, R. C. & Biklen, S. K. (1992). *Qualitative research for education: An introduction to theory and methods,* (2nd ed.). Boston: Allyn and Bacon.

Brodkey, L. (1987). Writing ethnographic narratives. *Written Communication, 4,* 25–50.

Brooks, J. (1991). Minimalist tutoring: Making the student do all the work. *The Writing Lab Newsletter, 15,* 1–3.

Burawoy, M. (1991a). Introduction. In Burawoy, et al. (Eds.), *Ethnography unbound: Power and resistance in the modem metropolis* (1–7). Berkeley: University of California Press.

Burawoy, M. (1991b). Teaching participant observation. In Burawoy, et al. (Eds.), *Ethnography unbound: Power and resistance in the modern metropolis* (pp. 291–300). Berkeley: University of California Press.

Cassell, J. (1980). Ethical principles for conducting fieldwork. *American Anthropologist, 82,* 28–40.

Cochran-Smith, M. & Lytle, S. L. (1993). *Inside/Outside: Teacher research and knowledge.* New York: Teachers College Press.

Cook-Gumperz, J. (1993). Dilemmas of identity: Oral and written literacies in the making of a basic writing student. *Anthropology and Education Quarterly, 24,* 336–356.

Davis, K. M., Hayward, N., Hunter, K. R., & Wallace, D. L. (1986). The function of talk in the writing conference: A study of tutorial conversation. *The Writing Center Journal, 9,* 45–51.

DeCiccio, A. C., Rossi, M. J., & Cain, K. S. (1995). Walking the tightrope: Negotiating between the ideal and the practical in the writing center. In B. L. Stay, C. Murphy, & E. H. Hobson (Eds.). *Writing center perspectives* (pp. 26–37). Emmitsburg: NWCA Press.

Delamont, S. (1992). *Fieldwork in educational settings: Methods, pitfalls and perspectives.* London: Falmer Press.

Deyhle, D. L., Hess, G. A., Jr., & LeCompte, M. D. (1992). Approaching ethical issues for qualitative researchers in education. In M. D. LeCompte, W. L. Millroy, & J. Preissle (Eds.), *The handbook of qualitative research in education* (pp. 228–291). Orlando, FL: Academic Press.

Eisner, E. W. (1991). *The enlightened eye: Qualitative inquiry and the enhancement of educational practice.* New York: Macmillan.

Erickson, F. (1986). Qualitative methods in research on teaching. In M. C. Wittrock (Ed.), *Handbook of research on teaching* (3rd ed., pp. 119–161). New York: Macmillan.

Fleischer, C. (1995). *Composing teacher-research: A prosaic history.* Albany: SUNY Press.

Freire, (1972). *Pedagogy of the oppressed.* New York: Herder and Herder.

Gee, J. P., Michaels, S., & O'Connor, M. C. (1992). Discourse analysis. In M. D. LeCompte, W. L. Millroy, & J. Preissle (Eds.), *The handbook of qualitative research in education* (pp. 228–291). Orlando, FL: Academic Press.

Geertz, C. (1983). Thick description: Toward an interpretive theory of culture. In R. M. Emerson (Ed.), *Contemporary field research: A collection of readings* (pp. 37–59). Prospect Heights, IL: Waveland Press.

Gould, S. J. (1981). *The mismeasure of man.* New York: W.W. Norton.

Heath, S. B. (1983). *Ways with words: Language, life, and work in communities and class-rooms.* Cambridge, UK: Cambridge University Press.

Hemmeter, T. (1990). The "smack of difference": The language of writing center discourse. *The Writing Center Journal, 11,* 35–48.

King, M. (1993). Introduction to section 11. In T. Flynn & M. King (Eds.), *Dynamics of the writing conference: Social and cognitive interaction* (pp. 17–23). Urbana: NCTE.

Lerner, N. D. (1996). Teaching and learning in a university writing center (Doctoral dissertation, Boston University, 1996). *Dissertation Abstracts International, 57,* 1060.

Lunsford, A. A. (1991). Collaboration, control, and the idea of a writing center. *The Writing Center Journal, 12,* 3–10.

Magnatto, J. N. (1991). The construction of college writing in a cross-disciplinary community college writing center: An analysis of student, tutor, and faculty rep-resentations (Doctoral dissertation, University of Pennsylvania 1991). *Dissertation Abstracts International, 52,* 2382A.

Miles, M. B. & Hubeman, A. M. (1984*). Qualitative data analysis: A sourcebook of new methods.* Beverly Hills: Sage.

Mishler, E. G. (1990). Validation in inquiry-guided research: The role of exemplars in narrative studies. *Harvard Educational Review, 60,* 415–442.

Moss, B. J. (1992). Ethnography and composition: Studying language at home. In G. Kirsch & A. Sullivan (Eds.), *Methods and methodology in composition research* (pp. 153–171). Carbondale: SIU Press.

Neuleib, J. W. & Scharton, M. A. (1994). Writing others, writing ourselves: Ethnog-raphy and the writing center. In J, A. Mullin & R. Wallace (Eds.), *Intersections: The-ory-practice in the writing center* (pp. 54–67). Urbana: NCTE.

North, S. M, (1984a). The idea of a writing center. *College English, 46,* 433–446.

North, S. M. (1984b). Writing center research: Testing our assumptions. In G. A. Olson (Ed.), *Writing centers: Theory and administration* (pp. 24–35). Urbana: NCTE.

Ray, R. (1992). Composition from the teacher-research point of view. In G. Kirsch & A. Sullivan (Eds.), *Methods and methodology in composition research* (pp. 172–189). Carbondale: SIU Press.

Roswell, B. S. (1992). The tutor's audience is always a fiction: The construction of au-thority in writing center conferences (Doctoral dissertation, University of Penn-sylvania, 1992). *Dissertation Abstracts International, 53,* 3830A.

Severino, C. (1992). Rhetorically analyzing collaborations. *The Writing Center Jour-nal, 13,* 53–64.

Spelling, M. (1990). I want to talk to each of you: Collaboration and the teacher–stu-dent writing conference. *Research in the Teaching of English, 24,* 279–321.

Spradley, J. (1980). *Participant observation.* New York: Holt, Rinehart & Winston.

Werder, C. & Buck, R. R. (1995). Assessing writing conference talk: An ethnographic method. In B. L. Stay, C. Murphy, & E. H. Hobson (Eds.), *Writing center perspec-tives* (pp. 168–178). Emmitsburg, MD: NWCA Press.

Wolcott, H. F. (1987). On ethnographic intent. In G. Spindler & L. Spindler (Eds.), *Interpretive ethnography of education: At home and abroad* (pp. 37–57). Hillside, NJ: Lawrence Erlbaum Associates.

Wolcott, W. (1989). Talking it over: A qualitative study of writing center conferencing. *The Writing Center Journal, 9,* 15–29.

Zaharlick, A, & Green, J, L. (1991). Ethnographic research. In J. Flood, J. M. Jensen, D. Lapp, & J. R. Squire (Eds.), *Handbook of research on teaching the English language arts* (pp. 205–225). New York: Macmillan.

II

Writing Centers as Sites of Institutional Critique and Contextual Inquiry

Writing Center Administration: Making Local, Institutional Knowledge in Our Writing Centers

Muriel Harris
Purdue University

In the literature of writing centers, there's a long history of debate about their marginalization. Some claim that writing centers are undervalued; others prefer the margins as places of freedom from institutional constraints; and still others proudly proclaim the writing center as cutting edge. It's not clear whether cutting edges are in the center or on the margins or even whether such spatial conceptions clarify or muddy the issues. But in such discussions, there is usually general agreement in calling for writing center research as an answer to strengthen whatever spatial context is being put forth as the writing center's appropriate place. Research, it is generally agreed, will give writing centers substance and weight and "centrality" in the field; writing center research will be the instrument of institutional change; writing center research will forge new paths. If arguments are to be made about writing centers as sites of substantive research, then we need to expand those discussions to include a type of writing center research—research on writing center administration—that is carried out with great frequency and effectiveness. There's a large body of knowledge being generated by this research, but it is less visible because it often does not employ empirical research practices, is local in nature, and is usually hidden under the rubric of "service" or "administrative responsibilities." Certainly, too many writing center directors fail to credit themselves when review time comes around for all the institutional research they do in order to run their centers well. And writing centers haven't exactly spotlighted themselves publicly as places with intense programs of institutional research. When such inquiry is noticed in the literature of writing centers, it is more likely to be devalued as "merely justify[ing] the center's existence to administrators" or as "responsible record keeping" (Severino, 1994, 51).

I describe writing center research on administration as localized because I want to distinguish such research from the studies done by those who investigate organizational or institutional structures in a more abstract or general way, displaced from their local contexts. Although writing centers could fruitfully be a source of highly interesting studies of an organization typically structured collaboratively and nonhierarchically (with innovative patterns of organizational communication among its personnel), the form of inquiry under discussion here is that type of research being done year after year, semester after semester, as part of a writing center administrator's work. It is the localized, contextualized inquiry in which a director studies aspects of his or her own center and institution as part of the process of shaping the writing center. To a degree even greater than is the case with composition programs, writing centers are—and must be—shaped to fit their particularized surroundings. In an essay arguing that "writing center personnel live and move and have their being within institutions on which they are dependent for their professional identity," Dave Healy (1995) notes, "It is difficult to imagine most writing centers divorced from their institutional context" (22–23). When creating a taxonomy of types of writing centers, Joyce Kinkead and Jeanette Harris (1993), in *Writing Centers in Context,* limited their case studies to 12 types, but writing centers are most successful when they are closely interwoven with the writing programs at their particular institutions. Thus, given the variety of structures of educational institutions at all levels, at least 12 more models could easily be added to Kinkead and Harris' book. Coming up with a universal picture of a writing center is not only impossible but also untrue to the nature of writing centers.

General theories, practices, and research on writing centers must all be worked into the decision-making processes of structuring and directing a center, but reality is much messier than theory, and the locality of each writing center has its defining features and constraints that impinge on the structure of the center and the solutions to the various problems and questions that arise. A well-functioning, effective writing center folds itself into and around the localized features, building on them. But how does the director know what those features are? That's where localized institutional research arises. By studying the particular place, with its particular staff, student body, institutional mission, administrative structures, and faculty needs, a writing center director makes knowledge—localized knowledge that is critically important as a basis for the administrative decisions that have to be made and problems that have to be solved. To dismiss the knowledge gained from such inquiry as mere record keeping or attempts to justify the center's existence is to misread the role—and importance—of this work, as well as its scope. To look more closely at this issue, I need to examine first the question of how and why institutional knowledge-making in writing centers is research, then to review topics and examples of such writing center research that have been shared in print, and—hoping I've made the case that there *is* such a form of inquiry—to argue for why recognizing and emphasizing this form of writing center research is important.

INSTITUTIONAL KNOWLEDGE-MAKING AS RESEARCH

Writing center directors regularly confront a number of administrative issues that are best answered when the directors have local, institutional knowledge at their fingertips. How does the writing center fit into the institution's mission? What is the best way to publicize the center? What do the faculty want to know in the notes tutors send to them? Writing center directors reading such questions will recognize them as ones that need answers (usually yesterday). They will also recognize how difficult it is to obtain data for some of the answers needed, because writing center administration is the process of solving the messy problems of the real world. Working in the realm of the real world is where Donald Schon (1987, 1993) finds the true challenge for the professional practitioner. On one hand, there are manageable problems, Schon explains, those that lend themselves to solutions through the application of research-based theory and technique. It is here that control groups can be set up and conditions for study can be isolated from the welter of factors that impinge in the real world. Traditionally, this research has been assumed to be superior to the work of practitioners, for its findings provide the base for practitioners. Or, as Stephen North (1987), describes this traditional hierarchy in *The Making of Knowledge in Composition*, researchers *make* knowledge, and practitioners *apply* it. Unfortunately, as Schon has argued at great length, such research hasn't helped a lot when practitioners move into the real world. Drawing on examples of doctors, engineers, teachers, architects, and others at work, he (1993) offers glimpses of practitioners facing situations of uncertainty, instability, uniqueness, and value conflict. The real world presents us with conditions unlike those in the tidy world of pure research. One of Schon's examples gives us a taste of working in the real world as he describes it:

> When professionals consider what road to build, for example, they deal usu-
> ally with a complex and ill-defined situation in which geographic, topological,
> financial, economic, and political issues are all mixed up together. Once they
> have somehow decided what road to build and go on to consider how best to

build it, they may have a problem they can solve by the application of available techniques, but when the road they have built leads unexpectedly to the destruction of a neighborhood, they may find themselves again in a situation of uncertainty. (1993, 40)

Schon describes this reality where practitioners work as a swampy lowland where we find the messy, confusing problems that defy neat, clean technical solutions. In real life, he notes, "problems are interconnected, environments are turbulent" (1993, 16) and the situations of practice are characterized by unique events. To add to the messiness, Schon reminds us that "practitioners are frequently embroiled in conflicts of values, goals, purposes, and interests" (1993, 17). The irony, as Schon repeatedly points out, is that the problems of the high ground, the manageable ones, tend to be relatively unimportant to individuals and to society at large whereas in the swamps lie the problems of greatest human concern. If the practitioner descends to the lowland, he or she must be prepared for doing nonrigorous inquiry (1987, 3). Inquiry of this form, which Schon terms the work of the "reflective practitioner," consists of reflection-in-action, questioning the assumptional structure of knowing-in-action, that is, thinking critically about something in the middle of doing it. This can lead to restructuring or to on-the-spot experimentation where new actions are tried, tested, and either affirmed or become the starting point for further reflection and experimentation (1987, 28). What is particularly important to writing centers is Schon's affirmation of the importance of acknowledging that we work in real, particularized settings where universal principles, theories, and findings from pure research may conflict or collide—or be of very little help. Other forces, those present in the particular situation at the particular time and particular place where the practitioner is practicing his or her art, dictate a different mode of response—if appropriate and valuable solutions are to be found. And this mode of response—reflection-in-action—is another type of research, differing from the pure form of traditional research. In "Practical Wisdom and the Geography of Knowledge in Composition," Louise Wetherbee Phelps (1991) points out that reflection-in-action "closely parallels academic research methods, but has a distinctive type of rigor" (873).

Thinking critically, or to use Schon's term, "reflectively," about real-world situations is, interestingly enough, becoming increasingly valued in composition studies as is evident in the rapid growth of the teacher-researcher movement. Books such as *The Writing Teacher as Researcher: Essays in the Theory and Practice of Class-Based Research*, edited by Donald Daiker and Max Morenberg (1990); *Inside/Outside: Teacher Research and Knowledge*, by Marilyn Cochran-Smith and Susan L. Lytle (1993); and *The Practice of Theory: Teacher Research in Composition*, by Ruth E. Ray (1993) provide eloquent and illuminating discussions of teacher-research in composition and its grounding in the particular classrooms where teachers practice their art. (Phelps extends this research to the arena of curriculum development while Irwin Weiser and Shirley Rose's collection of essays, *The Writing Program Administrator as Researcher: Inquiry in Action and Reflection* (1999), moves the discussion of institutionally oriented, reflective research into the work writing program administrators.) Chapter 3 of Ray's book offers sound arguments and a history of the teacher-research movement. The voices we hear in the Daiker and Morenberg collection offer guidelines that are immediately relevant to the work of the writing center director. For example, James Berlin (1990) notes that the aim of the teacher-researcher "is not primarily to publish" (9) but to "conduct her own research, to investigate the conditions of her own social setting in determining instructional content and strategies" (10). Yet, as Cochran-Smith and Lytle (1993) remind us, there is a rationale for making such work public: "When teachers study and write about their work, they make their own distinctive ways of knowing about teaching and learning more visible to themselves and others" (115).

In their chapter entitled "Learning from Teacher Research: A Working Typology" (Chapter 2), Cochran-Smith and Lytle (1993) offer an analytic framework for teacher research, defining it as "systematic and intentional inquiry about teaching, learning, and schooling carried out by teachers in their own school and classroom settings" (27). The first type of research in this framework is empirical investigation—using collection, analysis, and interpretation of data—and is conducted through journals, oral inquiries, and classroom/school studies. The other kind of research is conceptual—using theoretical/philosophical work or the analysis of ideas—and is conducted by means of writing essays recollecting and reflecting on what they see or read. The terms in Cochran-Smith and Lytle's working definition of teacher research are worth examining in more depth, because the words are carefully chosen and aptly characterize the nature of this kind of inquiry. Such research is "systematic" in that it follows ordered ways of gathering and recording information and analyzing events for which there may only be partial or unwritten records. It is "intentional" in that it is planned and not spontaneous, and can be characterized as true "inquiry" in that it stems from or generates questions and reflects teachers' desires to make sense of their experiences (23–24). But Cochran-Smith and Lytle refer to the work of Anne Berthoff to remind readers that, according to Berthoff, "it is not even necessary that teacher research involve new information but rather that it interpret the information one already has—what she calls 'REsearching'" (24). At a research conference on reading and English, Julie Jensen (1987) sought to broaden the view of what constitutes research: "I wish we could encourage a redefinition of the word 'researcher.' To the ranks of thesis and dissertation writers, assistant professors seeking tenure, . . . let's recruit anyone who has a question and a disciplined approach to finding an answer" (57).

KNOWLEDGE-MAKING IN ACTION
IN THE WRITING CENTER

Certainly, writing center directors have questions, and the information they seek out makes knowledge. Generally, the knowledge made in localized writing center research stays local, where it is constantly being used, and that may be the reason why this form of knowledge-making often goes unnoticed outside the center. But a typical example, one that was shared in print, illustrates the features of such research—Patricia Terry's (1994) "Things Your Mentor Never Told You: Discovering Writing Lab Identity in the Institutional Environment." In her essay, Terry details her work in defining her writing lab's place in the particular institution, Gonzaga University, where she began her new job as director. Quickly realizing that in order to understand whom it is that the lab serves, what services it should provide, what demands are being placed on the director, and how to fund and staff the place, she details for her readers the stages of her research. She investigated by means of questionnaires, interviews, surveys, and analyses of documents such as the institutional mission statement and financial aid systems. The result was that, as a director, she learned what she needed to know in order to begin functioning as an effective administrator. Even questions about how Terry might compensate tutors were answered by learning how students finance their education and what the campus policies on service are at Gonzaga. Books, articles, conference talks, even conversations with colleagues at other institutions were helpful, but finally, as Terry's story shows us, the knowledge she needed was scattered throughout her institution. She had to seek it out, realizing for herself the impact of Dave Healy's (1995) statement that "most discussions of writing centers eventually descend to the particular—or at least they should" (13).

The extent to which local knowledge is produced is particularly evident when we consider, in addition to the issues Terry notes, the vast range of other decisions a writing center administrator must make, the multitude of problems that have to be solved, and the number of structures the writing center administrator must build. What the particular center will focus on as its mission on campus depends on the institution it serves. Is retention an important issue on campus? If so, how does the writing center work to further this mission? Is distance learning important? What does the writing center do to accommodate students off campus who are involved in distance learning? Is research a valued part of the institution's mission? Is the writing center involved in basic research or contributing to research projects? Is outreach an institutional goal? If so, what types of outreach are being developed in the writing center? How well are any of these goals being met in the writing center? If the institution has other goals and missions, what are they? How do they impact the work of the writing center? A case study of the process of fitting a new writing center within the institution is described by David Schwalm (1995) as a "site-specific account" of "the values and concerns that a central administrator brings to the development of a writing center" (53). Schwalm, aware that his account is local and needs to be sifted, emphasizes the lack of transferability of the specifics but the usefulness of watching his story unfold: "Since sites provide different contexts and their administrators have different motives, the trick for the reader will be to separate the general from the particular, to determine what characteristics of this case study transcend the local circumstances and personalities" (53).

Much of what is valuable in Schwalm's account of the process is watching it in action. The topics of concern are universal (resources, student needs, administrative support, faculty interest, and so on) and the data for each is only useful locally, but the process by which Schwalm uncovers those specific realities reminds us that he is a researcher in action—in Jensen's definition, someone with questions and a disciplined approach to finding answers. His account, like Terry's, is offered as a case study, a form of inquiry that Thomas Newkirk (1992) reminds us is traditionally viewed as being in the minor leagues of research techniques, good for isolating variables and suggesting hypotheses, but not in the major leagues (130–131). Newkirk, however, finds great value in case studies, as their storytelling often contains what he calls "transformative narratives" whose authority comes from embedding sets of enduring cultural beliefs (134). Certainly, as we read the stories of Terry and Schwalm, we recognize and learn from patterns of academic culture embedded in those narratives, patterns we may not have been so acutely aware of without the narratives. Thus, case studies not only offer descriptions of processes for others to try, they also narrate patterns that, by their heightening in the flow of the story, are informative. These narratives tell us about the cultures we work in. But case studies, a form of inquiry particularly appropriate for institutional research, are not the only methods of inquiry to investigate our institutions. In a conversation on the electronic discussion group for writing center professionals, WCenter (WCenter posting, June 11, 1996), we read about Joan Mullin's use of surveys at the University of Toledo to learn the effects on grades of writing center tutorials, Jo Koster's use of surveys at Winthrop University to learn why students do or do not use the writing center and why faculty do or do not send students (WCenter posting, June 11, 1996); and Becky Rickly's use of case studies to determine the content of tutor training courses (WCenter posting, June 11, 1996).

And there are other issues in writing center administration to research as well. In addition to a writing center's need to define its role and mission within an institution, writing center administrators need to see how the center fits within and works with the writing emphases on that campus. If the center's goal is to work with the First Year Composition program, what is the center's role in this context? If classroom pedagogy emphasizes peer group work and reader feedback, then how does that impinge on tutorial work? Are the classes meeting and writing on-line? If so, how do tutor and student reinforce that emphasis and add it to the tutorial goals? How much of the center's resources (in both money and human energy and time) should be allocated to computers? What do teachers want from the writing center? How do they see it complement or supplement their teaching? What role are they consciously or unconsciously assigning the writing center? What resources do they seek in the center? What kinds of feedback do they need?

In order to learn how faculty defined the role of the writing center at his institution, Salem State College, Frank Devlin (1996) surveyed the faculty there. As a result, he reports, "We have already begun using the research to re-educate our campus about the writing center and its goals. The study immediately prompted us to revise our standard publicity flyers and to eliminate terms like 'writing difficulties'.... The first tangible result of the study was a careful editing of our own PR" (160). Devlin also used his findings in tutor training and as a source of information to forge closer links to the college's writing-across-the-curriculum program. Similarly, Lea Masiello and Malcolm Hayward (1991) surveyed their faculty's beliefs about the process by which students should learn to write. "These beliefs are instrumental in designing writing center programs that tap into the needs of the faculty and students" (74), they report, and their survey results were also used in designing publicity materials, redoing the report form sent to teachers, and redesigning their tutor training program. Where programs are structured from within, with little inquiry into the needs and preferences of users of that program, problems can arise, as has been the case with some OWLs (Online Writing Labs) that have been designed (Pemberton, 1996). Reports of less than runaway successes with attempts at OWLs and other Internet services in writing centers may be a representative case of planning and giving shape to programs without appropriate institutional inquiry (Blythe & Harris, 1998).

Fitting the center to the concerns of the institution's writing emphasis requires asking other questions as well. If the writing center's goal is to work with an active writing-across-the-curriculum program, what does this do to the writing center's structure? What role will the tutors play in various courses? Is helping with assignment design part of the writing center director's role? Or perhaps the campus has a writing assessment test with which the writing center assists. How does the center meet the need to offer assistance to students studying for those tests? The number of questions can be expanded indefinitely as writing programs themselves have unique shapes on each campus, but the issues involved in fitting the center to the writing emphasis on that particular campus require intensive inquiry before the director can help the tutors figure out what their tutorials should accomplish or what strategies are particularly useful. For example, realizing that the conferencing approach they were using at the University of Wyoming "provided inadequate assistance to an increasingly large group of writers in the disciplines" (12), which is an emphasis in their institution,

Judith Powers and Jane Nelson (1995) collected case studies to examine needed changes in their conferencing techniques. Powers and Nelson's analyses led to creating more effective strategies for working with writers across the disciplines. Following up that work with a pilot study to see what would happen with the new system they structured, Powers and Nelson came to some useful insights—and a better system of conferencing—based on their revised approaches. A later study by Powers (1995) focused on rethinking their approach to working with research writers, especially graduate thesis and dissertation writers. Again, reflecting on their conferencing methods and the needs of their students, they realized other changes that were needed and set up a new paradigm for tutorials, measuring the effectiveness of an approach they called "trialogues" by observing this technique with a small group.

There is yet another group of questions, concerning student population to be served, that must be answered before problems can be solved and decisions made. What demographics are needed? Is there a large percentage of ESL students on campus? If so, what are their levels of proficiency, and what will tutors need to be trained in to work with them? When are students on campus, and what hours should the center be open to serve them? What are the best ways to publicize the center so that students will hear about its services? What other writing tasks are students involved in that might take some extra tutor-training to be sure that appropriate help is provided? Before a center can plunge into computers and an OWL (Online Writing Lab), what are the facilities on campus available to assist an OWL? Is cooperation with the computing center needed, and if so, what is their view of a writing center's use of their facilities? (Will administrators in the computing center be happy to cooperate? Uneasy about overuse of their equipment? Uncomfortable with duplication of services which they see as their sphere of operation?) How ready are the students to benefit from online writing services? Are they computer literate and ready to engage in e-mail or MOO conversations, or are workshops needed?

Some of these student population questions concern attitude and awareness. What are student perceptions of writing centers? Does the center need to overcome any negative images? Given these students and their perceptions, how can that best be done? What goes into the reams of publicity the center sends out in its brochures, newsletters, bookmarks, posters, and flyers? (In other arenas, such as general advertising, seeking answers to these questions is called market research.) Is such publicity useful? As Joan Mullin found out from the questionnaires she distributed to students at the University of Toledo (WCenter, June 11, 1996), advertising was far less effective than class presentations, word of mouth, teachers, and bookmarks. When Wendy Bishop (1990) asked herself such questions, she stepped back a bit and began with questions about why students didn't come to her center. The survey she designed was sent to a group of English classes, and from the responses she learned a great deal about why students do and don't use the center and how little her advertising mattered in getting the students to come in. As a result of her research, Bishop encourages other writing center directors to use surveys as well because "they will benefit from surveying their own constituencies....[because] writing center coordinators and tutors will find confirmation for hunches, will spot trends, and will, ultimately, discover ideas that help them develop a stronger program" (40). Implicit here is Bishop's argument that although her findings may not be relevant to another campus, the method will be.

Tutor training is yet another administrative matter than cannot be structured arbitrarily, without recourse to learning about local conditions. If the student population is the source of the tutoring staff, what fields of study exist on campus and which might the best prospective tutors come from? How can they be reached to let them know about tutoring jobs and training courses? When are tutors available for training? What is their level of writing proficiency before they become tutors? Will they need some writing instruction prior to becoming tutors? What are the goals of tutor-training? Is a credit-bearing course feasible? If so, how can it make use of the resources of the center and its staff? What will the training topics be, that is, what do tutors really need to know and be skilled in? Deciding that it is necessary to "maximize [tutors'] effectiveness as conversants in a complex space" (4) Tom Hemmeter and Carolyn Mee (1993) conducted an ethnographic study to see how to train their tutors. If time is short and priorities have to be established, what is most important for the tutor to know and be able to do before plunging in? For the director and staff at Colorado College, the question was how to redesign a tutor training course to include concepts of ethnic identity. To do so, Peter Mulvihill, Keith Nitta, and Molly Wingate (1995) began by researching the relationships among minority students on their campus, their writing as perceived by faculty, and the Writing Center. What they found was that "the college's good, white, liberal attempts to *do* something create confusion, denial, and covert racism" (1). They then set up and looked closely at the training course they designed for tutors, reflecting on what happened and learning from their own reflections and later discussions with the tutors.

Other matters concerned with tutor training have to be scrutinized as well. How, given the particular setup of the center, will tutors be evaluated? To improve his tutor evaluation process, Richard Leahy (1994) spent 2 years tinkering with an audio-taping system to make it fit his situation and work effectively, and his essay describing his work is an apt picture of a reflective practitioner who notes results, reflects on new practices, and if needed, readjusts and tries again. As Schon (1993) explains, "The situation talks back, the practitioner listens, and as he appreciates what he hears, he reframes the situation again" (132). Writing center directors regularly confront problems that need solutions, and as solutions are tried, they are reworked and tried again in new forms. Building staff morale is a typical example of such non-static problems. Because the work is exhausting and tutors usually work at different hours, how does the director continue to build and sustain staff morale? What are some ways for tutors to be compensated? If the pay is low (as it too often is), what other compensations can be tried? What staff development needs to be undertaken in the center? For example, when Anne Mullin (1994) looked at how the Americans with Disabilities Act would impact the operation of the Writing Lab at Idaho State, she did a skills assessment of the staff to see what qualifications the staff had and what they needed, thus identifying areas for further training. She also located various university resources to assist them and looked at the lab's "modus operandi" to see if things such as lab scheduling of appointments were appropriate. Suggestions for answers to some of these questions are certainly available in the literature of writing centers, but each director has to take what is generally useful and adapt it to local conditions. And the adaptation requires local knowledge to see how this will be done effectively.

Although tutor training can also draw on a body of general literature, there are other matters that a writing center administrator must tend to that are purely local. How do administrators in the institution perceive the writing center? Where in the institution should the center be situated? Would it be to everyone's best interests to be housed in an English Department or as a service provided by Student Services or a Dean's Office, or is there some more appropriate home base for the center? When thinking about center policies, the administrator has to consider institutional policies as well. Is there an honor code or an official policy on plagiarism? If the spouse of a student walks into the center and asks for help, does the institution encourage or discourage this? Does it even matter to the institution what the administrator decides? Even the matter of determining how long tutorials should be can be a decision influenced by knowledge of whether or not the institutional structure that supports the center values high usage numbers (because the shorter the tutorial, the higher the usage stats will be). What should go into yearly reports, or should there even be yearly reports? To whom should such reports be directed? How and why should the center be evaluated? Without knowledge of the institution, such questions can only be shrugged off, but the answers are not easy to find. The better the writing center administrator's search techniques are, the easier it will be to locate the right places to search. Half (or most?) of the battle in good research is knowing where to look.

As we can see from gaining a perspective on the work that writing center administrators do, localized institutional research is conducted for the purpose of improving local practice, and it requires looking at unique situations and contexts. This is not, however, "lore" as Stephen North (1987) categorized it: the accumulated body of traditions, practices, and beliefs about what has worked, what is working, or what might work (22–24). Drawing on lore is a common practice, enacted in writing centers when one director hears of someone else's practice and adopts (or adapts) it to his or her own center on the assumption (or hope) that if it worked for someone else, it will work for her. Lore is, in fact, the reverse of local reflective inquiry, because anyone drawing on lore assumes that the same conditions pertain at his or her institution as did at the institution of the person adding the bit of practice to the storehouse of lore. Practitioner inquiry, another aspect of North's taxonomy, is different than practitioner use of lore as he describes it and also different from the institutional inquiry being described here. Practice-as-inquiry, in North's formulation, identifies a problem, searches for a cause (or causes), searches for solutions, tests those solutions in practice, validates the work, and then disseminates it. Practitioner's inquiry, as North envisions it, is not produced locally for local consumption because North still sees such inquiry as adding to the general pool of knowledge about writing and writing instruction. Dissemination is its last step, because it is supposed to be generally useful. In Ray's (1992) view of teacher-research, however, it stays local: "Teacher research is . . . teachers' *own* research into their *own* problems that results in modification of their *own* behaviors and theories" (174). Much of the writing center administrator's local, contextualized institutional research I have been focusing on does not produce results that have as their goal off-campus dissemination—though there is great need to disseminate it on campus. The *process* of such institutional research, however, can and should be disseminated publicly off-campus for use by other writing center administrators.

THE NEED TO ARGUE FOR WRITING CENTER ADMINISTRATION AS RESEARCH

One of the important outcomes of institutional research done by a writing center administrator is that the writing center becomes an effective, integral part of its campus. It serves that institution and that institution's students and faculty. A writing center actively involved in molding itself to the institution and furthering the work of that institution is therefore not some generic learning assistance program built in the mold of what Jeanne Simpson (1996) calls the "one-size-fits-all" program. Such programs do exist commercially, and as Simpson so eloquently argued in "Slippery Sylvans Sliding Sleekly into the Writing Center—or Preparing for Professional Competition," these commercial programs are being invited into our instructional systems. Educational institutions have en masse already outsourced their food services, and they are beginning to do so with learning assistance programs, as Simpson warns us. Such programs, like the one Simpson mentions, are commercial enterprises hired to provide learning assistance. Writing center directors know how inappropriate this is to work with writers, but administrators looking at cost-effective ways to provide such services may not know. A writing center director who has made the case publicly on campus for how and why that writing center is so appropriate for *that* campus and *those* students is also educating administrators as to why it is inappropriate to bring in some outside commercial service which does not understand the institution or its priorities or its students. In addition to using their institutional research to make the case against importing commercial instructional programs, writing center administrators also have to show their institutions that their writing centers are relevant to their institution. Such an outcome is easy to demonstrate, as it is the result of the institutional research that the writing center director has been doing. Clearly articulating this relevance is important because, as Simpson says, "the institutional reality is that writing centers depend for their existence on their ability to support the curriculum being offered, including non-credit and unconventional ones" (2). Showing how the writing center supports the curriculum is showing how the results of the writing center administrator's institutional inquiry were enacted.

Knowing how the center fits the institution and being able to demonstrate that it does may well be important in other ways too. If writing centers move toward an accreditation system, as has been discussed by the International Writing Centers Association and by Joe Law (1995) in his essay "Accreditation and the Writing Center: A Proposal for Action," documenting the writing center's fit will most likely be part of the process of acquiring accreditation. Those who choose to seek such accreditation, if such a system is developed, will also have to prove that their centers are doing what they claim. All of this will be much easier to do when writing center administrators have their institutional research well documented.

There is yet one more reason to argue for the importance of institutional research: writing center specialists need to upgrade the public perception of the requirements for a writing center administrator's position. We all know cases of faculty, staff, or part-timers who are asked to take on the responsibility of directing a center with no training for the job and little release time, if any. Directing a center is, unfortunately, too often seen as work that can be done in addition to "real" work or as the equivalent of teaching one course, at most. Yet, an effective writing center—one that incorporates the best from general principles of writing center theory and practice, and that weaves this into the specific needs and requirements and shape of the particular center that have surfaced through institutional inquiry—is a highly sophisticated organization. A director who regularly reflects on his or her practice and enacts the results of that reflection is doing complex work, work that demands a high degree of professionalism. If the position of a writing center director is going to be seen as a professional one, with the appropriate status in the institution and not as some minor extra task to be taken on, then the professional work of the writing center administrator has to be publicly understood. Educating campus administrators so that they realize that running a writing center requires the kinds of inquiry I have been calling institutional research is a step toward improving the status of writing center administrators. In sum, I am arguing for a movement among writing center administrators to parallel that of teacher research. Advocates of teacher research have been active—and successful—in raising public awareness and respect for teacher research, forcing the field to reconsider "it as an intellectual enterprise and a dynamic form of inquiry" (Ray, 1993, 186). Institutional research performed by writing center administrators deserves to be recognized similarly as a form of inquiry that is valid, necessary, and integral to the intellectual vigor of both the writing center and its institution.

REFERENCES

Berlin, J. (1990). The teacher as researcher: Democracy, dialogue, and power. In D. A. Daiker & M. Morenberg (Eds.), *The writing teacher as researcher: Essays in the theory and practice of class-based research* (pp. 3–14). Portsmouth, NH: Boynton/Cook, Heinemann.

Bishop, W. (1990). Bringing writers to the center: Some survey results, surmises, and suggestions. *Writing Center Journal, 10*(2), 31–44.

Blythe, S., & Harris, M. (1998). A discussion on collaborative design methods for collaborative online spaces. In C. Haviland & T. Wolf (Eds.), *Weaving knowledge together: Writing centers and collaboration* (pp. 81–105). Emmitsburg, MD: NWCA Press.

Cochran-Smith, M., & Lytle, S. L. (1993). *Inside/outside: Teacher research and knowledge*. New York: Teachers College.

Daiker, D. A., & Morenberg, M. (Eds.). (1990). *The writing teacher as researcher: Essays in the theory and practice of class-based research*. Portsmouth, NH: Boynton/Cook, Heinemann.

Devlin, F. (1996). The writing center and the good writer. *Writing Center Journal, 16*(2), 144–163.

Healy, D. (1995). In the temple of the familiar: The writing center as church. In B. L. Stay, C. Murphy, & E. H. Hobson (Eds.), *Writing center perspectives* (pp. 12–25). Emmitsburg, MD: NWCA Press.

Hemmeter, T., & Mee, C. (1993). The writing center as ethnographic space. *Writing Lab Newsletter, 18*(3), 4–5.

Jensen, J. M. (1987). Commentary. In J. R. Squire (Ed.), *The dynamics of language learning: Research in reading and English* (pp. 55–60). Urbana, IL: ERIC Clearinghouse on Reading and Communication Skills.

Kinkead, J., & Harris, J. (Eds.). (1993). *Writing centers in context: Twelve case studies*. Urbana, IL: NCTE.

Law, J. (1995). Accreditation and the writing center: A proposal for action. In B. L. Stay, C. Murphy, & E. H. Hobson (Eds.), *Writing center perspectives* (pp. 155–161). Emmitsburg, MD: NWCA Press.

Leahy, R. (1994). Using audiotapes for evaluation and collaborative training. *Writing Lab Newsletter, 18*(5), 1–3.

Masiello, L., & Hayward, M. (1991). The faculty survey: Identifying bridges between the classroom and the writing center. *Writing Center Journal, 11*(2), 73–79.

Mullin, A. E. (1994). Improving our abilities to tutor students with learning disabilities. *Writing Lab Newsletter, 19*(7), 1–4.

Mulvihill, P., Nitta, K., & Wingate, M. (1995). Into the fray: Ethnicity and tutor preparation. *Writing Lab Newsletter, 19*(7), 1–5.

Newkirk, T. (1992). The narrative roots of the case study. In G. Kirsch & A. Sullivan (Eds.), *Methods and methodology in composition research* (pp. 130–152). Carbondale: Southern Illinois University Press.

North, S. M. (1987). *The making of knowledge in composition: Portrait of an emerging field.* Upper Montclair, NJ: Boynton/Cook.

Pemberton, M. (1996, March). *Potholes on the infobahn.* Paper presented at the annual meeting of the Conference on College Composition and Communication, Milwaukee, WI.

Phelps, L. W. (1991). Practical wisdom and the geography of knowledge in composition. *College English, 53*(8), 863–885.

Powers, J. K. (1995). Assisting the graduate thesis writer through faculty and writing center collaboration. *Writing Lab Newsletter, 20*(2), 13–16.

Powers, J. K. & Nelson, J. V. (1995). Rethinking writing center conferencing strategies for writers in the disciplines. *Writing Lab Newsletter, 20*(1), 12–15.

Ray, R. E. (1992). Composition from the teacher-research point of view. In G. Kirsch & A. Sullivan (Eds.), *Methods and methodology in composition research* (pp. 172–189). Carbondale: Southern Illinois University Press.

Ray, R. E. (1993). *The practice of theory: Teacher research in composition.* Urbana: NCTE.

Schon, D. A. (1987). *Educating the reflective practitioner.* San Francisco: Jossey-Bass.

Schon, D. A. (1993). *The reflective practitioner: How professionals think in action.* New York: Basic Books.

Schwalm, D. E. (1995). E pluribus unum: An administrator rounds up mavericks and money. In B. L. Stay, C. Murphy, & E. H. Hobson (Eds.), *Writing center perspectives* (pp. 53–62). Emmitsburg, MD: NWCA Press.

Severino, C. (1994). The writing center as site for cross-language research. *Writing Center Journal, 15*(1), 51–61.

Simpson, J. (1996). Slippery sylvans sliding sleekly into the writing center—or preparing for professional competition. *Writing Lab Newsletter, 21*(1), 1–4.

Terry, (1994). Things your mentor never told you: Discovering writing lab identity in the institutional environment. *Writing Lab Newsletter, 18*(7), 1–3, 5.

Weiser, I., & Rose, S. (Eds.). (1999). *The writing program administrator as researcher: Inquiry in action and reflection.* Portsmouth, NH: Heinemann.

Chapter 6

Reading Our Own Words: Rhetorical Analysis and the Institutional Discourse of Writing Centers

Peter Carino
Indiana State University

Writing center history demonstrates that centers have long fought marginalization in the academy while simultaneously providing some of its most innovative instruction. As often the only organized one-to-one instructional service on campus, centers differ from the many traditional classrooms serving the academy's primary educational mission. On the one hand, this difference affords the freedom to innovate, to experiment, to play, to cross disciplinary and organizational borders—in short, to change the way things are usually done. On the other hand, difference contributes to marginalization because writing centers resist the traditional university structures of course or department; thus, they are often suspect. Some faculty, for instance, still suspect ethical misconduct, speculating that tutors write students' papers for them. Others question whether centers can help enough, asking if an English major can speak to a chemist or if peer tutoring is not the blind leading the blind. Composition instructors, although generally supportive these days, once feared that the establishment of a center implied they were not doing their jobs. Or, if these instructors were supportive, they sometimes wondered why tutors were addressing the same matters taught in class rather than merely tidying up students' grammar. Students have had their suspicions, worrying that peers might label them boneheads or doubting the value of spending an hour someplace where they would once again be asked to do their own work. And finally, when money is tight, administrators have questioned whether centers are worth the cost.

I could recite a litany of citations in writing center scholarship that document the community's responses to this history of marginality and innovation, but I would merely be repeating a tale that writing center professionals know too well. Suffice it to say that the most influential and most cited essay in writing center scholarship, Steven North's (1984) "The Idea of a Writing Center" is largely a manifesto against such marginalization and a plea for recognition of the innovative pedagogy writing centers offer. That North's plea remains largely unheeded is evident in Nancy Grimm's (1996) more recent "Rearticulating the Work of the Writing Center."

As a result of this positioning between innovation and marginality, we who work in writing centers, when talking to one another, often adopt the assertive attitudes evident in private conversations on WCenter, at conferences, and sometimes even in journals. In these spaces, we speak boldly about our potential as innovators and angrily against any attempts to marginalize us. That is, we often speak like outlaws plotting subversively in an out-of-the way tavern. As a metaphor, the outlaw encompasses the daring of our innovations and the outsider status of our marginality, because the outlaw as marginal, rather than be victimized, enjoys freedom outside the rules that circumscribe the law abiding, and, in our case, redistributes academic wealth—the center as a sort of Robin Hood or Bonnie and Clyde championing the oppressed and outsmarting the oppressor. However, on our local campuses, we must represent ourselves somewhat differently to colleagues and constituents, or risk blowing our cover. To borrow Grimm's language, "writing centers … occupy contested positions on their respective campuses" (523).

Situated thus, center directors must represent center work as integral to the institution's academic mission while simultaneously resisting the marginality that almost automatically adheres to any academic initiative not set in a classroom. Inhabiting such a difficult rhetorical space, directors must inform without confusing, must educate without condescending, must promise without bluffing, must assert without offending, and must offer help without promising servility. The rhetoric that directors produce tells much about how centers, individually and communally, have constructed themselves in the academy for themselves and others in light of their marginal status and innovative pedagogy. In this chapter, I would like to analyze the ways in which this communal sense of marginality and innovation in writing center culture shapes the ways centers represent themselves rhetorically in institutional discourse such as publicity materials and other communications with faculty, administration, and students.

Furthermore, I hope to demonstrate how such an analysis constitutes a method of research, a way of knowledge making.

METHODOLOGY

To illustrate these claims, I will be examining the rhetoric of promotional materials and in-house correspondence from 20 writing centers at various types of institutions, including 2-year colleges, small competitive private schools, comprehensive institutions with open or relaxed admissions policies, and large research institutions.[1] Although 20 may seem a small number given the many centers that exist today, the variety of the sample should enable some reasonable conjectures about how writing centers position themselves in the local contexts of their respective institutions and in relation to the writing center community as a whole. My efforts in reading the sample will attempt to make knowledge through rhetorical analysis—a methodology that primarily applies the reading methods of literary studies to non—literary texts, a method that, given this collection's intent, I feel compelled to define further before proceeding. In proposing rhetorical analysis as a method of writing center research, I locate myself within three methodological traditions: literary studies, Steven North's (1987) grouping of "the Critics" in The Making of Knowledge in Composition, and precedents in previous writing center scholarship. Bear with me as I digress to trace these traditions to establish rhetorical analysis as a legitimate and fruitful method for my comments on the institutional discourse of writing centers and, more broadly, for making writing center knowledge.

From the advent of the New Critics in the first half of this century, to post-structural criticisms such as reader-response and deconstruction in the 1970s, to more recent projects in new historicism and cultural studies, the stock and trade of literary critics, to greater and lesser degrees, has been rhetorical analysis, sometimes called hermeneutics or close reading, (although this latter term, as I hope we will see, designates only the starting point of the method invoked by the former). For the New Critic, analyzing the rhetoric of a literary text was limited to close reading, requiring meticulous attention to the text to foreground its aesthetic unity as well as to establish its authority in making meaning separate from the intention of the author, the response of the reader, or the text's status as a cultural production. As anyone who has studied literature in American universities from the 1940s to the late 1960s well knows, such reading entailed a search

---

[1] I would like to thank all of my colleagues who sent promotional materials from their institutions in response to my call on WCenter in December 1995. In characterizing these schools, rather than name them, I constructed designations of type based on ratings and admissions standards used in *Barron's Profiles of American Colleges* (1994). I do not claim that my designations are exact, but they do provide a general sense of context and means of differentiation for each institution.

for image patterns, symbols, and allusions, as well as irony and ambiguity (all supposedly intrinsic to the text) to reveal form and structure in the service of meaning. The purpose of this project was to celebrate the literary text as an aesthetically pleasing object and an intensified, enriched form of language.

Of course, post-structuralist criticisms undermined claims for textual authority and the privileging of literary language. Where New Critics saw ambiguity, post-structuralists saw indeterminacy (implicit in all language)—gaps filled in by, among other things, the reading subject, or absences evoked paradoxically by the exclusionary presences of the text. The text became less interesting as aesthetic object and more interesting as part of an intertextual transaction with readers and/or as a play (*jouissance*) of self-referential signifiers in a tenuous relation with their material signifieds. Simply (and necessarily reductively) put, post-structuralists exploited the gap between word and thing, reveling in the pleasure of the text.

In the 1980s, as cultural criticism and new historicism, long influential in Great Britain with the Birmingham School, began to take hold in the United States, post-structuralism was criticized as ahistorical, and its interests displaced by concerns with historicizing and contextualizing the text as cultural production, although these critics maintained the elusive nature of meaning central to post-structuralists and continued to practice the sophisticated methods of reading they had developed. Drawing on the Foucaultian argument that discourse and readers inscribe, are interpellated by, and are imbricated in cultural commonplaces, conflicts, and hierarchies, cultural critics advocated and practiced what Clifford Geertz calls "thick description," an enterprise entailing the close analysis of cultural events, practices, or productions (such as texts) to uncover the codes and patterns that invest them with meaning. Advancing a more historicized and politicized agenda than post-structuralism, new historicism, materialist feminism, cultural studies, as well as other "post-theory" methodologies, as Kurt Spellmeyer (1996) has argued, "share among themselves at least one identifying feature—a commitment to descending from textuality into the particulars of everyday life" (893). Spellmeyer here encapsulated the notion of rhetorical analysis I will attempt in moving from center discourse to the local and communal assumptions it encodes.

Given the training in literary studies of many first-generation composition (and many writing center) theorists, it is not surprising that rhetorical analysis underpins one of the methods of theorizing composition specified by North (1987). North identifies as "Critics" those theorists who follow in "the central mode of literary studies.... the tradition of textual interpretation" (116). He outlines the method of this group as beginning with establishing a body of texts for examination (in the case, of this chapter, center publicity materials) to situate textual patterns in a communal dialectic (in this case dialectics between marginality and innovation, and between local context and the writing center community).

North cites Kinneavy's *A Theory of Discourse* as the primary example of the method of the Critics, noting that Kinneavy wanted to create for expository texts "'norms parallel in a sense to the techniques of new criticism'" for reading literary texts (118). Examining Richard Fulkerson's "Kinneavy on Referential and Persuasive Discourses," North then demonstrates how critical works function in communal dialectic. He also included in the body of critical works those that take student texts as their starting point "to determine what and how particular texts mean as a function of the communicative context in which they were written" (125). Here North attributes to "the Critics" a more contextualized methodology than that which he finds in Kinneavy, for here the attention is on student texts in "communicative context"—an approach more aligned with cultural criticism than with the new critical bent attributed to Kinneavy.

The method North identifies in composition studies has parallels in writing center scholarship, most notably in Thomas Hemmeter's (1990) "The 'Smack of Difference': The Language of Writing Center Discourse" but also in Lex Runciman's (1990) "Defining Ourselves: Do We Really Want to Use the Word Tutor?"; Eric Hobson's (1994) "Writing Center Practice Often Counters Its Theory. So What?"; and some of my own work: (1992) "What Do We Talk About When We Talk About Our Metaphors: A Cultural Critique of Clinic, Lab, Center" and (1995b) "Theorizing the Writing Center: An Uneasy Task."[2] Analyzing the rhetoric of a large body of center discourse, Hemmeter argues that "no matter what the theoretical approach, theorists find themselves saying that the writing center is what it is because it is different from the classroom" (37). Hemmeter's project here is a kind of metatheorizing, a close reading of other theoretical texts to enter into a dialectic about identity politics. Hobson's "So What?" and my "Uneasy Task" adopt a similar method, close reading of a corpus of center discourse to raise questions and encourage dialectic about communally held assumptions—in Hobson's case to endorse practitioner lore as theory, in my own to question scholarship that attempts to construct a comprehensive theory of center work. Runciman's work zeroes in to interrogate a single term—tutor—and its historical and cultural baggage, while my "Clinic, Lab, Center" does the same with the designations by which facilities offering one-to-one writing instruction have called themselves. All of these articles begin with textual representations of

---

[2]Although I single out these few works as examples, I am aware of many more, but the necessary brevity of this discussion does not allow inclusiveness. In addition to those discussed, other obvious examples of center scholarship employing rhetorical analysis are Christina Murphy's (1994) "The Writing Center and Social Constructionist Theory," which tenders a detailed critique of Lunsford's (1994) "Collaboration, Control and the Idea of a Writing Center"; Alice Gillam's (1994) "Collaborative Learning Theory and Peer Tutoring Practice," which analyzes a student text in light of theory; or Anne Di Pardo's (1992) "Whispers of Coming and Going: Lessons from Fanny," which close reads the texts of a student and tutor to examine the multiple role conflicts in their relationship.

writing centers—rhetoric—as the object of their analysis, rather than, say, the WAC activities of a center, tutorial methods, tutor training, or the nature of a segment of center clientele, such as ESL or engineering students.

As I situate myself within the methodology of rhetorical analysis, I do so well knowing that I function not as an individual detached from the discourse I will examine, not as the objective observer the New Critics pretended to be. Rather, I occupy a subject position interpellated by the local context of 15 years as a center director and the communal context of writing centers as I construct it from experiences of attending writing center conferences, serving in a writing center organization, participating online in WCenter, and reading and writing center scholarship. Thus, I do not come to these publicity materials—these texts—innocently but with notions of the contested positions of writing centers as innovators and marginals. Nor do I enter this project assured of finding new information but rather seeking new ways of looking at old information—ways of questioning commonplaces that have become so lodged in the rhetoric of writing center culture that they inform centers' representations of themselves to those outside of the community. The analysis of these texts—the institutional discourse of writing centers—produces corroborative knowledge, rereading knowledge that most experienced writing center people know but hoping to enrich and complicate this knowledge and the identities that centers construct in light of it.

As would be expected, several issues recur in the institutional discourse of writing centers: the center's relationship to grammar instruction, the ethics of tutoring, the demographics of center clientele, and the qualifications of the center staff. While not the only issues, these were the most prevalent in the sample, and I will now approach them from the methodological stance sketched earlier.

THE CENTER AND GRAMMAR INSTRUCTION:
WE ARE NOT THE GRAMMAR GARAGE!

Probably the most embattled characterization of the writing center is that of the fix-it shop. Anyone who has worked in a writing center even briefly has fought this stereotype on campus and noted the many protests against it in center scholarship. One reason for this representation is that centers have usually grown in periods of change in higher education, and periods of change often involve the increased admission of groups without the standard dialect. The 1930s, the first decade when children of immigrants pursued higher education in large numbers, saw the establishment of some of the first entities we would recognize today as writing centers. Many more were set up in the 1950's when droves of returning veterans financed by the GI bill hit campus. The 1970s saw even more in response to open admissions initiatives and the public perception of falling literacy standards: Johnny can't read and Johnny can't write, the media clamored. Standards of literacy were equated with standards of correctness, and on numerous campuses centers and labs were charged to help students write standard English prose. Many centers initially embraced this mission, for it is certainly a noble calling to help newly enfranchised students. Some centers even housed non-credit or short courses in grammar and mechanics that students took concurrent with or before a remedial writing course. Some still do.[3]

Many centers, however, soon found that students wanted and needed more than grammatical instruction to succeed. Many other centers developed a distaste for having to serve as gatekeepers for an institutional discourse community where only those capable of wielding the standard dialect were welcome. Thus, as Dave Healy (1993) and Thomas Hemmeter (1990) have noted, turf wars often arose between writing centers and writing classrooms, with centers moving off the margins of grammatical supplementation and into rhetorical areas traditionally under the aegis of the classroom. While most composition instructors gradually and sometimes grudgingly accepted the writing center as a complement to their coursework, some maintained (and still do) the marginalizing image of the center as grammar garage. This problem repeated itself more subtly in the 1980s. As writing centers began to take larger roles in writing across the curriculum efforts, faculty in the disciplines often assumed that a student using the center would be producing grammatically pristine papers.

Given this history, it is not surprising that centers today often adopt a forceful rhetoric to explain where grammatical instruction fits into the center's work. The following statements typify those among the 20 sets of materials I examined:

> The lab is primarily for grammar problems. NO. Writers come mainly to work on rhetorical skills and the writing process. (From a list of "Misconceptions about the Writing Lab" in a memo addressed to inexperienced teaching assistants at a large research university)

> We focus first on large issues such as thesis, support, organization, and adherence to the assignment. Sentence construction, diction, and grammar come last after students have done their necessary revisions. (From a flyer addressed to faculty and students at a medium-sized competitive private university)

> Please tell your students that they are welcome to come to the _____ Writing Center to work on all stages of the writing process—planning, drafting, revising, editing. (from a memo to faculty campuswide at a small private college)

---

[3]These historical pressures are enscribed throughout writing center scholarship. For a more detailed discussion, see my (1995a) "Early Writing Centers: Toward a History."

Consultations can cover any writing problem—from how to generate ideas
about a particular topic [how] to figure[e] out how semi-colons work. (from a
brochure to students at a relaxed-admissions medium-sized comprehensive
university)

While these examples differ in force and tone, all emphatically ensure
that readers hear that grammar is only one of the center's concerns, and a
minor one at that. What they also share, I would argue, is the necessity still
felt to refute misconceptions about the center's role in enforcing the use of
the standard dialect. Subtextually inscribed in the rhetoric of all of them is
the writing center's history of marginalization and the struggle against it,
for the writers' collective need to assert themselves indicates both a feeling
of marginality and the courage to appropriate instructional areas primarily
assigned to the classroom. Indeed, the apodictic no of the first example,
coming from a two-page memo listing and refuting writing center myths, is
feisty to the point of belligerence as it almost renounces grammar
instruction to embrace rhetoric. The second example, although less
emphatic, certainly puts grammar in its place: It comes last. And the final
examples, though more even-tempered in tone, relegate grammar to one
among many concerns.

While each statement directly counters stereotype, each also tries to
educate its audience, assuming the role of innovator while simultaneously
deflecting the marginality of regulation. The forcefulness of the first,
addressed to novice instructors, sets them straight not only about grammar
but also about the clout enjoyed by the director who wrote it. Locating
grammar and editing as last steps, the second and third simultaneously
advance a stage model of the writing process and thus inform their
audiences while defining the center's relationship to grammar. The final
example, in placing semi-colon usage with generating ideas without
reference to stages or hierarchy, attempts to forward a more recursive, and
thus somewhat more complex, view of the writing process, but it is unlikely
an audience of students (or instructors outside of composition) will catch
this implication, leaving this final statement, despite good intentions,
probably less effective in educating the reader. Nevertheless, each, with
varying degrees of success, evidences a rhetoric of instruction, attempting
to inculcate a more sophisticated view of the writing process and the
center's role in teaching it.

I do not mean to say any one of these statements is "better" than another.
Each indicates the different views of the writing process held by those who
wrote them (or at least an assumption about what the audience can grasp),
as well as their political positions in communal and local contexts. All reject
the role of grammatical enforcer while revealing the anxiety of marginality,
the need to lay claim to pedagogy, and the desire for self-definition that are
recurrent themes in the writing center community. Given the audiences for
these statements, these directors evidently assume that these communal

issues obtain locally as well. Yet on closer inspection the statements reveal the further tracings of local context. For instance, the writer of the first must wield some power to write so forcefully and bear some battle scars to motivate such a contentious tone, while the writer of the second, although placing grammar last, employs a straightforward tone reflecting a more neutral context. In contrast, the writer of the third and fourth—their educative stance on the writing process not withstanding—approach their colleagues with much more deference, with one politely asking faculty to "please" inform students they are "welcome" and the other optimistically (and some might say, subserviently) promising to engage "any writing problem."

TUTORIAL ETHICS: WE DON'T DO STUDENTS' WORK

While centers constantly assert how much more they address than grammar, they simultaneously proclaim that they do not do students' work. The standard argument is that tutors work with, not for the student. Of the 20 sets of materials I examined, 17 included this type of statement, addressed to either students or faculty, or both. This stance results primarily from a tradition of Rogerian nondirective pedagogy advocated in writing center discourse since the 1940s (Sorenson) and maintained to the present day (Brooks, 1991). But it also stems in large part, I would argue, from communally held fears that others suspect writing centers are an institutionally sanctioned form of cheating—faculty worrying and students sometimes hoping that tutors will write papers or at the very least correct errors. As Lisa Ede (1990) and others have argued, much of this suspicion is tied to western cultural notions of the writer as individual voice, writing as a solitary act, and text as individual property, a position that ignores cultural studies and new historicist arguments that no text is totally singular. Compounding the problem is the usual prejudice against the newly enfranchised or nontraditional students that centers are often established to serve initially. Some faculty, still wanting to "guard the tower," as Shaughnessy (1976) put it more than 20 years ago, think these students just can't do the work and fear that centers will help them slip through.

Whatever the reasons, writing centers have found themselves in the unenviable position of feeling compelled to deny that they are doing students' work, often loudly, as the following excerpts indicate:

> Because our goal is to facilitate independence and competence in writers, <u>our staff will not proofread papers for students. Instead, we help students find strategies and build on strengths they already have</u>. (from a mission statement at a medium-sized comprehensive university, emphasis original)

In all situations, Writing Center Staff write WITH writers, never FOR them. (from a brochure to students and faculty at a small public competitive-admissions university, emphasis original)

Writing Center tutors will provide an audience for your work and suggest strategies for you to use. The tutors WILL NOT WRITE your paper, NOR WILL THEY PROOFREAD (i.e., fix your paper) or correct a text FOR you. (from a form students fill out to schedule tutorials at a medium-sized comprehensive institution, emphasis original)

All of these announcements display what classical rhetoric would term epanorthosis, that is, a correction as a means of reinforcing an argument. This move unmasks the communally held fear that center work will be perceived as so unconventional as to compromise academic integrity. The first example concisely encapsulates the center's philosophy, but the underscoring and the antithetical use of *instead* suggest the need to ensure that locally no one mistakes that philosophy. That this sentence appears in a mission statement of a long-established and highly progressive center uncovers the deeply entrenched worry that faculty and students might believe tutors do the students' work while doubting the claim of the second sentence. The uppercased emphases in the latter two examples point to a similar uneasiness. Ironically, the second example comes from a brochure that portrays this center as highly integral to the university's work, including impressive statistics on the number of students served, as well as glowing testimonials from both faculty and students on the value of the service—yet the writer still provides the bold disclaimer. The third example comes from the materials of a large WAC center, unaffiliated with any department. Charged with a WAC mission, this center obviously would have institutional support, but it nevertheless wants to warn students in bold type about what they can and cannot expect. This underscoring and uppercasing parallels the raising of one's voice in speech—usually a gesture of anger, fear, or insecurity.

I make these claims not to impugn the authors of these sentences (all are directors whom I admire) but to try to frame the causes. On the one hand, as mentioned, all of these representations of the writing center are struggling against Western culture's conceptions of individual authorship and American education's ideas of ethics—both of which are culturally ingrained in many faculty and students. On the other hand, I think they also indicate that writing center professionals, delivering instruction innovatively and unconventionally, are still trying to figure out what they do. Although center scholarship has at times expressed an almost dogmatic allegiance to nondirective tutoring—not holding the pen, always asking questions, constantly guarding against appropriating student texts—it has also questioned the degree to which the multiplicitous demands of tutorials enable a nondirective pedagogy. Ten years ago, Irene Clark's (1990)

"Maintaining Chaos in the Writing Center: A Critical Perspective on Writing Center Dogma" warned against etching nondirective pedagogy in stone. More recently, Deborah Burns and Linda Shamoon (1996), in "A Critique of Pure Tutoring," offered a master-apprentice model grounded in more directive methods, arguing that "the benefits of alternative tutoring practices are frequent enough to make us seriously question whether one tutoring method fits all students and situations" (139). Burns and Shamoon's article provoked much discussion on WCenter, with conversations struggling to come to terms with what constitutes directive and nondirective tutoring as well as the ethics of each for the institution and the student's learning.

I am not suggesting that tutors should be doing students' work for them, but I think, as these authors and practical experience with students indicate, the complexity of tutorials prohibits defining them in a rhetorical binary of working with or for the student, as is the case in these publicity statements. Providing a definition of this complexity is beyond the scope of a promotional memo or brochure, yet these materials suggest that the expectations of the center's constituents require such definition. And because center work is so different from the pedagogy of the classroom, directors often feel the need to raise their voices. Whether that feeling is justified depends partly on local perceptions of the center's place in the institution and partly on perceptions of writing center history as a story of marginalization. I am not recommending that all centers forego statements such as those quoted here. In an environment ignorant of or hostile to the center, such statements may be necessary for awhile. However, I would caution that before making them, directors carefully consider what they say about center work and what they say to those at whom they are directed.

In short, "Doth writing centers protest too much" That is, does the majority of the audience on most campuses assume that which these statements implicitly fear, or does their rhetoric contribute to raising suspicions by its very defensiveness? In preparing promotional materials, directors will have to answer these questions for themselves given their local situation, but opting to participate uncritically in communal anxiety grounded in a history of marginality could raise more problems than it solves.

CENTER CLIENTELE: WE ARE HERE FOR EVERYBODY!

These days, writing centers are directing their message and opening their doors to everyone. Of all the materials I examined, as would be expected today, none limited clientele to a particular group of students, such as basic, ESL, or freshmen writers, although some memos were targeted to faculty teaching particular groups from which the center might draw. Many

brochures simply designate their clientele as "all students" and leave it at
that; others feel they must state explicitly that they serve not only students
stereotyped as rhetorically and grammatically needy, or to specify the many
groups they target:

> We welcome all _____ students, full-time and part-time, undergraduate and
> graduate, matriculated and non-matriculated, in all disciplines. (From a
> memo to all faculty at a small selective private college)

> When students (undergraduate and graduate) visit the Writing Center, tutors
> are available to discuss almost any topic about writing. (From a memo to all
> faculty at a comprehensive relaxed-admissions university)

> We work with students from every level of writing, including beginning, ad-
> vanced and highly experienced writers. Our tutoring staff is highly skilled and
> trained to work with students from the sciences and the humanities, from biol-
> ogy as well as English. (flyer to faculty at an open admissions branch campus of
> a large research institution)

> Many people think of a writing center as a remedial facility for students with
> writing problems; however, our staff works with many very accomplished writ-
> ers, those who recognize that talking about writing and getting feedback will
> improve their work (from a flyer addressed to writing program faculty and stu-
> dents at a medium-sized competitive private university)

> We encourage students, faculty, and staff to use our services. Our tutors work
> one-on-one with writers on a variety of writing projects in a variety of courses.
> (from a brochure at a comprehensive institution)

Given the spread of WAC programs and the integral part centers have
played in them, this rhetoric of inclusiveness is not surprising, yet it
illustrates the need to specify potential clientele. The first two statements
ensure that the reader knows graduate students are welcome. The second is
even more explicit in crossing into the sciences and allaying the reader's
possible fears that the staff might not be up to serving specialized groups.
The fourth, with its audience limited to the writing program, nevertheless
distances itself from basic writers to include the more proficient. The final
example, in including faculty and staff as well as students, portrays the
center as widely inclusive.

Along with dissociating centers from remedial students, all of these
statements express an assertiveness and confidence bordering on daring.
When I read such statements, including the one in my own center's
brochure, I am heartened by the community's willingness to take on
difficult work. At the same time, I wonder if other directors are as nervous as
I am when a fairly inexperienced sophomore tutor must work with a
graduate student in physics. Fearing that maybe the center can't always
serve everybody, I find solace in Michael Pemberton's (1995) argument that

tutors can help students in disciplines unfamiliar to them by "encouraging [students] to confront issues of disciplinarity through pointed questions about style, tone, and format" (127). But in my other ear, I hear Richard Leahy (1992) saying, "We should question how much growth we want to encourage. How much can we grow and change and still retain our sense of community and purpose?" (44). Leahy's concerns were echoed in a discussion on WCenter in February, 1996, when a director who began her job primarily tutoring first-year students asked others to help her deal with the job overload and near burnout she was experiencing as a result of being charged with WAC responsibilities and other outreach projects. Indeed, although centers claim they are there for everybody, what would they do if everybody actually showed up?

I do not mean to imply that centers should turn away any student, but I wonder if claims of serving everyone are not motivated as much by institutional politics and a history of marginality as by altruistic motives or pedagogical confidence. As all directors know, writing centers are pressured to produce numbers. If students do not come to the center, funds dry up. If a center wants to grow, it must attract more students to justify more funds. These are simple equations. On the one hand, expansive impulses stem from a strong communal belief that all writers can improve themselves by talking with a sympathetic reader as well as from the center's willingness to develop innovative methods to accommodate a variety of writers. On the other hand, centers must ask to what degree inclusiveness is a kind of empire building to compensate for perceived marginality. Serving more students from more disciplines seems to be one way out of the margins, but directors must consider if they are not courting failure or job burnout by trying to do too much with too few resources rather than doing well that for which their resources provide.

In addition, although a rhetoric of inclusion may be necessary for purely informational purposes, centers need to be careful that their institutional rhetoric does not implicitly dissociate them from the students who likely need them most—struggling freshman. Although I agree with the community's general philosophy that all writers can benefit from tutors, I would argue that some need them more than others. In fighting marginalization, a tendency in center scholarship of the past 10 years is to play down work done with underprepared students. Indeed, it has become less prestigious to claim affinity with basic writers than to tout services for the more accomplished.

Again, politics are involved as much as pedagogy here, and the politics are complex. As legislatures in the 1980s became more fiscally and politically conservative, efforts perceived as remedial increasingly began to be looked on as expensive frills. Thus, centers needed to prove that they were more than a remedial service. However, in the 1990s, with the last of the baby boomer pool dried up, institutions increasingly have had to replace students, and recruitment and retention have become key issues with central administrations. Increasing and retaining enrollment often require taking a chance on students not traditionally admitted, and thus retention efforts involve remediation (although called something else). By dissociating themselves from remediation to combat marginalization, do centers run the risk of politically shooting themselves in the foot? Of course, writing centers do not want to contribute to stigmatizing a large segment of students by suggesting that they are deficient, so it is certainly politic to excise references to remediation in materials directed at students. But in today's institutional climate it is probably impolitic to suggest to administrators that the center welcomes all students if this effort comes at the expense of those who need the service most to stay in school. At the same time, centers need to demonstrate to administration that pedagogically they can serve all students if given the resources to do so.

I say all this fully knowing that some institutions, and likely those from which the previous excerpts come, have funded centers that indeed can serve a broad clientele, but centers that lack such resources, rather than follow the communal trend toward inclusiveness, should carefully think through the implications of what it means to welcome each and all. In short, local resources should override communal wisdom, although communal wisdom may function to help garner the resources needed to improve local conditions.

STAFF QUALIFICATIONS:
WE ARE COMPETENT AND KIND

As centers invite all students, and sometimes even faculty, through the doors, they like to ensure that the staff is up to the task. Here again, although implying much about local contexts, the rhetoric blends the communally held confidence and daring of innovation with an insecurity born of self-perceived marginalization:

> The writing center staff is comprised of undergraduate and graduate students who have passed a test and undergone a rigorous training program. Staff members are friendly, helpful readers who understand the difficulties writing can pose. (from a brochure aimed at students and faculty at a medium-sized relaxed-admissions comprehensive university)

> Visit the English Lab for free one-on-one tutorials with expert tutors in writing and grammar. (from a flyer to students at a small open-admissions 2-year state college)

> While the center provides the same type of assistance to both undergraduate and graduate students, instructional tutors with advanced degrees and advanced training are especially suited to deal with the often more complex writing projects graduate study requires. (from a brochure directed to faculty and

students at a medium-sized competitive-admissions comprehensive state university)

The _____ Writing Center offers one-to-one consultation to help you improve your writing with the guidance of an enthusiastic, competent, and welcoming staff (from a brochure directed to students at a private American-style university in Europe)

The first example, from my own writing center, I think combines paranoia and assurance. Although its purpose is to let faculty and students know that tutors are not just thrown into the breach, the mention of the "test" seems almost grave, particularly when the test is a series of three paragraphs about which I ask prospective tutors to comment. The larger criteria for employment are samples of their own writing, their potential for working one to one, and recommendations from faculty members or other students, things that should, and do, go without saying. Furthermore, in retrospect the reference to the "rigorous" training program seems overdone. In a worst case scenario, an audience might infer that I am subjecting tutors to urinalysis and boot camp, yet the tutors are somehow emerging friendly and helpful.

Granted, I exaggerate a bit, but this reading does uncover the paranoia encoded in my rhetoric, as well as in the others. The second example, from a 2-year college, shows similar tendencies with its dubious use of the word *expert*. Although I don't doubt that the tutors in this lab have a reasonable grasp of standard English, I question whether the claims to expertise are not hyperbolic, or even necessary. When I consider my own tutors, many of whom have taken a 3-hour grammar course required in the English major, I do not consider them grammar experts or even writing experts but instead reasonably competent writers with the ability to be receptive yet critical readers for other writers. In my mind, grammar experts are down the hall among the linguistics faculty. Nevertheless, I can see the local motives of the writer of this flyer. At the time the materials were written, this lab was only a year old and likely struggling for credibility, yet one wonders if the overstatement raised expectations that undermined the struggle. In the third example, the claim that graduate students need more highly credentialed tutors (not a claim center scholarship agrees on) and the promise they will get them reflects not only this center's philosophy but its need to broach the question of whether the center can handle the most sophisticated of clientele. There is irony here, for the implied expense of a staff that can designate advanced tutors for specific constituents evidences a strong financial and academic commitment from the university, but this commitment is not enough to allay the writer's communally informed anxiety. The final example differs from the others on the surface but contains a similar subtext. Appearing above a cartoon depiction of the staff grinning widely, drinking coffee, and eating donuts, it evokes the image of the center as a friendly, homey place. This image is often proudly upheld in center lore in references to soft couches, hot coffee, and crisp cookies, with the center the place, like Robert Frost's home, where "when you go there, they have to take you in." But even in constructing the center as such to students, it behooves this director to insert the word competent, subtly saying we are friendlier than other places on campus, but we still mean business.

In looking for the purposes and causes underlying this need for centers to wear their résumés on their sleeves, my first impulse is to be critical. Does the description of the biology department in our institutions' catalogues assure students that the faculty are qualified? At most it will list the faculty's names and degrees and maybe the institutions where they were earned. Do departments at research institutions where graduate assistants teach most beginning courses advertise how these neophyte instructors are trained? Certainly not. Why, then, do writing centers? As with the other issues, the answer, I think, lies in historical perceptions of centers as both innovative and marginal. Although not a conventional department, centers have the audacity (and the sanction, although sometimes less than wholehearted, of the institution) to provide a form of instruction that cuts across disciplines. This position can be a precarious, and one may feel anxious.

That's fine; to feel otherwise might be foolhardy, but I think centers also should carefully consider their position in their respective institutions before asserting claims about their competence—not because they can't live up to such claims, but instead because their assurances may increase rather than lessen doubt. When I wrote the sentence assuring students and faculty that our tutors had passed a test and undergone "rigorous" training, the center had just moved into a plush new facility and was in the process of transforming itself from a complement to first-year composition to a campuswide service. I suppose I was thinking that the local WAC clientele needed to be convinced we were up to the challenge. Was this an accurate perception of my local audience, or insecurity born of my knowledge of writing center history? I suspect more the latter, and when I revised the brochure, the reference to the test and "rigorous" training were excised because in serving students from hundreds of courses at all levels, the staff's competence should go without saying.

The four issues I have discussed in the institutional discourse of writing centers—the place of grammar instruction, the ethics of tutorial procedure, the nature of the clientele, and the competence of our staffs—appeared in nearly all of the materials I examined. Less prevalent but equally interesting were offers to visit classrooms to provide information or to tutor in the classroom. Related to these were promises of services to help faculty design writing assignments, and assurances that the center never displaces or even questions the faculty's authority. Some materials contained testimonials; that is, quotations from faculty or students touting the center's services, or lines from great writers that accentuated the center's philosophy. In sum, these additional concerns reflected much of the same tensions between the fear of being marginalized and the impulse to be innovative evident in the issues I have discussed.

CONCLUSION: WHAT CAN RHETORICAL ANALYSIS TELL US ABOUT OURSELVES?

I want to close by attempting to answer the question posed in this final heading. First, I believe rhetorical analysis, as a method of writing center research, enables us to engage in dialectic about our identities as shaped in communal and local context. Although I would like to claim definitiveness and certainty about my conclusions on the various issues discussed earlier, I realize that they constitute only one reading of a very complicated body of texts, and I hope (and knowing writing center folk, am certain) that readers will engage my own analysis with that of their own, filling in gaps with their own experiences, as well they should. As a method of research, rhetorical analysis does not provide certainty but dialogue. However, its failing is also its virtue, because it recognizes the post-structural dilemma that language is always representation and that generalizations must always be tentative and open to debate. In this light, I want to ask if in analyzing the rhetoric of our institutional discourse, we can generalize anything about writing center identity—writing center identity as we conceive of it singularly as when we speak of the writing center community—or is center identity always already largely determined by local context and the subjectivity of individual experience? I will sidestep the binary of this either/or question and simply answer affirmatively to both.

Certainly the institutional discourse of writing centers, as I hope my analysis has demonstrated, implies local identities, and if this study can offer any advice to new directors it would be to place local context before the consensual wisdom of the writing center community when designing publicity materials or other institutional communications. It is not wise, for example, to take a defensive position, as the community tends to, if no one is attacking on the local front. Conversely, communal wisdom can serve to pressure the local context when necessary. As for more general claims about the writing center, although I agree with Muriel Harris' (1990) claim that "the idea of a generic writing center makes us uneasy ... because [centers] have evolved within different kinds of institutions" (13), I think our institutional discourse collectively suggests commonalities. On the one hand, haunted by marginality, we can be insecure, curmudgeonly, and at times maybe even paranoid. On the other, we often turn these feelings of marginality to productive purposes, educating faculty about the process of composing, influencing writing programs in English departments and campuswide, and educating students to believe in the value and ethics of collaborative learning whether they are struggling remedials or advanced graduate students. In short, a history as marginals and innovators has given us the gumption to resist externally ascribed roles and can be fortifying when we negotiate the local terrain.

As we occupy this position, how do we then construct a rhetoric to represent ourselves in our institutional discourse? At the outset of this essay, I suggested that in speaking to one another writing center people often assume the identity of the outlaw, alleviating the pain of marginality with subversiveness. This outlaw image beckons, indeed romances, center professionals, motivating much of Terrance Riley's (1994) "The Unpromising Future of Writing Centers," a widely known caveat against seeking disciplinary status. In a lesser known but more openly provocative piece, Kevin Davis (1995) exhorted center workers to renounce professionalism to "maintain our personalities as renegades, outsiders, boundary dwellers, subversives" (7). He went so far as to suggest that "'writing center' is the ultimate misnomer; maybe we should be called the 'writing outland'" (7). Although not engaged consciously in rhetorical analysis, both Riley and Davis arrived at the representational space to which it leads, each opting to define writing center work metaphorically in personifications of the outlaw, or at least the outsider. But although our rhetoric contains the trace of an outlaw voice, it also shows that this metaphor does not construct us accurately. We are not hiding out; we are making ourselves highly visible, we are attempting to educate our constituents as we construct ourselves, and whether Riley and Davis like it or not, we are courting disciplinary status. As we cross borders into such heady air, do we leave the margins behind? Do we speak politely? Not quite, because our difference from traditional classrooms may always make us a little suspect and may ensure that our rhetoric carries a little chip on its shoulder. Maybe this is exactly where we want to be, a bit edgy but not quite the outlaw, because outlaws, although romantic, are ultimately destroyed.

At the same time, as we become less the outlaw and more a part of the institution, we need to ensure that our willingness to participate does not inadvertently result in the servility Grimm (1996) depicted in her metaphor of writing centers as housewives "supposed to make do with what they have, to keep the home tidy and put a perky ribbon in their hair when visitors come" (532). Although occasional traces of this servility are evident in our rhetoric, they are far outweighed by assertions of independence and self-determination. Thus, if we personify the center as housewife, this housewife is more likely rearranging the institutional furniture and taking lovers in the afternoon while the administrative patriarch is off earning money to foot the bills. In keeping with the literary roots of discourse analysis, I find metaphor a productive means of constructing writing center identity, of conceiving ourselves as constructed in our discourse, of making knowledge. But ultimately the outlaw and housewife fall short of representing what the rhetoric of our institutional discourse suggests.

If neither figure suffices, who does? If we can believe Jeanne Simpson's (1995) or David Schwalm's (1995) work on administrative views of writing centers, we have gained a place at the institutional table, neither outside, with nose pressed to the window like the outlaw, nor inside, serving the meal as the dutiful housewife. So rather than portraying us as outlaw or housewife, and keeping with the metaphor of the institutional table, I claim that our rhetoric more strongly suggests the shabby-coated dinner guest in the novel of manners, the one who lacks money and familial connections, the one who will say the wrong thing, the one who sometimes uses the wrong fork, but the one whose contributions to the gathering always ensure a return, if reluctant, invitation.

REFERENCES

Barron's Profiles of American Colleges and Universities, 20th Edition. (1994). New York: Barron's

Brooks, J. (1991). Minimalist tutoring: Making the student do all the work. Writing Lab Newsletter, 15(6), 1–4.

Carino, (1992). What do we talk about when we talk about our metaphors: A cultural critique of clinic, lab, and center. The Writing Center Journal, 13, 31–42.

Carino, (1995a). Early writing centers: Toward a history. The Writing Center Journal, 15, 103–115.

Carino, (1995b). Theorizing the writing center: An uneasy task. Dialogue: A Journal for Composition Specialists, 2, 23–37.

Clarke, I. (1990). Maintaining chaos in the writing center: A critical perspective on writing center dogma. The Writing Center Journal, 11, 81–93.

Davis, K. (1995). Life outside the boundary: History and direction in the writing center. The Writing Lab Newsletter, 20(2), 5–7.

Di Pardo, A. (1992). "Whispers of coming and going": Lessons from Fannie. The Writing Center Journal, 12, 124–144.

Ede, Lisa. (1990). Writing as social process: A theoretical foundation for writing centers? The Writing Center Journal, 11, 35–49.

Geertz, C. (1973). *Interpretation of Culture*. New York: Basic Books.

Gillam, A. (1994). Collaborative learning theory and peer tutoring practice. In J.A. Mullin & R. Wallace (Eds.), Intersections: Theory-practice in the writing center (pp. 11–18). Urbana, IL: NCTE.

Grimm, N. M. (1996). Rearticulating the work of the writing center. College Composition and Communication, 47, 523–549.

Harris, M. (1990). What's up and what's in: Trends and traditions in writing centers. The Writing Center Journal, 11, 13–25.

Healy, D. (1993). A defense of dualism: The writing center and the classroom. The Writing Center Journal, 14, 16–29.

Hemmeter, T. (1990). "The smack of difference": The language of writing center discourse. The Writing Center Journal, 11, 35–49.

Hobson, E. (1994). Writing center practice often counters its theory. So what? In J. A. Mullin, & R. Wallace (Eds.), Intersections: Theory-practice in the writing center (pp. 1–10). Urbana, IL: NCTE.

Leahy, R. (1992). Of writing centers, centeredness, and centrism. The Writing Center Journal, 13, 43–52.

Murphy, C. (1994) The writing center and social constructionist theory. In J. A. Mullin & R. Wallace (Eds.), Intersections: Theory-practice in the writing center (pp. 25–39). Urbana, IL: NCTE.

North, S. (1984). The idea of a writing center. College English, 46, 433–446.

North, S. (1987). The making of knowledge in composition: Portrait of an emerging field. Upper Montclair, NJ: Boynton/Cook.

Pemberton, M. (1995). Rethinking the WAC/writing center connection. The Writing Center Journal, 15, 116–133.

Riley, T. (1994). The unpromising future of writing centers. The Writing Center Journal, 15, 20–34.

Runciman, L. (1990). Defining ourselves: Do we really want to use the word tutor? The Writing Center Journal, 11, 27–34.

Schwalm, D. E. (1995). E pluribus unum: An administrator rounds up mavericks and money. In B. L. Stay, C. Murphy, & E. Hobson (Eds.), Writing center perspectives. (pp. 53–62). Emmitsburg, MD: NWCA Press.

Shamoon, L. K., & Burns, D. H. (1995). A critique of pure tutoring. *The Writing Center Journal*, 15, 134–151.

Shaughnessy, M. (1976). Diving in: An introduction to basic writing. *College Composition and Communication*, 27, 234–239.

Simpson, J. (1995). Perceptions, realities, and possibilities: Central administration and writing centers. In B. L. Stay, C. Murphy, & E. Hobson (Eds.), Writing center perspectives. (pp. 48–52). Emmittsburg, MD: NWCA Press.

Spellmeyer, K. (1996). After theory: From textuality to attunement with the world. College English, 58, 893–914.

Chapter 7

Student-Centered Assessment Research in the Writing Center

Jon Olson
The Penn State University

Dawn J. Moyer
Adelia Falda
Oregon State University[1]

We have written this essay for an audience that includes the writing program administrator who said, "Assessment is just frightening, no matter who is at the other end doing the evaluation" (Mullin, 1997, 8). Assessment doesn't have to be frightening, nor does it have to require a lot of time, energy, and money. When assessment occurs, the future of the writing program doesn't have to be at stake. Furthermore, assessment need not represent a quantified, numerical point of abstraction far removed from human interaction. Moreover, it doesn't have to be boring. Rather, assessment can be the very thing that reveals and enacts the reason why writing programs exist in the first place: to improve communication between writers and readers. In other words, assessing a program can be like tutoring a writer—addressing questions, through conversation, that help people see more clearly what they've been doing so they can then do more effectively what they need to achieve. Assessment activities can

[1]We thank John Young, Chester Bateman, Lisa Ede, and Cheryl Glenn for their support in writing this essay.

111

represent the best of what happens when writers interact and learn from one another.

In this essay, the three of us suggest a research-oriented, student-centered application of assessment that is low pain and high gain for the writing program administrator. To that end, we discuss writing programs, writing centers in particular, as sites for student research, taking inspiration and caution from assessment experts such as E. M. White (1990) and M. Waldo, J. Blumner, and M. Webb (1995). We address two reasons why assessment often prompts negative reactions in administrators, reactions ranging from boredom to fear: (1) the terms "assessment" and "evaluation" often get confused or conflated; (2) a focus on the assessment of writing *programs* can easily become distorted by issues having to do with the assessment of *writing*. Although we discuss assessment within the context of a writing center,[2] we think the approach we outline works with any writing program.

What we suggest is this: One of the most basic, most familiar forms of research to students and teachers alike, the research paper assignment, can be a valuable source of program assessment, especially when those research papers are written in classrooms across the curriculum, not just in the writing program's disciplinary home. We urge administrators to offer their programs—in our case, the writing center—as sites for cross-disciplinary student research. We illustrate this assessment approach by showing how three graduate students in an anthropology class conducted a research project that culminated in a paper on a writing center. They used the ethnographic strategy of Rapid Assessment. For those readers who might want to use this assessment strategy themselves, we define Rapid Assessment, show how it was applied within the research site, and describe the results. In our conclusion, we take issue with the conventional wisdom that scholars in one discipline should not assess programs in another discipline, and we consider the importance of looking outside of one's disciplinary home for assessment perspectives on one's program.

Student-centered assessment research is worthwhile for administrators because it provides a simple, stress-free way to get information that can help them improve their program. It is worthwhile for students because the assessment research enables them to be both learners and experts.

TOWARD A DEFINITION
OF ASSESSMENT RESEARCH

Before going further, we should define assessment. Consider a definition published on the WCenter e-mail listserv discussion group by writing center director K. Davis (1996). Davis was trying to focus a discussion that was

---

[2]The Oregon State University Writing Center is one of the programs within the Center for Writing and Learning directed by Lisa Ede.

blurring the lines among writing center assessment, outside evaluation, and accreditation: "Assessment is what *we* do in *our* writing center (classroom, department) to verify that *we* are accomplishing *our* goals. The goal is to improve our performance. Assessment itself is never threatening, providing formative data, not summative" (emphasis his). The definition relies on who is using data for what purpose. Davis also defined outside evaluation: Outside evaluators are "people *we* bring in to assess *our* assessment. They make sure that *we* are not fooling ourselves. They help *us* see that *we* are looking at the big picture. Outside Evaluators are meant to help *us* improve *our* performance so that *we* can continue to improve" (emphasis his).

Davis defines assessment and outside evaluation in contrast to accreditation. Accreditors carry the kind of pass/fail power for programs that writing-assessment evaluators have for student writers. According to Davis, accreditors do not provide assessment information that writing program administrators can use as they choose. Accreditation "is something *they* do to a program. *They* decide what a program should look like, what it should include, and if the program being studied is looking close enough to the ideal," says Davis. He continues, "Even if *they* are members of the profession, appointed by the members themselves, *they* can dictate changes to a program which the program may not, indeed, want" (emphasis his).

At a summer Council of Writing Program Administrators Workshop, workshop leader S. I. Fontaine (1998) presented a handout defining assessment terms. This handout was one of several discussion prompts to help small groups, initially, then all workshop participants, try to reach consensus on definitions. On the handout, assessment is defined as "the task of understanding how a student, a program, and/or an institution is doing" (1). This jibes with Davis' definition, and at the workshop it was noted that this definition did not include the word *evaluation*. However, when *kinds* of assessment were defined, evaluation *was* used synonymously with assessment: "Formative assessment: evaluation that helps students develop, evaluation that feeds back into the on-going curriculum (e.g., responding to drafts and revisions)"; "Summative assessment: evaluation that provides a final, summary judgment"; "Multi-modal assessment: an evaluation that relies on both qualitative and quantitative ways of knowing" (1). Of the six small groups that reported their definitions, all but one conflated evaluation and assessment. This conflation appeared to have been done unconsciously, without a sense of what would be gained by distinguishing assessment from evaluation.

We distinguish the terms because evaluation carries with it an act of judgment that may or may not be based on assessment. Whereas assessment usually leads to evaluative judgment, it does not always lead to judgment from the outside; yet, the two words in the phrase *outside evaluation* often pull together automatically in the thinking of writing center administrators, as Davis' definition illustrates. When *outside evaluation* takes on characteristics of accreditation and is then used synonymously with *assessment*, we all too often find the perception quoted at the start of this essay, where one administrator says to another, "Assessment is just frightening, no matter who is at the other end doing the evaluation."

How can we rid assessment of fear and link it with values often embraced within writing centers, such as the peer tutoring relation, generative dialogue, and collaborative learning? One way is to first separate assessment and evaluation, as Davis has done, thereby freeing assessment from the assumption of outside judgment; and then to bring evaluation back into assessment in a supportive, nonthreatening way. Student-centered assessment research combines the best of both: the safety and self-determination of assessment and the fresh perspective of outside evaluation. We think student-centered assessment research can provide nonthreatening, formative, outside data that can help us understand how we are doing without presuming to tell us what to do.

ADVANTAGES OF STUDENT RESEARCHERS

Student research projects can provide research data from a position somewhere between outside evaluation and self-assessment. In our view, the data provided by student research can hardly be said to be evaluative in the sense of upper-case judgment, as Davis seems to use the term *Evaluators*. Although these student researchers may be *outside* in a disciplinary sense and may be as evaluative as the Outside Evaluators Davis invokes, they provide assessment data with which program administrators can do as they like. The students work with authority, but they lack the power of accreditors that can seem so menacing. The future of the program does not rest on the results of the student research. It is okay if the research provides only partial views of the program; each assessment research project does not need to render a complete picture. Program administrators can take the results, leave them, or "fool themselves" with them at will. The political stakes are low and the expense negligible. The student researchers are likely to use methods that address a writing center's data from different angles (for example, from the angle of user expectations) rather than a method that policy-minded administrators might think to take themselves. New perspectives yield fresh insights into familiar practices. Moreover, a research methodology from another discipline can have the detachment one would expect from an Outside Review; yet, it retains the comfort built into Davis' definition of assessment.

Importantly, this assessment approach situates students productively, placing them in the roles of both learner and authority. Assessment research becomes an additional opportunity for a writing center to enact dialogue among student writers where everyone learns something—where authority and control are dynamic and negotiable, not static and univocal.

Student-centered assessment research in a writing center increases an investment in issues of writing improvement for students both inside and outside a writing center staff. This research situation places the writing center personnel in an important rhetorical position vis-à-vis the sociopolitical practicalities of writing across the curriculum, that of listener and learner rather than the more commonly perceived position of all-knowing missionary of writing. Furthermore, it can increase the cross-curricular visibility of the writing center, within both the student body and the faculty, as the student researchers share their work back in the classroom where the research assignment originated. And not least, this form of assessment is very little work for the writing center administrators.

Conventional wisdom, however, says that writing centers should assess themselves. In "Writing Centers and Writing Assessment: A Discipline-Based Approach," Waldo, Blumner, and Webb (1995) built on White's (1990) "Language and Reality in Writing Assessment" to argue that disciplines must assess *themselves* because every discipline speaks and writes a specialized language. A method of assessment that works for one department is not likely to work for another (39). They are all talking about assessing writing, not writing programs; yet, their arguments seem to hold for assessing programs, too. When that view is applied to program assessment, as we think it often is, the writing center administrators would seem to be the best assessors of their own writing centers. Indeed, these busy administrators commonly resolve, year after year, to move beyond, say, staff self-assessment and responses from writers who use their center, and to conduct more rigorous and comprehensive research that determines accurately how well the program is accomplishing its goals. Writing center administrators who take this view might consider, for example, bringing in a team of outside evaluators to assess the writing center. These would be fellow writing program administrators—such as Waldo, Blumner, and Webb—who would speak the language of the writing center and would understand the writing center's context. Such plans for discipline-insider assessment, however, usually require a heavy investment in time, energy, and expense. (The useful—and lengthy—1980 self-study outline provided by the WPA Board of Consultant Evaluators contains 76 comprehensive questions.) Unless mandated by a higher administration, such plans for assessment can easily get postponed, and often are. Moreover, a unidisciplinary focus on *us, ourselves, myself* for assessment research can lead administrators to overlook the simple win-win option we advocate for gaining user-friendly assessment data—student research assignments. This student-centered assessment approach combines an outside "expert opinion" with an inside application of local data and therein fulfills a criterion of what S. Witte and L. Faigley (1983) might call an adequate theory of program assessment.

Let us describe our experience with cross-curricular student assessment research.

AN APPLICATION OF ASSESSMENT RESEARCH

The research originated in an anthropology classroom, a graduate-level class called Uses of Anthropology. Three students—Dawn J. Arthur,[3] Chester Bateman, and Adelia Falda—approached their university's Writing Center Coordinator—Jon Olson—saying they had to do a project for their anthropology class using research methods that are important to developing skills of anthropological inquiry. Their project involved writing a paper applying ethnographic Rapid Assessment strategies. Could they please assess the Writing Center? They wrote a proposal, which the Center for Writing and Learning (CWL) Director and the Writing Center Coordinator approved. They designed their methodology (they did not negotiate their survey questions with the Writing Center Coordinator or the CWL Director), went ahead and completed their work, and, at the end of the term, gave the Coordinator a 10-page paper titled "The Writing Center: A Study of Perceptions." Some of the observations were more useful than others, and some recommendations might not have been made if a history of the center and its position within the university had been fully in view. However, the outside view contained in the paper was so interesting to the Coordinator and to the Writing Assistants on the staff (two of the researchers, Arthur & Falda, presented their findings at a staff meeting) that the Coordinator decided to solicit such writing-centered research periodically.

RAPID ASSESSMENT

The graduate students in the Uses of Anthropology class were assigned the task of performing a Rapid Assessment of an organization in the community in order to gain experience in the skills useful to anthropologists conducting qualitative research. The class readings included articles by J. Beebe (1995), J. M. Fitchen (1990), and R. T. Trotter (1991). These articles highlighted research methods such as ethnographic interviewing techniques, considered the advantages and pitfalls of using survey data, and discussed the basic concepts of analysis and of establishing procedures to elicit an insider's perspective of an organization. Students were expected to work in small groups and conduct what the course syllabus called a "quick and dirty research project on an applied topic."

Using Beebe's (1995) "Basic Concepts and Techniques of Rapid Appraisal" as a guide, the students established three main goals to accomplish their tasks:

---

[3]After the assessment research paper was completed and as this essay was being prepared for publication, Arthur married and took the name of Moyer.

1. Develop an understanding of a system's perspective (determine the "players" involved: the administrators of the center, the students working at the center, the students using the center, and the faculty referring students to the center).
2. Ensure the triangulation of data collection (make sure to include multiple perceptions and research methods).
3. Use an iterative process to shape the direction of the research (use the collected information to guide the research, produce a tentative hypothesis, and use findings to refine it).[4]

The students were to enact these goals in a brief but intense period of assessment/appraisal while performing participant observations, conducting formal and informal interviews, distributing surveys, and reviewing written information on the chosen organization. The research process would conclude when a written report detailing the hypothesis, methods, and findings of the research was presented to the professor and to the organization studied.

THE STUDY

The researchers determined that the purpose of their study was "to evaluate the relationship between the image that the Writing Center conveys to the public and other factors that influence perceptions of its role in the community" (1). Arthur, Bateman, and Falda (1996) wrote in their introduction:

> In order to encourage the freedom of exploration for its use, the Writing Center has chosen to convey a loosely defined statement of purpose to the public. By looking at perceptions of users and nonusers affected, our goal is to determine whether this idea of a broad statement has the desired effect or if it contributes to misperceptions about its purpose. By employing a Rapid Assessment approach, we generated the qualitative data to assess and compare the variability of perceptions of the Writing Center on campus. (1–2)

---

[4]It may be helpful to explain further this iterative process. James Beebe (1995) stated, "The iterative nature of the process allows for the discovery of the unexpected. Rapid appraisal can be thought of as an open system using feedback to 'learn' from its environment and progressively change itself" (48). The researchers enter an environment with some preset ideas and try to look at the situation from the viewpoint of those who are in this environment all the time. The researchers meet often during the assessment, and they look at the information they are receiving from their key consultants to see if they should review and/or revise their methodology. They may decide to change their questions, as well as the direction of the research, depending on the information they are receiving from their interviews, observations, and so on.

Methods

The researchers used a variety of methods in order to "compile a 'mosaic'" of perceptions (2):

- They conducted ethnographic *interviews* with 2 administrators (J. Olson and Assistant Coordinator D. Shaw), six Writing Assistants, and six student writers.
- They received written *surveys* from 29 faculty members, 20 student writers, 14 Writing Assistants, and 99 students from an undergraduate writing-intensive anthropology class.
- They *observed* day-to-day interactions among Writing Assistants, writers, and the two administrators.
- They conducted *informal discussions* with the administrators and an unspecified number of faculty members, Writing Assistants, student writers, and other students in the university community.
- They implemented a *class exercise* in which the 99 students from the writing-intensive anthropology class "participated in the development of a 'mental map' or a diagramming of ideas related to the resources and purposes of the Writing Center" (3–4).
- They *analyzed texts* including their questionnaires, interview transcripts, observational notes, the "mental map," the Coordinator's year-end reports, the university's *Student Guide to Life*, and Writing Center promotional materials (noting the visibility and accessibility of these materials).

Results

When they had completed their field research and analysis, Arthur, Bateman, and Falda noticed "several patterns that may affect the communication of the Center's goals to the OSU community" (1996, 4):

1. *Lack of visibility (physical and cognitive) within the OSU community.* They found that when people were asked to describe the Writing Center, "descriptions included 'dark,' 'inaccessible,' and 'great resource, but practically invisible.' Due to its location in the basement of Waldo Hall, we found that many students were not aware of the Center, or if they knew of it, did not know where it was housed" (4).

2. *Elusive definition of the mission statement.* They observed that "in order to include a wide variety of . . . users, the Writing Center has chosen to use a 'loosely defined' mission statement. Consequently, users and non-users alike have divergent perceptions of the Center's role in the community. The lack of specific objectives

precipitates user-generated definitions of both the role and purpose of the Center" (6).

3. *Confused name recognition.* The CWL includes the Writing Center, a
Study Skills Program, a Conversant Program, and a Community
Outreach Program.[5] The names Writing Center and Center for
Writing and Learning were often confused and used interchangeably. The researchers concluded, "Students and faculty associated
the Writing Center with instruction because of the connection with
the Center for Writing and *Learning,* which houses a study skills
program" (6).

4. *Inconsistent professionalism and protocols.* They observed "significant
variations in Writing Assistants' protocol at the Center." For example, there seemed "to be a 'casual' atmosphere in the entryway that
at times bordered on 'chaotic.' During busier periods, first-time users and patrons of the Center were sometimes not acknowledged
when they arrived in the reception area" (5).

5. *Discrepancies in theory versus practice.* When they asked the Coordinator about his philosophy and goals for the Writing Center, they
write that he introduced them to "the idea of a 'parlor' atmosphere;
the center aspires to have a 'welcoming' atmosphere where writers
can meet to 'generate and focus' ideas in the writing process." They
write that he also "mentioned the 'writer-to-writer' aspect of the
'parlor,' where the relationship between the writer and assistant is
not [an instructional monologue] but a [learning] dialogue." In
contrast to the Coordinator's theorizing, they found that:

interviews with Writing Assistants . . . generated a variety of responses to questions designed to elicit attitudes and beliefs about the "role" of the Writing
Center. The staff felt pressured to deviate from the stated goals of the Center
(i.e., perform a proofreading service). Most Assistants acknowledged performing such services, though they told us they subscribed to the philosophy
of a "writer-to-writer" dialogue and not one of "teacher-to-student" instruction. (5-6)

The researchers found discrepancies in approaches used to implement
the mission and aim of the Center:

Students' ideas are shaped by recommendations by faculty ("improve your
grade"), misconceptions based on hearsay from friends ("make sure you ask
for someone who proofreads"), and an overall lack of information ("I didn't
know it existed"). Some Writing Assistants made their personal philosophies

---

[5]At the time of this research, the CWL's Study Skills Program, Conversant Program, and
Community Outreach Program were coordinated by Moira Dempsey.

clear in a consultation ("we don't proofread here"), while others varied their services at the request of the writer. (6)

"This lack of continuity," they concluded, "compounds the problems of mixed perceptions and hampers the effectiveness of the Center" (6).

Recommendations

1. *Develop a clear and concise mission statement.* "Take into account practical constraints and special considerations in the development of the mission statement . . . . Lack of clarity in a mission statement allows for misconceptions that may reflect goals contrary to philosophical aims" (7).
2. *Increase faculty awareness.* "Inform . . . faculty about the stated purpose and objectives of the Writing Center. Schedule speaking engagements, use electronic media, and determine effectiveness and circulation status of printed materials" (7).
3. *Improve name recognition.* "Consider a study of the associations and confusions that occur because of the inadvertent association with the Center for Writing and Learning. . . . Many survey respondents did not differentiate between the Center for Writing and Learning and the Writing Center" (7).
4. *Implement a two-tiered approach to provide needed services (proofreading).* "Acknowledge demand for proofreading in strategic planning. Consider establishing a separate service to address these needs" (7).
5. *Sustain professionalism.* "Establish a clear protocol for roles in the daily operations of the Center. Include in the introductory training of Writing Assistants a special emphasis on professionalism in all aspects of the Writing Center" (8).
6. *Emphasize team building in weekly meetings and group e-mail discussions.* "Incorporate a professional 'team building' component to each meeting. Emphasize continuity in information shared with the public (i.e., the image projected to the [university] community)" (8).
7. *Explore other media to promote mission statement.* "Develop a Web home page that is well advertised in the community. This home page would dispel many of the 'myths' shared by the public" (8).

Assessment Conclusion

The following two paragraphs reach a firm conclusion while acknowledging the complexity of the Center's context:

> Although our research focused on discrepancies and inconsistencies within the Center, it did not find that the Center was not presently beneficial to the

community. Many of our observations and discussions involved interested and helpful attitudes, knowledgeable students, and satisfied writers. Statistics indicate that 90% of visitors to the Center plan to return; it has clearly provided a needed and welcome resource for the university community. With a large volume of users (particularly at the end of each quarter), significant changes might necessitate a larger working area and staff. The constraints that are presently placed on the Center (budget, volunteers) dictates much of the policy that affects its viability. Increased public awareness could potentially burden the resources currently available. An increased awareness, however, could provide university administration with an incentive for expansion. The decision is complex, and we do not purport to answer such questions with this report.

The [Writing Center's] effort [is] to provide a comfortable, non-judgmental atmosphere where visiting writers need not feel intimidated. By structuring the Center's format to allow for the greatest amount of flexibility, the Center has attempted to avoid being 'pigeon-holed,' and thereby exclusive. The difficulty, however, lies in the dissemination of information that will both attract students and shape their ideas enough to make their visits productive. Without a clear idea of the purpose, writers' perceptions are often shaped more by a lack of information and external influences than they are by current information generated by the Center for Writing and Learning. (9)

RESPONSE TO RECOMMENDATIONS

In the case of each recommendation, the Writing Center Coordinator either took the advice, was already working on it, or continued to think hard about it:

1. *Develop a clear and concise mission statement.* When the researchers asked if there was a mission statement, the Coordinator said, "Sure," and then he couldn't find one. The only thing he came up with was a CWL mission statement from 1992 that was similar to the Communication Skills Center mission statement from 1986. (The name of the learning center was changed in the spring of 1990.) The Writing Center didn't have its own mission statement, and the Writing Center was indistinct within the one for the CWL. The Coordinator wrote a statement for the Writing Center immediately. (Appendixes A and B show these two mission statements.) Until now, his stance had been, "Let's not waste too much energy worrying about everyone's different expectations of the Center. We'll take writers any way we can get them, and we'll focus our energy on winning them over once they're here." After the Rapid Assessment, he decided he had been too flexible.

2. *Increase faculty awareness.* Before the Rapid Assessment, the Coordinator had thought a system was in place whereby a Writing Center flyer was included in the orientation packet of every new faculty member; he also thought the same flyer was automatically included in the packet of materials provided at Writing-Intensive Curricu-

lum (WIC) Program faculty seminars. Following the Rapid Assessment, he investigated to make sure this was happening, and, in
each case, it wasn't. Those flyers were not getting to faculty. The Coordinator also realized he wasn't writing to faculty as often as he'd
done in earlier years to announce Writing Center hours, procedures, and innovations. He figured everyone already knew about
the Center and wouldn't want to be pestered with junk mail. The
Rapid Assessment happily disturbed his complacency.

In response to the Rapid Assessment's recommendations, the
Coordinator designed and printed bookmarks with Writing Center information on them, and every first-year student living in a
residence hall received one. He sent a bookmark in a letter to all
English department and Writing-Intensive-Class faculty telling
them about the Writing Center in much more detail than he had
ever done, going as far as to suggest ways faculty should *not* talk
about the Writing Center with their students. (Appendix C shows
the letter.) As a result of that letter, invitations increased for writing assistants or himself to visit classrooms across the curriculum.
In addition to the letter to faculty who had curricular interests in
writing, announcements went to campus periodicals and to faculty e-mail lists in various colleges within the university. The coordinator also made small Avery-label stickers (return-address sized)
saying "Writing questions answered: writingQ@mail.orst.edu" to
publicize the Writing Center's writing hotline, and these stickers
were distributed on campus for placement on computers in computer labs, residence halls, computerized classrooms, and departmental offices, as well as off-campus locations with online
computers such as high schools, elementary schools, and the public library. In addition, a public service announcement about the
Writing Center was placed in rotation on the local cable television
network.

3. *Improve name recognition.* There seems little to be done about the
name confusion between the Writing Center and its parent unit, the
Center for Writing and Learning. Even in the 1980s, faculty sometimes used "Writing Lab" and "Skills Center" interchangeably. One
of the reasons why the names were changed in 1990 was to help dis-
place the perception that the Writing Lab's mission was merely to
remediate discrete writing skills. When the Coordinator and/or
Writing Assistants talked to classes following the Rapid Assessment,
they decided to simply refer to the Writing Center and not mention
it was part of a larger learning center with a Study Skills Program.

4. *Implement a two-tiered approach to provide needed services (proofreading).*
In orientations for new staff members, the Coordinator reconsid-

ered the dangers of the abrupt rejection of "We don't proofread." After all, *proofreading* isn't a bad word in this center. Writing Assistants have always needed to work with proofreading. At issue is who does the proofreading and at what point in the writing process. After the assessment, the Writing Assistants tried to be more eager to help writers proofread their own work while avoiding doing the proofreading *for* the writers.

5. *Sustain professionalism.* The Writing Center continued to strive for professionalism in a 30-member staff made up usually of slightly more undergraduates than graduate students, a staff that changed dramatically every term and featured a majority of volunteers. It benefited the staff to see, through the researchers' eyes, how what they thought of as a relaxed and homelike atmosphere could easily seem *un*inviting and cliquish to clients who were new to the process of openly discussing their writing and who weren't as comfortable in writing situations as the Writing Assistants were.

6. *Emphasize team building in weekly meetings and group e-mail discussions.* "Team building," broadly defined, continued to be a goal in the weekly staff meetings and in the staff's e-mail discussion list. The Coordinator wondered if the "team building" terminology might have originated from Total Quality Management (TQM), a management philosophy that was being adopted in certain areas of the university at the time. He suspected the inclusion of TQM language in the recommendations may have reflected a philosophical bias of one of the researchers. He was therefore especially interested to look at the research data to study what had prompted the team-building recommendation (see the "lost data" item later in this chapter, under the "Disadvantages of Student Researchers" heading).

7. *Explore other media to promote mission statement.* At the time of the Rapid Assessment, the website was little more than a list of services provided by the CWL. A year later, the website was more fully developed, featuring the mission statement, information about the center and staff, reference resources and exercises, and a link to the online Writing Hotline where writing questions are answered; moreover, plans had been initiated to enable writers to send in a document and then make an appointment to meet a Writing Assistant in an online synchronous chat space to discuss the writing. The CWL Director hired a graduate student in computer sciences to assist the Writing Center staff in doing this technological work. As mentioned earlier, thousands of labels with the hotline address and a three-word description were placed on computers in various locations on and off campus, and the hotline was promoted to the uni-

versity staff and faculty, as well as to writers in the surrounding community. The hotline received more questions from faculty and staff than from students. Notes of appreciation abounded ("This is a great service for the Writing Center to provide!"), and no complaints had been received up to the time this chapter was written. On the writing resources website of the university's College of Business, there had previously been a link to a writing center—Purdue University's Online Writing Lab. Now, that resource page links to the writing center on its own campus, too.

Each recommendation prompted useful thinking and action.

DISADVANTAGES OF STUDENT RESEARCHERS

There *were* a few occasions for raised eyebrows; yet, any problems that came with the student assessment research seem relatively insignificant.

1. *Lost data.* Most significantly, the findings could not be verified because the boxful of raw data was lost. Although a definitive explanation was never rendered, the data seemed to have been inadvertently recycled shortly after the end of the term, despite the Coordinator's requests to have those materials and despite the university's regulation that the materials from research using human subjects must be saved for 3 years after the research project is completed. Such a loss of data might have been less likely had the assessors been hired professionals or were themselves the program admininstrators. Yet, because of the low stakes involved in the assessment project, the findings did not necessarily need to be verified in order for the Writing Center staff to benefit from the finding's insights. If, for example, the Writing Center had been under pressure to adopt a TQM style of administration, and if the research recommendations had been distributed more widely than to the classroom professor and the Writing Center Coordinator, the loss of data would have been a greater disadvantage (see item 6 under the "Response to Recommendations" section, found earlier in this chapter).

2. *Negativity.* The possibility of bad press is probably the main thing that makes outside evaluation scary for administrators. The negative orientation of the Rapid Assessment findings ("our research focused on discrepancies and inconsistencies" [9]) and the use of double negatives to express a positive result (the research "did not find that the Center was not presently beneficial to the community" [9]) didn't quite seem to jibe with the enthusiasm the researchers expressed in person for the work done in the Writing Center. The

assessment experience was a distinctly positive one, however, even though the researchers looked for negative characteristics (that may have seemed easier to document than positive ones). Because no budget decisions hinged on the results of the research, there was no need for the findings to present what the Coordinator might think was a balanced view of both positive and negative features. While negative findings can be unsettling no matter who finds them, the findings in this study led to constructive results. The Writing Center Coordinator and the CWL Director were confident enough in the Writing Center's benefits that they were willing to risk any "bad press" that might result from the students reporting to their classmates about Writing Center problems. The administrators were eager to learn, and they gained a new perspective on how they were doing without feeling forced to do things in a way that compromised their values. The Writing Center was better for having had the anthropological Rapid Assessment. The criteria of Davis' (1996) definition were met: "assessment itself is never threatening, providing formative data, not summative."

To illustrate our point about the lack of threat from negativity, we can review a recommendation that contradicted the program's stance of promoting collaborative learning *among* students rather than directive teaching *to* students: "Acknowledge demand for proofreading in strategic planning. Consider establishing a separate service to address these needs" (Arthur et al., 1996, 7). In order to appreciate the low-stress nature of recommendations from student assessment research, imagine the difference between hearing that recommendation from students and hearing it from a team of outside evaluators whose professional qualifications are impressive enough for, say, the Department Head, the College Dean, and the University Provost to fund the program assessment. The professionals probably wouldn't say exactly what the students said; they'd use different language, maybe something like the following, which is taken from an article by I. L. Clark and D. Healy (1996), two writing center administrators who would themselves be well-qualified evaluators of writing centers. In their article, Clark and Healy evaluate what they see to be the status quo writing center, such as the one in this study, which aspires to what they call an "orthodoxy" of nondirective, dialogic, collaborative learning: "In its current form, the writing center, out of a misguided sense of ethical responsibility, has catered to ill-founded fears and outdated epistemologies, and consequently has not ethically served its clientele" (45); its "noninterventionist policy" is "increasing the center's marginality, diminishing its influence, and compromising its ability to serve writers" (32).

The students' recommendation is likely to prompt a knowing smile from a writing center administrator (from having known many students who would rather have someone fix their papers for them instead of engage them in active learning), a smile likely to be followed by continued thought and dialogue. The professionals' assessment, representing as it would the opinion of hired experts, is likely to prompt a conflict that would end with either the successful defense of the program's policy or a mandated change in approach. It could well be that the confrontation of the second scenario would benefit a writing center the most in the long run; our point here, however, is that the fear of such conflict can lead administrators to put off assessment and miss the benefit of outside perspectives on their programs.

CONCLUSION

Student-centered assessment research is more readily available to writing centers than administrators might at first realize. Many writing center administrators have probably had students interview them about what they do in their work. Students are often given the research assignment to interview a faculty member and to use the information in a paper or an oral report. If writing center administrators are astute, they can initiate research contacts that help not only students but also the administrators. Such collaborative learning spans the academic hierarchy. If writing program administrators were to approach research-oriented classes—within the social sciences, business administration, or systems engineering—that are likely to assign projects that could address a topic of importance to a writing program (marketing, user and staff perceptions, patterns of use, customer satisfaction and confidence, etc.), this centered research could be more readily and systematically available for writing center assessment.

As we've prepared this article for publication, other student research projects have been conducted in the Writing Center. A group of researchers from a lower-division business writing class investigated the Writing Center to find out what it contributed to the university and non-university communities. In addition, a graduate student from a sociology class did an ethnographic research project in the Center. Her focus was on the Writing Center staff's perceptions. And when the Writing Center Coordinator in this study left to direct a program at another university, he continued to welcome student-centered assessment research in his Writing Center. A student of speech communication earning a Master of Arts in Teaching English as a Second Language videotaped tutorials with ESL writers, performed discourse analyses, and distributed a survey to find out what tutors, student writers, and ESL teachers think is a successful tutoring session.[6]

We worry, however, that writing program administrators might not recognize the assessment opportunities afforded by student research projects from across the curriculum if those administrators believe that only discipline-based assessment strategies are valid.

We do understand the importance of that wisdom, appreciate its application to writing programs, and recognize the reasons why it is thought to be true: misunderstandings about goals and outcomes can develop; damage can result when writing and/or teaching and/or programs within one discipline are assessed according to the methods and values of another discipline, especially when one discipline thinks in terms of quantitative measurement while the other is primarily interested in qualitative data that are difficult to measure. White (1990) describes the different approaches taken by writing researchers (who are usually from English departments) versus what he calls "measurement specialists in the assessment movement" (who are usually from the social sciences): he argues that

> Our disciplinary and professional divisions, with their own languages, form equally distinct ways of seeing that divide us from each other in destructive ways. . . . The choice of an evaluator [from outside the program's discipline] often means the selection of a unique set of assumptions and definitions that emerge out of the language of the evaluator's world; the implications of such a choice, particularly when made without much attention to this issue, can be profound, affecting the funding or even the survival of the program. (189)

Unfortunately, discipline-based assessment can sometimes lead to discipline-centric narrow-mindedness and lost opportunity. Much can be gained by seeing ourselves from another perspective, one outside of ourselves. Writing center tutors and administrators broaden their understanding of assessment practices when they see how students from other disciplines select methods, define terms, and answer such questions as: What do you want to know? Why do you want to know it? Who is the audience for your findings? How will you know if the assessment succeeds?

If assessment is to serve a writing program, then assessment options should be accepted, adapted, or rejected according to their usefulness, not according to their disciplinary point of origin. White (1990) warns us what

---

[6]The results of these three subsequent assessment research projects share a problem: none of them were submitted to the writing center administrator as promised (though there is reason to hope that the research paper on ESL tutorial assessment will be received eventually). When students turn in their research projects at the end of a quarter or semester and then go on to graduate or to jump into a new round of classes, they easily forget about the administrator who provided the research site. Administrators need to follow up assertively in order to receive research results. Note that in the Rapid Assessment research assignment, which we have featured in this essay, giving a copy of the paper to the client was required by the professor.

can happen when a university's central administrators—such as a dean of admissions who values numerical positivism and thinks in terms of categories—talk about assessment strategies with writing teachers and tutors who value holistic or portfolio assessment and who think in terms of individual students (189, 193). Despite the dangers, though, White concludes that a blend of perspectives is important: "Program evaluation ought always to be the responsibility of a *team*, representing different discourse communities, and, just as certainly, any such evaluation should require multiple measures" (199). The same holds for program assessment. In fact, when student researchers from different discourse communities are invited to assess or evaluate a writing center, the aims of evaluation and assessment (as we have distinguished those two terms using Davis's definitions) tend to merge: the summative acuity of evaluation becomes nonthreatening, formative assessment data. The students gain valuable experience as researchers and consultants; the writing center administrators and tutors gain useful, nonfrightening perspectives on their program. We urge writing program administrators to consider using student-centered research to assess their programs.

REFERENCES

Arthur, D. J., Bateman, C., & Falda, A. (1996). *The writing center: A study of perceptions.* Unpublished manuscript.

Beebe, J. (1995). Basic concepts and techniques of rapid appraisal. *Human Organization, 54*(1),42–51.

Clark, I. L., & Healy, D. (1996). Are writing centers ethical? *Writing Program Administration, 20*(1–2), 32—48.

Davis, K. (1996, September 25). Re: Slippery sylvans sliding sleekly—reply. *WCenter Listserv* [Online]. Available E-mail: WCenter@ttacs6.ttu.edu archive [1996, September 25].

Fitchen, J M. (1990, Spring). How do you know what to ask if you haven't listened first?: Using anthropological methods to prepare for survey research. *The Rural Sociologist*, 15–22.

Fontaine, S. I. (1998, July 15). *Assessment terms.* Unpublished handout from the Council of Writing Program Administrators Workshop, Tucson, AZ.

Mullin, J. (1997). NWCA news from Joan Mullin, President. *Writing Lab Newsletter, 21*(7), 8, 16.

Trotter, R. T. (1991). Ethnographic research training at a national park. *Practicing Anthropology, 13*(4), 7–10.

WPA Board of Consultant Evaluators (1980, Winter). Writing program evaluation: An outline for self-study. *Writing Program Administration, 4*, 23–28.

Waldo, M. L., Blumner, J., & Webb, M. (1995). Writing centers and writing assessment: A discipline-based approach. In B. L. Stay, C. Murphy, & E. H. Hobson (Eds.), *Writing center perspectives* (pp. 38–47). Emmitsburg, MD: NWCA Press.

White, E. M. (1990). Language and reality in writing assessment. *College Composition and Communication, 41*, 187–200.

Witte, S. P., & Faigley, L. (1983). *Evaluating college writing programs*. Carbondale: Southern Illinois University Press.

APPENDIX A: CWL MISSION STATEMENT, MAY 1992

It is the mission of the Center for Writing and Learning

—to provide developmental programs in reading, writing, and learning skills essential for students at all levels to function effectively, efficiently, and confidently in the academic environment.

—to enable students to apply reading, writing, and study skills in classroom learning and testing situations.

—to offer individual and small-group consultations in reading, writing, and study skills which are specifically tailored to individual students' needs.

—to administer appropriate diagnostic tests so students can assess their proficiency in reading speed and comprehension, vocabulary, spelling and language use.

—to provide opportunities for pre-professional training in one-to-one and small-group writing conferences for students who act as writing assistants in the writing center.

—to offer international and U.S. students opportunities to improve their conversational skills with partners from cultures other than their own.

—to provide faculty with services and resources to improve teaching and to affirm the importance of writing as a means of learning.

APPENDIX B: WRITING CENTER MISSION STATEMENT, MAY 1996

The Oregon State University Writing Center, a program within the Center for Writing and Learning, is dedicated to helping writers take advantage of all the opportunities for learning inherent in the writing process. OSU students, staff, and faculty, as well as members of the nonuniversity community, are encouraged to make a half-hour or hour-long appointment with a Writing Assistant for one-to-one discussion of any writing project at any stage in their writing process. Small groups working on collaborative writing projects may also schedule group appointments.

Writing Assistants are committed to helping writers generate and focus ideas at the prewriting stage; responding to rough drafts after having writers read them aloud; helping writers discover their strengths and weaknesses; helping writers develop specific writing skills; suggesting possible ways to strengthen papers (leaving it up to the writer to accept, reject, or modify those suggestions); and helping writers find answers to specific questions regarding mechanics, wording, usage, or sentence structure, explaining the rule or concept in the process. For writers who do not wish to have one-to-one or small-group conversations about writing, self-study modules in spelling, vocabulary, and language use are also available

APPENDIX C: LETTER TO FACULTY PROMOTING WRITING CENTER SERVICES

10 October 1996

Department of English and Writing-Intensive Curriculum Faculty
OSU Campus

Dear Colleague:

Now that the term is underway and your students are writing, please consider mentioning to them the value of getting peer response in the Writing Center of OSU's Center for Writing and Learning. We're open Monday through Thursday, 9–7; Friday, 9–4. Writers can call 737-5640 to make a half-hour or hour-long appointment. If you'd encourage your students to try us, I'd appreciate it.

The Center is designed to increase opportunities for student-centered learning based on two well-known educational principles: 1) students learn from each other, often the very concepts and ideas that resist the direct instruction of classroom teachers; 2) when students help other students, they sometimes learn more than those they are helping. A Writing Assistant (who is an undergraduate or graduate student from across the curriculum) will help your students become more adept at such things as analyzing the rhetorical demands of the writing task; understanding the material to be written; planning, organizing, revising, and editing papers; overcoming writer's block; and preparing for oral presentations.

You might tell your students about the Center in several ways: 1) distribute in your classes a flyer or the enclosed bookmark (I can send copies); 2) invite me and/or a Writing Assistant to come to your classroom for a few minutes and talk about the Center; 3) bring your students to the Center for a visit during a class period; 4) mention the Writing Center in your syllabi; 5) build the Writing Center into an assignment: "Bring your draft to the Writing Center before Oct. __ to see whether your explanation of these concepts is clear to a lay reader"; 6) when returning a paper, say something like, "This paper might have been more effective if you'd made your point clearly at the beginning and focused your discussion more narrowly. Next time, please consider taking your draft to the Writing Center to work on these areas."

Please don't imply that the Writing Center is only for weak writers by saying something like, "Everyone with a C or less should go to the Writing Center for the next paper." Discussing and revising papers is a normal part of the writing process, not simply something weak writers do. (Indeed, it's something weak writers rarely do.) If the Writing Center is perceived to be remedial, many students will be reluctant to use this resource. Fortunately, many strong students regularly use the Center. We want to familiarize all students —weak, developing, and strong writers —with the opportunities the Writing Center offers them.

You can reach me at my office in 139 Waldo Hall (7-3712) if you have questions about the Writing Center. If you have questions about other resources of the Center for Writing and Learning, such as the Study Skills Program, the Outreach Program, or the Conversant Program, contact Moira Dempsey (7-3709).

Sincerely,

Jon Olson, Writing Center Coordinator
olsonj@cla.orst.edu

Enclosure

Chapter 8

Capturing Complexity: Using Grounded Theory to Study Writing Centers

Joyce Magnotto Neff
Old Dominion University

Nancy Grimm (1996) and Muriel Harris (1995) remind us of the promise that writing centers hold as sites of literacy research. In these articles, they caution us that studying literacy in writing centers is not an easy task. My own experiences as a tutor and writing center researcher have taught me that writing tutorials cannot be reduced to Likert scales and statistical significances. Nor can they be represented adequately by simple descriptions and anecdotal evidence. Neither can writing center ideologies and institutional relationships be explained satisfactorily through deductive theorizing. My ongoing quest for better methods of studying literacy practices in writing centers eventually brought me to grounded theory, an interpretive methodology originally developed by sociologists who wished to simultaneously describe and theorize the complexities of human interactions. Social scientists use grounded theory to study such phenomena as chronic illness, status passages, remarriages, and professional socialization. Researchers and practitioners in anthropology, psychology, nursing, and education have also embraced grounded theory because of its general "way of thinking about and conceptualizing data" (Strauss & Corbin, 1994, 275).

When Bernie Glaser and Anselm Strauss (1967) developed grounded theory in the late 1960s, they were studying the medical treatment of

133

terminally-ill patients and wanted a methodology with the working capacity
to produce theory that would be faithful to the data in which it was
grounded—a methodology that would provide practical as well as
conceptual information. They wanted to depict the multiple levels of
interaction in the treatment of the terminally ill at the same time that they
theorized about the actors, contexts, and causal agents involved in such
interactions. Conceptualizing complex activities and developing theories
about them are desirable outcomes for writing center research, too. For
instance, the issues that Harris and Grimm and other researchers raise
about writing centers often concern delicate balancing acts, tensions rather
than binaries, and "messy problems of the real world" (Harris, this volume,
chap. 5). Some of those research questions are: In what ways do tutors
balance higher-order concerns against a student's pressing need for editing
and proofreading? How do tutors navigate that uneasy space between being
teachers and being students? When and how might local writing center
knowledge influence institutional policy? What should be done when
conflicting notions of literacy compete within a writing center or between a
writing center and its institutional host?

My purpose in this chapter is to explore the suitability of grounded
theory for literacy research, and to reflect on my own and others' use of the
methodology in studying writing centers. To that end, I introduce the
basics of grounded theory, review recent projects that used the
methodology, reflect on its limitations, and lay out its potential. I conclude
with a call for additional use of grounded theory for several reasons. First,
grounded theory produces a dialogue between description and theory, a
dialogue that does not privilege one over the other. Second, it provides
systems for managing and displaying the complexity of social practices such
as literacy interactions. Third, it supports situated research as well as
collaboration among researchers and practitioners. Best of all, in the
grounded theory paradigm, there is a place for our experiences as writing
center staff and administrators. The experiential knowledge that
researchers and practitioners bring to grounded theory studies forms an
integral part of the database and is consciously woven into the descriptive
and theorizing phases of each project.

WHAT IS GROUNDED THEORY?

In their useful handbook on qualitative methodologies, Miles and
Huberman (1994) discuss three approaches to qualitative data analysis:
interpretivism (hermeneutics, ethnomethodology, semiotics), social
anthropology (ethnography, ecological psychology, grounded theory), and
collaborative social research (critical ethnography, action science). These
approaches use similar methods of analysis such as coding, constant
comparison, returning to the field to further test emerging patterns,

working toward a small set of generalizations, and constructing theories to explain selected phenomena. (8–9).

Grounded theory is a "style of doing qualitative analysis" that works especially well for "understanding interaction processes and social change" by encouraging "conceptual development and density" and by requiring the researcher to maintain a critical tension between empirical data and explanatory analyses (Strauss, 1987, 6). Grounded theory is also a methodology that asks researchers, practitioners, and theorists to combine their talents. The process begins with collection, classifying, coding, and interpretation of data—with multiple opportunities for input from participants in the study. The research team also explores the larger significance of what they are describing and interpreting during theory-building phases of the process. Periodically, the researchers return to the database and to the participants, to test emerging theory against its sources. The process is recursive and requires a juggler's agility. The balancing act of keeping empirical data and explanatory analyses in the air nicely parallels the balancing acts or tensions the researchers are exploring in the scene that they are studying.

HOW GROUNDED THEORY WORKS IN PRACTICE

Space limitations prevent an extensive account of grounded theory here,[1] but I will show briefly how coding operates and explain the data-theory dialogue so that readers can better evaluate studies using the methodology and can consider its potential for their own research agendas. I use my recent study of a televised writing course (Neff, 1998a) as an illustration. In that study, I was curious about how students might or might not develop as writers in distance education and what the contributing factors might be. I kept a teaching journal and saved as many materials from the course as I could (student papers and responses, tablets used instead of chalkboards, videotapes made of the live productions).

Coding

In grounded theory, as soon as the researcher starts collecting data, the coding process begins. Coding occurs multiple times and from multiple perspectives. The data are subjected initially to *open coding*, then to *axial coding*, and then to *selective coding*: "Coding represents the operations by which data are broken down, conceptualized, and put back together in new ways. It is the central process by which theories are built from data" (Strauss & Corbin, 1990, 57).

Open coding involves making comparisons and asking generative questions until the researcher is able to chunk events or interactions or phenomena in the data. A few weeks into the semester of the televised course, I reviewed my teaching journal, used open coding to brainstorm

---

[1]For detailed descriptions of grounded theory as a methodology, see Miles and Huberman (1994); Strauss and Corbin (1990); Neff (1998b).

categories, and drafted "memos" capturing my reflections. Meanwhile, I informally interviewed my teaching assistant, several students, the technician responsible for broadcasting the course, directors at the distance sites, and others who "mediated" the instruction. Figure 8.1, an open coding memo on the teaching journal, shows my notes from an open coding session.

Open coding is a heuristic strategy for the researcher. As Strauss (1987) says, "It is especially important to understand that these initial open-coding sessions have a 'springboard' function. The analyst does not remain totally bound within the domain of *these* data, but quickly jumps off to wonder or speculate or hypothesize about [other] data, and phenomena" (63).

Axial coding is "a set of procedures whereby data are put back together in new ways after open coding, by making connections between categories" (Strauss & Corbin, 1990, 96). The connections are made when the researcher asks questions about the categories—questions that cover the conditions, contexts, actions, interactions, strategies, and consequences surrounding the phenomenon under investigation. In the television research, by asking the same questions of each phenomenon, I added

MEMO: Whose Perspective?

5/13/96

Now for another pass through the teaching journal. Entry 10: "peer review are normal for me, but site directors don't know and must be kept informed so drafts don't get returned." Entry 11 is a note about a student saying how valuable peer groups are.

Right away I think of the "new" intermediary in the pedagogical process—the site director. Categorically, this fits in with the "open door'" of television versus the autonomous traditional classroom, There's also something here about not only having observers, but observers who are active and therefore must be "trained" or educated about what they are seeing happening, so they can make non-traditional choices such as not returning papers just because the names on the papers don't belong to students at their sites. There's something about ownership and the idea of an author here and ideas of schooling as being a relationship between the student and the teacher. The master-student metaphor versus the community of learners metaphor.

Entry 18: "B.C. wonders why I don't call. I should remind students at mid semester or I should incorporate a set conference." This entry suggests a traditional master-student idea of school and a passive or waiting game played by the student. Actually, that strategy is what gets rewarded in traditional schooling-don't bother the prof too much, but let him know who you are.

Fig. 8.1   Open coding memo on the teaching journal.

density and precision to the analysis. Figure 8.2 shows an axial coding memo on "timing" as a potential category name.

Two analogies between coding processes and writing processes may help explain coding here. First, open coding reminds me of invention techniques such as applying the topoi to a subject or doing a cubing exercise. In grounded theory, the researcher looks at the phenomenon to be coded many times, considers the phenomenon from several perspectives, and asks questions of the phenomenon until a provisional name or label can be applied to it. This process foregrounds everything the researcher knows about the phenomenon, both consciously and subconsciously, in much the same way that invention exercises foreground what writers know about their subjects.

MEMO: Timing as a Category Name

5/13/96

Who is involved in timing during a televised writing class?
The list is long: the engineer lets the class go on air and stops it; the technological connections (wind, electrical problems) can delay or stop transmission to one or more sites; the students because of the time it takes to press the mikes and to speak; the teacher because of his or her power to control content; the site director who may not return or distribute papers to teacher or students.

When is timing a factor in a televised writing class?
All the time! Waiting for sites to check in takes time at the beginning of class. Waiting for students to press microphones or reminding them to do so takes time throughout the class; spending my time on cover sheets for returning papers takes time,

What is "timing" for a student/writer?
I can't find direct references in the data for this question.

Why is timing important?
The teaching journal is full of my complaints about how time-consuming teaching on television is. My lesson plans are scripted with time guesses in the margins, much less free-flowing than classroom teaching.

My difficulty with these questions leads me to think that timing isn't necessarily a core category but may be a dimension of whatever the core category is, from a "lot of time" to a "little time." Constructing writers in virtual and material reality is more intriguing to me. So, I will try the axial coding questions for "constructing a writer."

Fig. 8.2: Axial coding memo on timing.

The second analogy is to webbing or mapping, an invention strategy that pushes writers to see relationships among topics and subtopics and then to test the holding power of the relationships. In grounded theory, axial coding requires the researcher to probe provisional relationships among concepts and subconcepts and among categories and subcategories of concepts. Through the process of specifying differences and similarities among and within categories, the researcher creates a map or web or other graphic representation of the connections in much the same way that a writer adds to and changes a provisional mind-map or web of a topic. See Figure 8.3 for a graphic from the television study.

The Dialogue Between Data and Theory

Concept development and relationship analyses as previously described are important steps in grounded theory, just as they are in many qualitative methodologies. A researcher using grounded theory must move back and forth between empirical data and emerging sets of relationships: "Proposed relationships have to be supported over and over again in the data" (Strauss & Corbin, 1990, 112). In grounded theory,

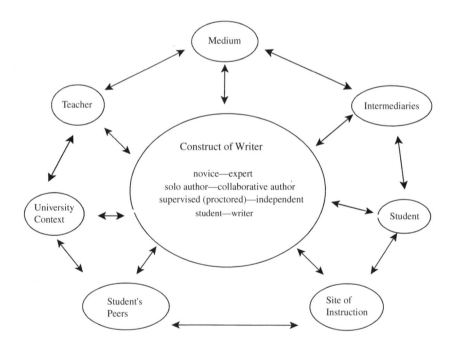

Fig. 8.3   The "construct of writer" in an interactive, televised writing class.

a third process, selective coding, follows open and axial coding. It is this process that further distinguishes grounded theory from other methodologies.

Selective coding is similar to axial coding but at a higher level of abstraction. During selective coding, the researcher refines and develops provisional category relations until the core category is firmly established and other categories are placed in relationship to it. Then the researcher explicates the story line of the core category by further validating causal conditions, contexts, intervening conditions, interactions, and consequences surrounding the phenomenon. In other words, the researcher now delineates a "grounded" theory about a particular event, process, or social practice by writing the story of the event and showing it graphically. Visuals, such as the previous one in Figure 8.3, and balancing matrices, such as the one in Table 8.1 (discussed later in this chapter), display relationships among categories and help a reader see a complicated phenomenon in broad brush strokes that supplement the written theoretical account. Matrices are a refreshing change from binary oppositions, and they allow researchers to indicate the complexity of situated social practices such as writing center tutorials.

Writing Up The Research

Writing is an integral part of grounded theory methodology. Researchers write memos for all coding sessions and periodically write summative or integrative memos after rereading parts of the data collection and the memos related to those data. By the summer following my semester of televised teaching, I was putting together sections of the research report. Some sections came verbatim from my coding and integrative memos; others were written reflectively now that the project was drawing to a close. I shared rough drafts with the participants in the project and continued to revise until I submitted the report to the grant sponsors and to a journal for publication. Of course, the work is never really finished. I am currently preparing conference papers and completing a follow-up study based on further investigations into how writing is taught on television.

GROUNDED THEORY AND WRITING RESEARCH

The ERIC database from 1982 to 1996 lists 12 studies of writing in which researchers used grounded theory. All are about perceptions of the subjects under study: for example how sixth graders define themselves as readers (Guice, 1992), how veteran teachers reconceive the value of dialogue journals when confronted with student responses to the journals (Gross, 1992), how novice researchers redefine themselves as they produce a dissertation using grounded theory (White, 1992), and how two researchers view their efforts at collaborative writing (Smith, 1982). The researchers

TABLE 8.1

Representations of College Writing

	Student Representations	Tutor Representations	Faculty Representations	Writing Center Constructs
Audience	Teacher as examiner	Teacher as examiner, Interested, nonexpert readers	Teacher as examiner	Teacher as examiner Tutor as interested reader Writer as reader
Purpose	To earn a grade by satisfying a professor	To display knowledge To learn content To learn to write To communicate one's ideas	To test learning To teach content To assist student learning	To satisfy the professor/institution To meet writer and reader needs
Products	Content and form are separable; writing is right or wrong	Content + form; Professors want deductive, thesis–driven essays, relatively free of error	Formal products "count"; writing–to–learn products "uncountable"; Ideal texts vs. Student texts	Institutional constraints determine form and content
Process	Linear, mysterious, painful, constrained by slippery rules, solitary; revision = polishing	Recursive, messy; HOCS & LOCS; revision = meaning–making	A means to the product rather than a means of developing the writer	Collaborative and social; strategies can be taught and learned by moving between the particular and the general
Student as writer	Students are students, not writers	Students can also be writers	Unexamined dimension	Students can be constructed as writers

chose grounded theory for its appropriateness to their research questions, its flexibility as a methodology, and its insistence on keeping data and theory related to one another.

Dissertation Abstracts Online lists approximately 50 studies that make reference to grounded theory, education, and writing. Several of these studies concern childhood language acquisition. More pertinent to this chapter are those that explore relationships among teacher training, curriculum decisions, and writing instruction at the secondary and college levels (e.g. Cain, 1982; Carter, 1993; Dinkler, 1991; Edsell, 1996; Gallow, 1987; Matranga, 1995; Pippen, 1991; Roswell, 1992; Spigelman, 1996; Weitz, 1995). Weitz (1995), for example, analyzed student writing to formulate a grounded theory about how a college writing curriculum can help learners become "agents of meaning." Carter (1993) compared instructors at the secondary, community college, and university levels to determine similarities and differences in writing instruction. Pippen (1991) used several methods from naturalistic research (including those of grounded theory) to analyze a peer group of three English education majors taking their last writing class before becoming writing teachers themselves. Edsell (1996) explored the dissonances between his graduate study in composition theory and his classroom practices.

GROUNDED THEORY
IN WRITING CENTER RESEARCH

So far, the number of studies applying grounded theory to writing centers is small. Spigelman's (1996) work concerned peer writing groups in classrooms rather than in writing centers, but her findings shed light on tutorial exchanges. Spigelman examines the tension between a writer's personal investment in his or her own work and relinquishing that investment to make use of peer responses. Furthermore, Spigelman situates her findings in an historical review of textual ownership practices and ethics, issues of recurring interest to writing center tutors. Roswell (1992) uses methods from ethnography and grounded theory to examine authority positions in writing center conferences. She concludes that "tutor preparation will be most effective when it examines the ideological conflicts tutors encounter and problematizes the assumption that writing centers are institutionally autonomous" (vi).

A Closer Look At One Writing Center

In 1990, I used the writing center at a large, metropolitan community college where I was teaching at the time as a site for exploring two questions (Magnotto, 1991): How do students and faculty-tutors represent writing in their writing center discourse? What are the implications of their representations for writing across the curriculum? The cross-disciplinary center was staffed by faculty-tutors from math, computer science, psychology, English, foreign languages, and philosophy. The center benefited from administrative support and was closely connected to the writing-across-the-curriculum (WAC) program at the college. There was no lack of clientele who wanted tutoring, nor of faculty who wanted to learn to tutor. Even a nearby government agency paid for tutoring time for its employees.

My research questions led me to grounded theory as a methodological framework, because it did not force a choice between description and theory. At the time, others were compiling excellent narratives about writing centers and WAC programs (e.g., Fulwiler & Young, 1990; Harris, 1986), but few were theorizing about either movement, and no one was developing writing center or WAC theory that was grounded in careful empirical work.

The grounded theory procedures I followed are similar to those explained previously. Data were collected during a 1-year period and included field notes, assignment sheets, student papers, tape recordings of 27 writing center conferences, and interviews with tutors and students. Data analysis began early in the study with open and axial coding of conference and interview transcripts.

Throughout data analysis, I returned to the writing center to observe additional conferences and to talk with tutors about the emerging findings. I also sampled archival documents (writing center handouts and forms, records of tutoring sessions, collections of assignments and responses kept in the files). As Strauss (1987) suggests, I drew on my experiential knowledge as a teacher, student, tutor, and writer to interpret and to interrupt the emerging findings, always remaining aware that I was the agent of the analysis (see Silverman & Torode, 1980).

The findings emerged over time as I wrote integrative memos and added details to the matrix of "representations" I was developing (see Table 8.1), The matrix allowed me to display multiple, and sometimes conflicting, representations of a concept. As Table 8.1 shows, students simultaneously represent college writing as ordinary, anxiety producing, and problematic. They believe writing is a solitary act, yet they seek help from tutors. Students know the instructor is the audience, yet as one confessed, "I don't know who I've been telling it to, I've just been putting [words] down" (Magnotto, 1991, 92).

In Table 8.1, the boxes in the matrix summarize the predominant assumptions that a group of individuals hold about various dimensions of writing (audience, purpose, product, process, student-as-writer). The matrix shows that faculty and faculty-tutors often represent a dimension in ways that differ from how students represent the same dimension. One interesting comparison can be seen across the bottom row, which summarizes assumptions about students being (or not being) writers. Students did not represent themselves as writers in their tutoring sessions; faculty did not represent students as writers in assignment sheets or in comments on student papers. Fortunately, faculty-tutors did represent students as writers during tutoring sessions, and many writing center documents represented students as writers.

As I further analyzed data from tutoring sessions, the discursive interruption or "aha" moment emerged as a core category. In one tutoring session after another, I found "aha" moments, which I then analyzed for their causal conditions, contexts, intervening conditions, interactive strategies, and consequences. Eventually, I wrote the storyline for "aha" moments in writing center conferences, defining them as times when one person realizes that the other holds different assumptions about writing and therefore represents writing differently. My claim is that "aha" moments signify the presence of tensions within and across discursive representations. When those tensions are recognized as differences, they can be addressed through further tutoring.

"Aha" moments and what happens in tutoring sessions following "aha" moments provide empirical evidence of learning taking place. In that empirical evidence, I can ground my theories about talk, writing, and learning. For example, one type of "aha" moment occurs in several conferences in which a student assumes that a professor is his or her only audience. In the writing center session, the student meets an additional audience discursively represented by the tutor—the audience as an interested, nonexpert reader. In the "aha" moment, the student realizes that his or her writing can be read in ways other than for a grade or judgment. Ideally, the tutor represents a writer/reader talking to a writer/reader throughout the conference. But it is not that simple—the tutor also represents the institution and the faculty. Thus, the tutor is in a position of tension that leads to additional "aha" moments on his or her part. These moments raise questions for tutors about who does and does not belong in college, about the levels of abstract thinking students are capable of, about where in the academy writers can find places to write about their own ideas and tell their own stories, and about how "unwriterly" students feel in school settings. Equally important for writing center research is the absence of tension. The finding that faculty do not represent students as writers is a prime instance of an absence of tension needing additional study.

The analytic methods used in grounded theory encourage a researcher to examine multiple viewpoints, assumptions, and interpretations. It is understood that additional data or additional analyses can be used to further refine and enrich a theory; the conversation is ongoing.

LIMITATIONS OF THE METHOD

Grounded theory is not a panacea. The most obvious problem is time. The methodology requires months and even years because the processes of interviewing subjects, collecting data, cycling findings to participants, negotiating meanings, and returning to the data for theoretical sampling are both recursive and intensive. I started my study of the televised writing course in the fall of 1994, and by the spring of 1998 was still revising a journal article on the findings. The study of the writing center was 2 years in the making. After collecting the original data and analyzing them, I tried out early findings on tutors, students, and writing center administrators. Their responses sent me back to the data collection to rethink the core category and propelled me forward to previously unconsidered sources such as archival records.

As such scenarios suggest, grounded theory produces so much data that physically managing and intellectually manipulating them is difficult even with software programs for assistance. For each of my grounded theory studies, I had more than filled a file drawer with printed data in less than 2 months. Add audiotapes and videotapes to the data collection, and one is soon overwhelmed. Setting up a data management system becomes a priority.

Fortunately, too much data and not enough time to analyze them are problems that can be solved. More troubling are epistemological and professional issues. To do grounded theory, I found that I had to reimagine myself and my relationship to the academy. My background in English studies had caused me to construct myself as a solo researcher who dealt with written texts by interpreting them and then developing arguments to support my interpretations. An adversarial stance was part of that image. Grounded theory, on the other hand, is best done collaboratively; it is field based, uses coding and classification systems derived from the social sciences, requires graphic as well as textual reporting of results, develops theory from data, and tests theory through negotiation. To move to grounded theory I had to reexamine my assumptions about research and knowledge. Only because my questions about writing and teaching were so pressing, and only because other methods I tried forced me to simplify the complex acts I wished to study or to choose between description and theory, was I willing to reconstruct myself as a grounded-theory researcher.

And there's the rub. Once I had embraced grounded theory as an appropriate and useful methodology for my research questions, I had to face its lack of credibility in English departments. Its social science roots and its collaborative bent are problematic to scholars working out of different epistemologies. Even rhetoric and composition colleagues, if they have not been trained in field research, need to be convinced of the value in grounded theory. Qualitative researchers often find themselves outside certain conversations in English studies, and that limits their access to publication. One solution is to build new communities, such as the special interest group on qualitative research, which meets at the Conference on College Composition and Communication each year. This group supports beginning and experienced qualitative researchers and operates an active listserv on topics such as human subject review boards and research ethics. One can also take heart in the recent publication of collections such as this one and *Under Construction* (Farris & Anson, 1998), both of which feature a chapter on grounded theory. Keeping the potential of grounded theory in mind through the struggle is another way I remind myself that the struggle is worth it.

THE POTENTIAL OF GROUNDED THEORY FOR WRITING CENTER RESEARCH

In spite of its limitations, grounded theory has been invaluable to me when I grapple with questions about writing, teaching, and learning. The methods tease out complexity and invite dialogue. At present, the potential of grounded theory in writing center research is largely untapped but nonetheless very promising for the following reasons:

- *Grounded theory as praxis can bridge the gap between researchers and practitioners so that those who study writing centers and those who work in them are in direct communication.* As I collect and code data for my studies, I cycle my early interpretations to study participants. Their reactions promote additional teasing out of institutional, political, and social issues such as gender, ethnicity, and access to technology. The analytic procedures in grounded theory make space for these data. Multiple interpretations and perspectives are welcomed, and "subjects" become "agents" in analysis phases of a project. For example, when writing tutors listened to tapes of their conferences in one of my studies, their responses helped me add density to the "aha" concept.

- *So much of the work done in writing centers is collaborative that a collaborative research paradigm seems logical for studying that work.* Grounded theory, having been designed for the social sciences where research teams are the norm, is well suited for a team approach. Even when grounded theory researchers collect and code data individually, they write coding and integrative memos and visuals, building a continuous and accessible record that supports group progress.

- *Grounded theory works as meta-analysis.* It requires the researcher to document the connections between investigating a scene of writing and interpreting that scene. Plus, grounded theory offers a means of meta-analysis across case studies and is excellent for long-term research agendas.

- *Grounded theory supports the use of multiple data collection methods and multiple reporting formats.* Spigelman (1996), for example, uses argument, historical narrative, and case studies to report her results. The flexibility means that an initial investment in a project can have multiple payoffs and can produce multiple research reports geared to particular audiences.

- *Grounded theory shows promise for cross-disciplinary research* (see Nye, 1995; Smith, 1996). Center administrators wanting to study writing improvement across the curriculum will find that they can use both quantitative and qualitative data and can, through education and negotiation, develop analytic categories in concert with team members trained in different paradigms.
- *The results of grounded theory "fit" and have great "working capacity" to explain things to both researchers and practitioners* (Glaser & Strauss, 1967, 4). Through the dialogues that are part of grounded-theory projects, writing center staff and administrators can parlay initial findings into ongoing research agendas.

Writing centers are sites of complex social practices. Our years of experience with them have convinced us of their educational value for students, tutors, and faculty. Unfortunately, others who make policy and funding decisions about writing centers do not have our day-to-day experience, nor do they give much credibility to our wealth of stories and practitioner lore about how writing centers work. Grounded theory is one productive solution to this dilemma. It allows researchers and practitioners who wish to address particular questions about how, why, and when writing centers work to do so by combining their years of experience with a rigorous research tradition. At the same time, grounded theory meets administrative expectations about research. The methodology has a successful history in the social sciences and in education. Experts in the method have developed guidelines for evaluating both the processes and products of grounded theory studies (Strauss & Corbin, 1990). The methodology supports an "inclusive" rather than "exclusive" search for answers to the many meaningful questions we can pose about writing centers. It lets us look carefully at our centers and theorize productively about how they work.

REFERENCES

Cain, B. J. (1982). *Form fluency in transactional discourse of college freshmen: An exploration toward a grounded theory.* Unpublished doctoral dissertation, University of Southern California.

Carter, S. D. W. (1993). *A case study of the comparable patterns in writing instruction between a secondary school instructor, a community college instructor and a four-year institution instructor.* Unpublished doctoral dissertation, University of Arkansas.

Dinkler, P. D. (1991). *Recursive composing in freshman composition: Case studies of four student writers in search of the self-made writer.* Unpublished doctoral dissertation, Ohio State University.

Edsell, R. J. (1996). *Enacting theoretical practice: Construing constructivism in the teaching of college composition.* Unpublished doctoral dissertation, New York University.

Farris, C., & Anson, C.M. (Eds.). (1998). *Under construction: Working at the intersections of composition theory, research, and practice.* Logan: Utah State University Press.

Fulwiler, T., & Young, A. (Eds.). (1990). *Programs that work: Models and methods for writing across the curriculum.* Portsmouth, NH: Boynton/Cook.

Gallow, D. (1987). *Fiction as a transition between personal narration and exposition: Implications from interviews with professional writers and college student writers.* Unpublished doctoral dissertation, University of Southern California.

Glaser, B. G., & Strauss, A. L. (1967). *The discovery of grounded theory: Strategies for qualitative research.* Chicago: Aldine.

Grimm, N. M. (1996). Rearticulating the work of the writing center. *College Composition and Communication, 47*(4), 523–548.

Gross, P, A. (1992, December). *Shared meaning: Whole language reader response at the secondary level.* Paper presented at the Annual Meeting of the National Reading Conference, San Antonio, TX. (ERIC Document Reproduction Service No, ED 359 491)

Guice, S. (1992, December). *Readers, texts, and contexts in a sixth-grade community of readers.* Paper presented at the Annual Meeting of the National Reading Conference, San Antonio, TX (ERIC Document Reproduction Service No. ED 369 071)

Harris, M. (1986). *Teaching one-to-one: The writing conference.* Urbana, IL: National Council of Teachers of English.

Harris, M. (1995). Talking in the middle: Why writers need writing tutors. *College English 57*(1), 27–42,

Magnotto, J. N. (1991). *The construction of college writing in a cross-disciplinary, community college writing center: An analysis of student, tutor, and faculty representations.* Unpublished doctoral dissertation, University of Pennsylvania.

Matranga, J. F. (1995). *Writing process and change: Studies of teachers implementing a writing workshop approach.* Unpublished doctoral dissertation, University of the Pacific.

Miles, M. B., & Huberman, A. M. (1994). *Qualitative data analysis: An expanded sourcebook* (2nd ed.). London: Sage.

Neff, J. M. (1998a). From a distance: Teaching writing on interactive television. *Research in the Teaching of English, 33,* 136–157.

Neff, J. M. (1998b). Grounded theory: A critical research methodology. In C. Farris & C. M. Anson (Eds.),*Under construction: Working at the intersections of composition theory, research, and practice* (pp. 124–135). Logan: Utah State University Press.

Nye, E. F. (1995). *"The more I tell my story": Writing as healing at an HIV clinic.* Unpublished doctoral dissertation, University of Michigan.

Pippen, C. L. (1991). *A social scene of writing: The peer group talk of three women English-education majors enrolled in an advanced composition class.* Unpublished doctoral dissertation, University of Pennsylvania.

Roswell, B. S. (1992). *The tutor's audience is always a fiction: The construction of authority in writing center conferences.* Unpublished doctoral dissertation, University of Pennsylvania.

Silverman, D., & Torode, B. (1980). *The material word: Some theories of language and its limits.* London: Routledge & Kegan Paul.

Smith, L. (1982, March). *Teaching tales and theories: An ethnographic next step?* Paper presented at the Annual Meeting of the American Educational Research Association, New York. (ERIC Document Reproduction Service No. ED 225 227)

Smith, S. L. (1996). *Making sense: Journals as tools for learning and representing student experience in a field-based doctoral program.* Unpublished doctoral dissertation, Oregon State University.

Spigelman, C. (1996). *The dialectics of ownership in peer writing group.* Unpublished doctoral dissertation, Temple University.

Strauss, A. L. (1987). *Qualitative analysis for social scientists.* Cambridge, England: Cambridge University Press.

Strauss, A. L., & Corbin, J. (1990). *Basics of qualitative research: Grounded theory procedures and techniques.* Newbury Park, CA: Sage.

Strauss, A. L., & Corbin, J. (1994). Grounded theory methodology: An overview. In N. K. Denzin & Y. S. Lincoln (Eds.,), *Handbook of qualitative research* (pp. 273–285). Thousand Oaks, CA: Sage.

Weitz, A. L. (1995). *Agents of meaning: A study of college writers and their representations of self.* Unpublished doctoral dissertation, New York University.

White, K. (1992). *Themes to theory: A data analysis process.* (ERIC Document Reproduction Service No. ED 352 167)

[1]For detailed descriptions of grounded theory as a methodology, see Miles and Huberman (1994); Strauss and Corbin (1990); Neff (1998b).

Chapter 9

The Portfolio Project: Sharing Our Stories

Sharon Thomas
Julie Bevins
Michigan State University

Mary Ann Crawford
Central Michigan University

When we established our Writing Center several years ago, we were determined to make research and reflection an integral part of our work. We encourage graduate student writing consultants not only to manage the particular projects they oversee, such as coordinating classroom presentations, teaching a linked course, and developing the use of technology, but also to study these projects. We encourage undergraduate writing consultants to reflect on their experiences and write about and present their ideas in articles in our newsletter, *Peer Review,* and in presentations at local and regional conferences. Eight years ago we also began the Portfolio Project, a longitudinal study of the writing done by a group of students during their 4 years as undergraduates at our university. In the following story about that project, we want to share not only what we are learning by listening to the students in the Portfolio Project, but also the transformations that are occurring in our thinking about writing center work, about our consulting practices, and about the way we articulate our role in the institution.

GETTING STARTED

The project began in the fall of 1993, when our university was preparing for a North Central Accreditation Association study. One area of particular interest to this committee was the writing program on our campus. This interest provided the opportunity for establishing the Portfolio Project. In a transition from terms to semesters, the writing requirement had been transformed from a 1-year series of composition courses to a vertical writing program. The first-year writing course became a one-semester course that is followed by a writing-intensive, sophomore-level course and Tier II writing-in-the-disciplines courses. At the same time, the Writing Center was established in order to provide writing workshop support both to the faculty who were developing these new courses and to the students who were enrolled in them.

As part of the preparation for the North Central study, the provost's office asked several units to research and document their work. Unwilling to be satisfied with either quantitative studies or one-time snapshot ethnographies, we suggested and received funding for an in-depth qualitative research project in which we would study the writing of a group of students throughout their undergraduate program. We began this project with two research questions: How are these students using writing to learn, and what are they learning about writing? In this work, we wanted to emphasize the student perspective, and we wanted to provide the students with multiple opportunities for reflection to help us understand their writing and learning experiences: oral interviews, small-group discussions, and written reflections in addition to sharing samples of their writing. We envisioned a descriptive study composed of detailed narratives of the undergraduate writing experience that we thought would enable us to understand the culture of writing in our university from the perspective of those who live, study, and work in that culture—the students.

Although we believed firmly in our student-centered approach, we undertook this longitudinal study with some trepidation. We knew that this project would require an ongoing commitment of our energy and time. We also recognized that our research project differed significantly from other projects in our center because it was not a study of writing center practices. Nevertheless, we could not have predicted the impact this project has had, and continues to have, on all of our work. It has influenced not only how we understand and carry out our mission to provide support both to faculty who wish to integrate writing into their courses and to the students enrolled in those courses, but on all facets of our work, from consulting to research to outreach to how we envision our role in the university. We'll begin at the beginning.

THE PROJECT

At first, we attempted to garner a statistically selected, random sample of first-year students, but letters sent to that group resulted in only a few responses. However, when we advertised for volunteers in the first-year composition classes, we had 34 responses. Thus, all the students in this study are self-selected volunteers who received no compensation, other than a few pizzas, for their participation in the project. In the fall of 1994, we invited another group of students to join the project, bringing the total number to 42, 27 of whom remained in the project until its conclusion.[1]

Our emphasis on the student perspective for this research comes from Loren Barritt. In "Practicing Research by Researching Practice," Barritt (1983) defines educational research as "studying an educational experience from the point of view of individuals who lived through it" (80). Thus, our research design for this project relied heavily on collecting both the writing these students did while they were undergraduates enrolled in our university as well as their reflections on that work. During the 4 years of this project, students participating in this study kept all of their writing, both formal and informal, in files in the Writing Center. They also agreed to come to the Writing Center at least once every semester to write about, talk about, and reflect on their writing experiences, sometimes in one-on-one interviews and at other times in groups, and to let us tape-record and transcribe those sessions.

In a few instances, one of the graduate student researchers, Julie Bevins, also visited the students' classes and conducted follow-up interviews with those students about their writing and learning in those classes, but for the majority of these students we neither visited their classes nor interviewed any faculty. If we could repeat this study, we would probably add a more systematic classroom observation component.

Throughout the study, the principal researchers, as well as other members of the Writing Center staff, met regularly to study the materials we were collecting from the students. At the end of the year, we asked the students to meet with us in small groups to reflect on their experiences: to look over the materials in their folders, to write in response to a particular prompt, and then to discuss their reflections with one another. From our study of the transcriptions of these sessions, categories began to emerge. During both the third and fourth years, as part of our small-group meetings, we reported our tentative conclusions to the students and asked for their reactions. During the final year of the project, the researchers met weekly to revisit all of these transcriptions once again and to use the merging categories to explore other data—transcriptions of individual meetings with students, notes kept about meetings with these students, and the writing in the students' portfolios.

THE RESEARCH

During the first couple of years of the project, as we were collecting materials, holding meetings, transcribing tapes, and writing reports for the

---

[1]We wish to extend our sincere appreciation to all the students who have participated in the Portfolio Project and especially to those whose voices are included here. To preserve anonymity, all names have been changed. Transcriptions are verbatim except where edited for ease of readability.

vice provost, we continued to go about our other activities, including reading and discussing various articles in our weekly meetings with the graduate teaching assistants who work in our center. One of those articles was Marilyn Cooper's (1980) "Really Useful Knowledge: A Cultural Studies Agenda for Writing Centers," in which Cooper describes a writing center "as a site for inquiry and critique, where tutors not only are helping students learn how to improve their writing but also are developing better practices of teaching writing and really useful knowledge about the experiences of students writing in college and in our society" (146).

We discussed Cooper's article in terms of our consulting practices, but at the time, we made only limited connection between that article and our work with the participants in the Portfolio Project. We were pleased to discover that Cooper believed tutoring/consulting ought to be built on the experiences of students writing in college, but we were somewhat concerned about her suggestion that "rather than learning to sit across from the student and not write on their papers, tutors learn to critique the social and institutional setting of writing pedagogy and to reflect on their practices in light of theories of writing and language" (146). What might such a critique mean for the Portfolio Project? We made a note to return to this article after we had completed our study, and we went on about our business.

The drawers in the writing center continued to fill up with student papers. The transcribing of tapes moved on at its usual snail's pace. We began to do presentations on our findings. We shared our "really useful knowledge" with our colleagues, and we invited some of the students to do a readers' theater performance of a script constructed from transcriptions of their conversations, juxtaposed to present a variety of students' voices and insights.

As we entered the final year of the Portfolio Project, we were reading and discussing two articles by Nancy Grimm, one published in *The Writing Center Journal* in the fall of 1996 and another one from the December, 1996 issue of *College Composition and Communication*. In these two articles, Grimm argues that "writing center workers and composition teachers continue to talk about their work as that of enabling students to understand and enter the academic community" (1996b, 528).

Grimm (1996b) goes on to suggest that the way for writing centers to rid themselves of their usual regulatory role, a role that emanates from the typical "service" mission of most writing centers, is for writing centers to become "sites of articulating practice." According to Grimm,

> such writing centers will be less tuned to helping writers master community conventions and more tuned to developing the capacity of the staff to entertain multiple perspectives, to resist binary alignments, to think in systematic and complicated ways about literacy practices, to manage emotional reactivity, to gather evidence, and to explore the contradictions in literacy work. As places of research and knowledge-making, writing centers are uniquely situated to invite undergraduates into the intellectual work that makes a difference. (546)

Even though Grimm is talking here about those undergraduates who come into writing centers as clients and we were studying undergraduates who might never have come to our center for consulting, we were pleased to find some affirmation for our project. The "regulatory" part, however, was troublesome. Were we, we asked ourselves, merely describing the successes of a group of self-selected, primarily middle-class students? Would the end result of this study simply be more of the same? Would our work be interpreted as a blueprint for preparing ever more students for entrance into the academic community of the dominant class? Would our findings be used to vindicate those who always assume it's the student who must change (or be changed), not the faculty or the institution?

We began to make more connections among the authors we were reading, the discussions we were having, and the research projects in which we were engaged. Grimm and Cooper helped us remember Stephen North's warning that institutional-initiated research can be dangerous, that "the writing center's institutional potential may actually mask its complicity in what Elspeth Stuckey (1994) called the violence of literacy" (15). We needed to be reminded that institutions generally support research that validates prevailing institutional policies. Documenting the ways successful undergraduates adapt to institutional forces could lead to the conclusion that all is well in the world and that a relatively open admissions policy, augmented by a writing center to repair the underprepared, constitutes responsible policy and practices, even when that institution is situated in a democratic and multicultural society.

Shortly after these concerns surfaced, we began to meet weekly to take another look at the students' work as well as our understanding of that work as we had constructed it in various annual reports and conference presentations. In these meetings, we often found ourselves using the insights we had developed from reading Cooper and Grimm as the lenses through which we could review the first 3 years of the project.

Year 1 (1993–1994)

In our summation of the first year of the study, we kept our focus narrowed to a discussion of the students' "efforts to situate themselves within the academic culture of the University" (Writing Center Portfolio Project). We began with small-group discussions in which we asked students to talk about composing by asking them two questions: What are you learning about writing? How are you using writing to learn? This was a discourse we understood. It reinforced our own ideas and values about writing and our service role in a research institution. At this point, the students, with few prompts from us, were already beginning to describe the conflict between writing about topics that interested them—something they often referred to as "personal' writing—and writing to satisfy a course requirement—what they called "academic" writing.

Now, when we began to take another look at those comments, this time using Cooper and Grimm as lenses, we could begin to understand more fully the students' struggles with the constraints of academic writing. We could also see their desire to claim a position within the academic community at the same time that they held onto the personal connections that meant so much to their writing. We thought about Cooper's (1980) argument that if students "are to achieve agency in writing, they must learn how to challenge these constraints productively in the service of their own goals and needs" (140). In that first year, students often talked about the tensions they felt between academic and personal writing; by Year 2, they had already begun to challenge those constraints.

Year 2 (1994–1995)

In our annual report on the activities of the second year, we continued to describe the students' developing competence as writers in academia, and we praised the students for becoming "more capable of discussing the act of composing itself" (Portfolio Project, 1995). Once again, however, the students were well ahead of us. We were looking for ways that they worked "to acquire the discourse of the academic community" while the students were praising "those contexts in which they were encouraged to write and learn and to claim that learning and writing for themselves" (Portfolio Project, 1995). Students revealed this search for "agency" in their discussions about the motivations and limitations that affected their writing and learning. For example, one of the problems that students talked about was their "propensity to correct too soon in the writing process" (Portfolio Project, 1995). This propensity occurred, the students argued, when teachers overemphasized form and structure. In comparison, the students "applauded faculty who had helped them unlearn these hypercorrection behaviors. The opportunity, these students claimed, to do more than adhere to the textual form and mechanics of a paper offered them the most motivation for growth and change in their writing"(Portfolio Project, 1995).

When we took a second look at these statements, we began to understand more clearly what Grimm (1996b) meant when she suggested that motivation and engagement were what students needed rather than another software program to improve study skills or review grammar troubles. In fact, she noted that a preoccupation with quick fixes can "be a distraction from the real thing—a relationship that motivates learning" (539).

Year 3 (1995–1996)

A look at the report from the third year revealed that we had begun to shift our focus toward the particular relationships that motivated these students to learn. Because students were moving into their majors, we saw a greater variety of contexts for the writing they were doing. This variety encouraged us to ask more open-ended questions to elicit responses generated by particular contexts. In her meetings with individual participants, Bevins suggested: "Using your portfolios as a guide, look through your work and tell me the story of 'you.'" Reshaping our own understandings of the project allowed us to reshape the questions we asked, a strategy that gave the students greater agency in their responses, which we, in turn, were able to hear and understand in new ways.

Instead of describing their composing processes or how they were using writing to learn, the participants shared particular characteristics they thought described them as writers. Then they began to describe the way writing is also "shaped by the context in which it occurs" (Portfolio Project, 1996). As they moved into their majors, students began to mention a need to alter their writing for various fields, disciplines, and audiences, and this necessity for change produced new difficulties. At this point, we began to see that the once-parallel courses of our many different areas of writing center work were beginning to converge. When we studied these students' descriptions, we began to understand Cooper's (1980) suggestion that tutors/consultants "can best help students become agents of their own writing by helping them . . . understand . . . how various institutional forces impinge on how and what they write and how they can negotiate a place for their own goals and needs when faced with these forces"(139).

Once we made this connection, we saw the necessity of returning to earlier data from this project to rethink the issues the students had been talking about: for example, their discussions of academic versus personal writing. We ended the 1995–1996 report with the following statement:

> As in other years of the investigation, the issue of personal versus academic writing continued to be a strong theme. Many students maintain they cannot produce "good" academic writing if they are not connected personally in some way to the topic. They need to be able to make connections between topics and their professional development and/or life experiences in order to write effectively. Conversations with Portfolio Project students seem to suggest that students use their areas of interest to inform their writing; they figure out what is significant to them and how that interest can play itself out in their academic projects. (Portfolio Project, 1996)

As Grimm (1996b) has pointed out, one of the things we need to do is "listen, and think about the implications of what our students might have to teach us" (546). We were learning to listen.

CONVERSATIONS WITH STUDENTS

Over the past 5 years, a number of themes that we are continuing to study have emerged from this project: the value of talk, the importance of the students' own intellectual projects, the value of portfolios as benchmarks for student writers. For this chapter, however, we want to focus on the way our understanding of the tensions between academic and personal writing developed as a result of this project. We want to look more closely at the way students negotiate between the unifying "centripetal" and destabilizing "centrifugal" forces of language that Alice Gillam (1991), citing Bakhtin, noticed in her work with students who came to their writing center, and what we see as an interplay between academic accommodation and personal resistance. In particular, we were struck by the fact that students express a strong desire to accommodate to the academic culture. That is, they exult in becoming members of particular academic communities, and they are interested in learning and contributing to the various discourses in their respective fields. Heidi, for example, explains that she has discovered that her major, biochemistry, "is just like you're learning a different language, and it's just exciting to be able to talk in that different language and to be able to talk with other people and understand what they're saying . . . . Once you really understand it, if you can understand it, it's exciting, it's fun, and you want to learn more" (Portfolio Project, 1995).

Pam, a music therapy major, agrees with Heidi, adding that "there's lingo in music, there's lingo in biochemistry, there's lingo everywhere, and if you either force yourself or are forced to be within or are just sucked within the environment, you start using it. You just start using it" (Portfolio Project, 1995).

Despite the difficulties of learning a new "lingo," these students are eager to become associated with the discourses that help define them as "biochemists" or "music therapists." Connie, a psychology major, is thrilled when, after allowing a friend to read one of her papers, he tells her, "Oh, you can tell you're a social science major!" "That made me feel good," Connie notes, "because I WROTE like a social science [major], you know? That was neat to know that" (Portfolio Project, 1995). Bob, a telecommunications major with a strong interest in scriptwriting is also interested in accommodating to the academy (or, in his words, becoming more of an "intellectual"), describing the development of his interest in academic writing by comparing such writing to playing chess:

> Do you have anything that you do occasionally and you know that there are people out there that do it so much better than you, but it doesn't matter because it's just something you do? You know, like playing chess. You know you'll play chess every once in awhile but you're not gonna read all the books and ... and then I came in here [the Writing Center], and people are like, "You know, we're gonna take some time and really learn how to play chess." And I started playing it, and I was like, "Hey, this is pretty cool, so let's keep going." (Portfolio Project, 1996)

Once students are interested, connected to what they are studying—be it biochemistry, social science, or writing—they are motivated to join the community of individuals who speak the "lingo" of that field. They willingly submit to learning the discourses of that environment even if, as Connie reminds us, it "is hard, to be as straightforward as they [people in the field of psychology] want you to be. It's very, it's a challenge, and I haven't reached that yet" (Portfolio Project, 1995). Karesh, a communications major, tells us, "The pain to me is equal to the gain. It's no pain, no gain kind of thing, and I want my degree" (Portfolio Project, 1995).

However, even as students tell us they are willing, often eager, to accommodate, their stories illustrate the power of their desires to further their own goals within the academy. As Patricia Stock (1996) has reminded us in the *Dialogic Curriculum,* students often come to their schoolwork with already-conceived intellectual projects and, if they are given the opportunity, they will develop and explore their own themes. For example, Nicki, who majored in both science and history, often found ways to bring to her writing her desire to become a veterinarian, not only in her science courses but in her history courses as well. In looking through her portfolio one day, Nicki commented:

> This was written so long ago, yet, you know, it's got veterinarian written all over it, *all* over it. Everything I've written has "vet" written—I mean, ever since I was *little*. It's got animals galore, you know? That's kind of cool that they can see that theme if they, you know, if a person wants to read through here. That's all I ever talk about is vet medicine, vet medicine. (Portfolio Project, 1996)

The stories told by the Portfolio Project students also show these students resisting forces that they see as subverting those goals. Although they are willing to accommodate, to some extent, to the demands of institutional forces, many of the Portfolio Project students insisted that they would do so only insofar as this accommodation does not interfere with the progress of their own projects, and they found ways of inserting their own decisions into academic expectations.

For Nicki, constructing herself as a veterinarian hinges solidly on her ability, in effect, to write herself into that role in her own way. Because Nicki needs "to internalize all the information myself," she insists that in writing, "[I] will use evidence, but I refuse to use quotes." Although she paraphrases other authors and often cites sources, Nicki avoids all direct quotations in her papers—in spite of some instructors' urgings to the contrary—because she believes that quoting detracts from her ability to make sense of what she has read and learned. Nicki is aware of the great demands placed on her as a pre-vet student: our university's veterinary school is highly competitive and, to be accepted, she must perform well academically, not only in her science courses but also in her history courses. Although she wishes to become a part of the academic community in veterinary medicine, she sets limits on how far she will go to meet institutional demands. As eager as she is to talk the talk of the veterinarians, Nicki wants to control the way she shapes her writing and, thus, the way she shapes herself.

Likewise, Jane, a student with a double major in journalism and English, tells us early in her college career, "I don't have a problem questioning authority" (Portfolio Project, 1995). She exemplifies this confidence by confronting a professor who had given her a lower grade than she thought she deserved on a paper. Her confrontation resulted in a grade change.

In this instance, "authority" for Jane resides in the persona of her instructor, and she is willing to challenge that authority when it conflicts with her sense of what is—as she puts it—"right." She displays this resistance, even though she wishes to join the academic community her journalism professor represents. She also recognizes the differences between journalism and English discourse conventions and the conflicts created in switching from writing articles for her journalism classes to writing papers for her English courses. When she describes the writing of journalists, she says, "All their paragraphs are one sentence long!" Then, when she has difficulty producing the more developed paragraphs required by her English professors, she said, "So I've started writing English papers, and it's like, 'Learn how to paragraph!'" (Portfolio Project, 1995). As Jane progresses in her majors, she becomes more and more concerned with her representation of herself as a writer and more resistant to the "authority" of these different discourses—much in the same way she once resisted her instructor's authority. At the end of her junior year, she describes the way she has started to reshape her writing by blending journalistic and English conventions:

> For the *State Journal*, I am using more of my English skills than I used to. It used to be kind of like the pyramid for journalism writing: newsworthy stuff on top, and then it just trickles down. But now I am using more detail[ed] writing, especially with features, and it's becoming so that it's more important to me.... I get a better article if I'm looking at the whole picture and not just what's important. Because when I first started doing journalism, [it was] like, these are the rules for journalism, and this is what I am going to follow, so that is what I did.... I think now that I'm a bit more advanced in my major areas, I can use some of my English skills because I feel a bit more like I can challenge a pyramid concept and get more out of my articles. (Portfolio Project, 1995)

Like Nicki, Jane sets limits for herself regarding how far she will go to meet the institutional demands placed upon her by her academic or professional community. She resists the "pyramid" structure in writing her news articles; she adds her English experiences. By blending the discourses of journalism and English, Jane not only gets "more out of [her] articles," she also develops agency as a writer.

Nicki and Jane are examples of how some students in the Portfolio Project are both accommodating to and simultaneously resisting academic forces. We might call these forms of resistance "negative," not in a pejorative sense, but in the fact that they are student *refusals*. That is, Nicki will *not* use quotations, and Jane will *not* neatly separate the discourses of journalism and English. When we think of students resisting academic forces, we often conjure up "not" tales like these. But what Portfolio Project students tell us they are "not" doing most of all is unquestioningly accepting all aspects of the academic culture into which they are "accommodating" themselves. Thus, accommodation and resistance are not necessarily antithetical. For Nicki, being able to look through her portfolio to see how she positions herself, through her writing, within the academy and within the field of veterinary medicine, gives her a sense of agency among institutional forces. As Cooper (1980) has explained, "Agency in writing is not simply a matter of taking up the subject positions offered by assignments but of actively constructing subject positions that negotiate between institutional demands and individual needs" (140).

Deborah, a social relations major, demonstrates this act of negotiation for us further when she talks about recognizing her area of interest in Latino issues:

> When I opened [my portfolio] up this time I was curious to see what I had considered significant pieces of writing. I could see several papers had a common focus or similar focus and I realize that the topic of those papers is what has become my main area/topic of interest in my college experience. At first the writings I did were topics my professors chose, but after my freshman year I began to choose what I wanted to focus on in my writing.... I have found a definite area of interest, or focus, in my writing. I am very interested in the immigrant experience, specifically of the Latino population, and social conditions of the Latino community. And these are the areas I want to continue to focus on in my graduate studies. In fact, Latino immigrants and their experiences in the U.S. are the focus of my summer research project. (Portfolio Project, 1997)

This self-selected focus on Latino experiences—a theme that Deborah tells she has chosen for herself (no longer allowing professors to choose "topics" for her) and a theme that she returns to and re-examines from multiple perspectives in several different papers—becomes her way of negotiating a space for herself within her particular academic community. She is no passive recipient of her professors' "choices"; she is, instead, an active participant in her construction of herself within the social relations community. Here we can see, more fully, the significance of Portfolio Project students' comments about their need to be connected "personally" to their academic writing, something they have told us since their first year as undergraduates. Such connections allow students to try on the various "new languages" or "lingoes" of the academy with some degree of familiarity, but they also provide a way for students to position themselves within these discourses, to claim spaces for themselves that ensure they are not simply carbon copies of their professors or of other professionals in their fields. Now, more than ever, we can understand what Rachel, as a first-year pre-med student, meant when she talked about writing as a way of exploring academic interests in a particular subject:

Profs of all courses should allow students to explore the realness of that subject. It is not just a biology course, of learning which animals have an open circulating system; you have to have feelings about this subject or you wouldn't be pursuing that field. Teachers should allow more writing instead of just being a sponge, sucking it in and spitting it out, because it just passes through instead of meaning something to you. (Portfolio Project, 1994)

Rachel is describing for us how students can use writing to process their understandings in relation to a particular field so that they can then position themselves among institutional forces. This understanding leads students to setting the kinds of limits that Nicki and Jane describe. In *Writing and the Sense of Self*, Robert Brooke (1991) suggests that

we see writing as part of a larger and more basic activity: the development and negotiation of individual identity in a complex social environment. Like any social activity, writing does not have meaning or value in itself. Rather, human beings assign it value (for the self, for the community) when it helps them position themselves relative to one another in ways which are important to them, when it helps them understand and interact with their community. (5-6)

In our work with the students in the Portfolio Project, we have come to see this writerly positioning of the self at work in the ways students represent themselves as both accommodating and resisting academic forces in their various fields of study. Accommodation and resistance are not either/or strategies for these students; if students simultaneously accommodate and resist as writers and learners in the academy, as Portfolio Project participants have informed us that they do, then it becomes our responsibility to support students in this both/and relationship. Portfolio Project students are teaching us that we must, indeed, avoid becoming the "silent" writing center that Grimm (1996a) warns us about, a center that will "maintain silence in order to protect students; maintain the *status quo*...; ensure viability of their work" (540), a center that avoids the issues of accommodation and resistance that students confront.

As the students sort, shape, and reshape their portfolio pieces, they talk about the variety of positions and meanings they discover and the selves they represent in various contexts, for different purposes, with limits and constraints but also with choices. Through the Portfolio Project conversations, these students maintain that they have come to understand more clearly the decisions they made, the positions that they have occupied, and the both/and conflicts they continue to negotiate. As we have listened to the students' process of shaping and being shaped, we have also had to consider and reconsider our writing center's "relationship of service to institutional practices of literacy" (Grimm, 1996a, 6) and our efforts at making both useful knowledge and knowledge useful to our community.

CONVERSATIONS WITH OTHERS

Advocating what she calls an "articulatory practice," Grimm (1996a) argues that writing centers ought to move toward greater dialogue with faculty. We need to share what we have learned from those students we have been studying and those with whom we work. As Grimm has suggested, "Rather than engage in unproductive and frustrating dialogue with those resistant to change, articulatory practice encourages us to apply what we know in areas where change is being considered" (22). The problem, perhaps, is that we do not always recognize those areas. The story of our work with a professor from the College of Education and his graduate students is not only typical of our interactions with most faculty, but it also illustrates the assumptions under which those of us who work in writing centers often operate.

The professor, in charge of a large 100-level education course taught by close to 20 graduate students, contacted us for assistance. The students in this course (mostly first- and second-year university students) began the semester by writing personal narratives about their own learning. Because the students were having difficulty moving from telling the stories to analyzing them, the professor looked to us for some rubric or set of guidelines for analyzing narratives—a typical example, we thought, of locating the problem in the students and assuming the students had to change, not the course or the institution.

Based on our belief that teachers need to experience what they ask students to do, we suggested a workshop with his graduate student teaching assistants (GSTAs) in which they would write and then analyze narratives about their own learning as a way of helping them understand the difficulties the undergraduates were experiencing. The professor was not convinced the GSTAs needed to write narratives, but he did agree to the workshop. It was probably at this point that we assumed this was not one of Grimm's (1996a) areas "where change [was] being considered" (22). When the GSTAs came to our writing center, we asked them to write about a significant learning experience and, when they were finished, to write another paragraph in which they explained why that experience was so significant. After they had written and then worked in groups to tell one another their stories, we put some of the themes they had generated on the board and asked them to share other stories that illustrated those themes, or suggest other themes that fit their stories. Although we managed to get four or five themes and about 10 stories on the board, we noticed that moving from description to analysis wasn't exactly easy for the GSTAs either. Like the undergraduate students, the GSTAs liked telling the stories. When we discussed the possibilities of applying a similar strategy with the students in their classes, the GSTAs wondered whether their students would come up with the necessary "important" themes, but they also considered the possibility that it might be interesting to find out what the *students* thought was important and universal about the stories they told. The GSTAs discussed the possibilities of publishing the students' stories as a way of making the students' voices part of the class conversations and of making the narratives available as examples for the pedagogy and theory they would be reading in the course. At this point, the professor told the GSTAs to ignore his two-page handout with directions for writing and analyzing the narratives. The GSTAS, having lost the security of the professor's handout, raised other issues. What should they do if one of the students couldn't find a theme for his or her story? What would happen if, as they continued to discuss course content through the semester, the principles they had generated so early in the semester had to be revised?

We concluded the session by sharing some of what the Portfolio Project students had told us about accommodating and resisting authority, about finding ways to position themselves in academia, and about wanting opportunities for exploring their own interests and goals. We parted with promises to continue the conversation.

Conducting research, especially university-initiated research, results in both benefits and risks. This research has given us greater insight into the writing culture in our university, but it has also put greater demands on us to find ways to share what we learn and to keep the dialogue, and so the potential for change, going. In order to recognize those places where change might occur, we will need to remain open to possibilities. Rather than simply assuming that most faculty are not ready for change or that we know which ones are, we might want to withhold judgment a bit longer than usual.

We learned long ago that students frequently do not ask for what they really want. Thus, they often ask us to "edit" their papers, when they really want to know if we understand what they are trying to say. Perhaps we should be equally tolerant of faculty. When faculty come to us with complaints that locate the problem solely within the students, perhaps we should not be so quick to assume that they mean what they say. In the case of the education professor and the graduate students, we clearly had made a judgment too soon. When the professor withdrew his handout in favor of allowing the categories for analysis to emerge from the students' own stories, we were more than pleased. Perhaps we should not be so sure that we always *know* where potential areas of change are located.

CONVERSATIONS AT HOME

When we began the Portfolio Project, research seemed to be simply another of the multiple activities and projects going on in our writing center. Because it was university-wide research, it gave us some amount of power in the institution: We were a repository of information, a marketable product in the academy. At the same time, we were aware of the possible conflicts involved in using that information to critique the institution that supported us. Quite possibly, because of those potential conflicts, it took substantially more time for us to see the project's relationship to our daily work. Only later, as the project was ending, could we turn our attention to the conversations that need to occur at home, in our writing center, and these often proved to be the most difficult conversations of all.

In his study of consulting practices in our center, William McCall (1996) discovered that the student writers he interviewed claimed that they were working to find a position between the personal and the academic. However, he could find no evidence of this negotiation in the consulting sessions. McCall describes three different writing consultants as they worked with student writers. In addition to analyzing the videotapes of these writing conferences, McCall also interviewed the writing consultants and the students (one from each of the first-year writing programs on our campus: the general writing program and both the science and the social science residential colleges), as well as their professors. Immediately after the consulting sessions, the students and the consultants also wrote about their conversations with one another. In a description of the efforts of the students and the consultants to move away from mere summary and toward analysis, McCall points out that this emphasis on analysis often took on "a personal tone and meaning." "For consultants and clients," McCall says, "analysis does not always or even usually mean a denial of personal response." As one of the writing consultants pointed out, "I think to be good at analysis, you have to realize that the way I'm reading isn't just, you know, the way that my brain works. It's also the way I live, who I am, where I've been, what I've done and stuff, and what my past is" (102).

In the interviews, all three student writers described ways they worked to bridge the gap between personal connections and the subject matter of their courses. The student writing a paper on a cultural aspect of the 1950s interviewed her mother, who had been a teenager in the 1950s, in order to develop her understanding of *Homeward Bound*. The student who was doing an analysis of *The Awakening* spent much of the interview comparing her own assertiveness with Edna's lack of assertiveness as part of her attempt to understand the obstacles Edna had faced but that, living in a different time, the student had not. Even the student who was writing a scientific paper on Mendelain genetics using fruit flies as subjects described to McCall (1996) the ways in which he "worked hard to personalize his paper" (104). He described his process as follows:

> I could write all this stuff and I could include 15 quotes and that would proba-
> bly show that I'm interested, you know? Or I could even put a personal con-
> nection in there but the format probably wouldn't allow it. Or something
> along that line, but definitely if you're not interested sometimes, a lot of times,
> you can tell in the paper. There's just no life in the paper basically. (105)

This student is very aware of the limits of the form for scientific writing within which he must work. Nevertheless, in the interview, he told McCall that "every paper I write is part of me. I see myself as part of how I write. I have my own style" (105). Even though McCall found clear examples from the interviews that these student writers *were* working to "negotiate a place within the confines of writing assignments for interests and abilities that arise out of their experiences" (Cooper, 1980, 146), the lack of documentation of this activity in the consulting sessions is disturbing. Except for the few instances when the science major halted the writing consulting session to work out the particular word choices that he claimed were part of his "style" and that he believed would convey to his professor his enthusiasm for the topic, McCall could find no evidence of negotiation between the assignment and the student's interests and ongoing intellectual projects in the transcriptions of the tapes of the consulting sessions.

If, as the Portfolio Project students claim and as McCall's student interviews document, so many students are working to negotiate places for themselves in the assignments they are given, why is this work not part of the dialogue that occurs between the writing consultants and the student writers? As Cooper (1980) has pointed out:

> All students and tutors know how institutions coerce them in writing classes. They know that students in writing classes are offered and can exercise little or no control over such things as the topic or genre of their papers, the argument structure or organization of their papers, the length of their papers, and the style or register of the language in their papers. Students know that in order to get a good grade they must carefully follow assignments that specify these things.... (139–140)

How, then, can we encourage undergraduate writing consultants to take up these matters in their conversations with the students who come to our writing center? How can we encourage them in their work with student writers to acknowledge the institutional constraints they both encounter and to introduce the possibility of challenging those restraints?

According to Cooper (1980), undergraduate tutor/consultants are capable of this work because their writing center work brings them into close contact with students, they are familiar with composition theory, they "have little investment in disciplinary beliefs and practices, and they are thus less responsive to its standards and expectations than they are to the needs of and experiences of their peers" (144).

Because the undergraduate writing consultants who work in our writing center consult with an average of 10 student writers a week, they do, in fact, have considerable experience working with student writers. Nearly all of these consultants have also taken a semester-long course on composition and consulting, so they are at least somewhat conversant with composition theory. We would argue, though, that because they themselves are undergraduate students, they *do* have "an investment in disciplinary beliefs and practices"(Cooper, 1980, 14) and, like the Portfolio Project students, they are also actively seeking their own niches within those disciplines.

When Nicki recognizes that "everything" she has written has veterinarian "all over it," she sees both the effects of institutional forces and her own responsibility for shaping herself as a student within the academy. Likewise, when Jane establishes her own priorities within the context of her academic work, understanding that her choices do not necessarily adhere to "conventions," she negotiates a space for herself within what Portfolio Project students have repeatedly called "personal" and "academic" and what Gillam noted as the "centripetal and "centrifugal" forces of language.

We want to argue that the undergraduate writing consultants in our writing center bring to their work their own experiences as students in a large research university, and it is these experiences, we think, that can best inform their work as consultants. We must be careful not to "train" tutors simply by asking them to read composition theory and pedagogy. Rather, as we have done with the Portfolio Project students, we need to start with the writing consultants' own experiences—with their stories of their own work as student writers in the university.

Only slowly have we come to this realization, and our attempts to introduce this understanding into our conversations at home in our writing center meetings have not been entirely successful thus far. For example, after the graduate students read Cooper's article, two of them decided to develop a presentation for the undergraduate writing consultants. Given Cooper's (1980) assurance that she *was* talking about undergraduates when arguing that "tutors help students negotiate a place within the confines of writing assignments for interests and abilities that arise out of their experiences" (146), the graduate students were hoping to move the writing consultants toward a "critical reading of the syllabuses and assignments that students are given" in order to help them "see what subject positions are being offered to them in these texts and what spaces are left in which they can construct different subject positions" (146) rather than continuing to obey North's (1994) dictum of supporting "the teacher's position completely" (441).

What we learned was an important lesson in the difficulty of maintaining conversations without a common ground of experience. If we had started by inviting the writing consultants to share their own stories of negotiating assignments, we might have been able to move to a discussion of subject positions. We didn't, and the discussion became focused on what teachers should not do rather than on how to support students in their efforts to find spaces for themselves in their assignments.

If we invite the writing consultants to do the same kind of reflection on their roles as student writers as we have asked the Portfolio Project students to do, if we start with the writing consultants' stories about their own struggles with institutional forces, maybe we will have more conversations about these issues. Then we might begin to develop a higher level of awareness of these issues so that consultants can make such topics an integral part of their consulting sessions.

Susan Miller (1991) claims that she came to "understand the politics of writing by learning that power is, at its roots, telling our own stories. Without 'good' stories to rely on, no minority or marginalized majority has a chance to change its status.... " (1). As we have reflected on the stories that the Portfolio Project students have told, we have begun to understand more deeply the politics of writing and writing centers and the kinds of conversations that can make change possible. Such conversations rely less on the information or "findings" that research can provide (although those are certainly valuable) and more on valuing the stories that students share with us, stories from which we can learn, and stories we can share with others.

REFERENCES

Barritt, L. (1983). Practicing research by researching practice. In P. L. Stock (Ed), *FForum: Essays on theory and practice in the teaching of writing* (pp. 79–85). Upper Montclair, NJ: Boynton/Cook.

Brooke, R. E. (1991). *Writing and the sense of self: Identity negotiation in writing workshops.* Urbana, IL: NCTE.

Cooper, M. (1980). Really useful knowledge: A cultural studies agenda for writing centers. In C. Murphy & J. Law (Eds.), *Landmark essays on writing centers* (pp. 135–147). Davis, CA: Hermagoras.

Gillam, A. M. (1991). Writing center ecology: A Bakhtinian perspective. *The Writing Center Journal, 11*(2), 3–11.

Grimm, N. (1996a). The regulatory role of the writing center: Coming to terms with a loss of innocence. *The Writing Center Journal, 17*(1), 5–29.

Grimm, N, (1996b). Rearticulating the work of the writing center. *College Composition and Communication, 47*(4), 523–548.

McCall, W. (1996). *Academic discourse: Tradition, challenge, and destabilization.* Unpublished dissertation, Michigan State University, East Lansing.

Miller, S. (1991). *Textual carnivals: The politics of composition.* Carbondale: Southern Illinois Press.

North, S. (1984). The idea of a writing center. *College English, 46,* 433–446.

North, S. (1994). Revisiting "The idea of a writing center." *The Writing Center Journal, 15*(1), 7–19.

Stock, P. L. (1996). *The dialogic curriculum.* Portsmouth, NH: Boynton/Cook.

Chapter 10

Computer Literacies and the Roles of the Writing Center

Dànielle DeVoss
Michigan State University

> Technology does not drive change per se. Instead, it merely creates new options and opportunities for change. It is our collective response to technologies that drives change.

—Paul Saffo

Peter Carino (1998), in "Computers in the Writing Center: A Cautionary History," poses a twofold challenge to writing center staff: (a) to develop pedagogy to respond to the changes that technology generates, and (b) to take an active stance as computing technologies emerge and take stronger and stronger roles in shaping our institutions. Two of the changes that computer technology has pushed to the forefront are, first, our understanding of how text has evolved (and is evolving from traditional paper texts to media-rich hypertexts), and, second, our understanding of how research and writing are complicated by the texts that exist within new electronic realms. Students are now expected not only to research online, but also to publish hypertext. Writing center theory and practice must likewise evolve so we can situate ourselves as crucial stakeholders, working toward a more complex and critical use of computing technologies and computer-related literacies.

In this chapter, I describe one possible approach to meeting Carino's challenge, that is, the development of the Internet Writing Consultancy,

167

which began at the Michigan State University Writing Center in fall 1996. I will discuss the research practices we used to develop and refine the consultancy and the process through which the Writing Center came to develop its approach to electronic texts and electronic literacies. Changing notions of what literacy is and what it does foregrounds this discussion. Based on our experiences with Internet consulting, I describe new roles for the writing center to consider adopting. To conclude, I pose questions for future research, important questions and considerations for those of us who would like to see writing centers at the center of discussions of and research on computers and writing.

IN THE BEGINNING

To meet the literacy demands of a technologically driven society, most colleges and universities have implemented some sort of technology initiative; however, beyond providing some new software and installing some new computers, the peopleware aspect of technologizing is often ignored. There's an "if you build it, they will come" sort of mentality and an "if they come, they will learn" expectation. However, without support and training, few students, faculty, and staff will learn, especially those students who have not had access to technology in their homes or in their previous schooling and whose literacy practices might not have prepared them for interactions with computing technologies.

In May of 1996, the president of Michigan State University (MSU) implemented a technology guarantee (<http://www.msu.edu/events/techinfo/>), promising all students an excellent and diverse technological education while at MSU. This guarantee included space on the university's main server for publishing student web pages. As more and more instructors incorporated web-focused assignments in their classes, the Writing Center began addressing more writing-related questions, such as:

- How do I cite a URL using MLA?
- How can I tell who the author of this web page is and if the information is worth using in my paper?
- My instructor expects us to publish a web page; how do I make one?
- How do I include a graphic in my web page and where should I put it?
- If I create a link on a web page I wrote for a class to another person's web page, am I plagiarizing?

To address the demands of an increasingly large number of students researching, writing, and publishing on the internet, specifically the World Wide Web, we launched an Internet Writing Consultancy. Without trained and committed individuals to reinforce the purpose of such technology guarantees and to enable users to develop the literate practices necessary to use such technologies, the technology guarantees don't mean much; they become the empty rhetoric so common in a society that privileges technologies while downplaying the needs and interests of the people affected by the technologies.

THE DEVELOPMENT OF THE INTERNET
WRITING CONSULTANCY

The Internet Writing Consultancy was a necessary development in addressing new questions about online research and publication. In fact, ignoring the demands arising from the shift in literacy skills that are demanded of students would have alienated the Writing Center from the important work done within the university community and would have marginalized students who otherwise had no source of support for the new work they were expected to undertake.

Other sources of support did, in fact, exist, but we found that many were either inaccessible to students or privileged the technology more than the academic endeavor of writing. Michigan State University had a Computer Center with a customer help desk, but, as the name might indicate, students were often treated as customers, not necessarily as learners negotiating new skills and literacies. Although services were free, a wait of up to an hour was to be expected when one stopped by the help desk. Consultants were often trained in computer sciences and specialized in hardware, software, and network troubleshooting. This was not the place for a student to go to inquire about how to conceptualize and then write for the global audience that the World Wide Web supposedly offers.

Sources of support did exist within departments. Inevitably, however, each department had one or two frazzled instructors identified as "specialists" or "techies" who were called on for every task related to computers, from changing toner cartridges in printers to answering student and faculty questions about how to appropriately cite electronic resources. The staff of the Writing Center recognized the demanding realm in which these techies worked; realized that they needed a source of support for the writing-related advice they were providing; and also recognized that important links could be fostered among faculty members, their departments, and the Writing Center. These interdisciplinary ties created a web of interaction, access to new departmental connections, and new sources of dialogue, support, and funding for the Writing Center.

The Writing Center had long before established a graduate research assistant position of Technology Projects Coordinator. Each new graduate student who took the post gave it his or her personal touch, and the position had meandered from focusing on data entry of client demographics (collected for each session), to moderating and maintaining the Writing Center's email lists, to developing the Center's web site. Because the graduate student in this position maintained the Center's computer system and worked on innovative approaches to integrating computers and writing, this person was identified as best to coordinate the unfolding Internet Writing Consultancy. I was the technology projects coordinator at the time this decision was made. Although our research and development team didn't stop at the doors of the Center, I worked closely with Sharon Thomas, the acting director of the Writing Center; with Keri Hungerford, another interested graduate student; and with the consultants interested in becoming Internet Writing Consultants.

None of the first set of Internet Writing Consultants (IWCs) were computer "experts," but all had their own individual strengths and knowledge; this situation made for an exciting dynamic, as they learned to play off one another's skills and to work together to solve problems and address the questions of faculty and students. None of the IWCs were hired strictly as IWCs; all were writing consultants who had undergone traditional writing center training. But because of their interest in computers and writing, hypertext issues, and web-based research and publication, they had been striving to increase their familiarity with computers and to help the Writing Center work toward a sustainable culture of computers and writing. Their interest in these issues was identified at several places: on their private e-mail discussion list, during informal discussions inside and outside of the Center, and in the course they were required to take to become full-fledged consultants in the Center. At one time, approximately 12 of the 22 undergraduate writing consultants the Writing Center employed were identified as both traditional writing consultants and IWCs.

THINKING ABOUT WRITING,
THINKING ABOUT THE WEB

After identifying an initial group of consultants interested in developing the Internet Writing Consultancy, our initial euphoria diminished a bit as we had a better idea of the bigger picture. There was lots of work to be done and, first and foremost, we needed a stronger idea of current research and theory on how text and reading were changing in order to sculpt new consulting practices. Then, we had to focus on specific approaches and tactics to move us toward our goal of supporting students who found themselves facing new literacy challenges posed by electronic realms for research and writing.

As the Internet Writing Consultants came to learn—and as contemporary work in composition studies, in writing center theory, in rhetorical theory, and in other realms indicates—(see, e.g., Bolter, 1991; Joyce, 1995; Landow, 1994; Lanham, 1993), the notion of what we consider a text to be is shifting. Davin, one of the IWCs, noted that one of his goals in an internet writing session was "to familiarize clients with HTML and the idea of hypertext as another form of communication, a very unique form." No longer is a text always a paper document. No longer are the more privileged texts peer-reviewed and formally published. With web access, HTML familiarity, and server space, students have access to a powerful new publishing medium, one that may make their texts as available and—in some ways and for some audiences—as important as the print texts we privilege. These are complex texts, sometimes with new and unfamiliar attributes. Expanding notions of visual literacies, hypertexts, nontextual compositions and the like are shifting the way we approach the notion of text.

Further complicating new approaches to texts and the new approaches we were exploring was the fact that few research models existed regarding computer use in the writing center, and, as Blythe (1998) notes, such studies are often contradictory, due to local-issue diversity in different writing centers. Blythe addresses networked computers specifically, but this diversity characterizes all writing center work with newer technologies. Although we are a disparate lot, the common thread here, of course, is the technology and it is important within this diversity not to privilege the technology, not to see users as merely *users*. Instead, it is crucial to formulate research approaches that recognize students and faculty relying on technologies as partners engaged in a dialogue with and about technology (105).

Without models, and feeling as if we were negotiating a new realm on our own rather than deciding on a strict research methodology, we instead formulated some general questions that helped guide us as we explored possible practices and theoretical frameworks for our Internet Writing Consultancy. These questions included the following:

- What would be the best way to shape our approaches? What types of feedback did we want to seek, who would be best served (and who would best serve us) by taking part in our teasing out and testing of approaches, ideas, materials, and so on?
- What basic "computer literacy" skills could we presume most students to have? Could we support students who required training in basic keyboarding skills and computer use? If so, how could we best support these students?
- How might we address students' diverse and complex literacy practices? How could we borrow from their past literacy practices to help them acclimate to new literacy practices and discourses?
- Would our traditional writing consulting practices be affected by the new consulting practices we wanted to incorporate? If so, how would internet writing consulting change our practices?
- How could we best formulate new consulting approaches? Specifically, how could we support students as they came to reading and writing in new and quite different realms?

With these questions—and many, many others—in mind, we began our work. Our approaches evolved as our thinking evolved; our research practices were hybrid, dynamic, and continually unfolding.

CREATING APPROACHES, TESTING POSSIBILITIES, REVISING OURSELVES AND OUR WORK

We had decided that one of the best ways we could support students was to accompany our one-to-one internet consulting with handouts students could take with them and refer to when they returned to web work on their own. Handouts had always been a contentious topic in our Writing Center; some feared that if students could merely walk in and grab a handout, they'd avoid the important interpersonal experience with our writing consultants. We decided to make the handouts available anyway, hoping that most students would choose to make an appointment with an IWC and spend some time working with a consultant, rather than walk in and walk right out, handout in hand.

Many of us had struggled to learn web-based research and web-page creation on our own and felt we could anticipate possible questions or problems students might have. We created handouts on a variety of web-related topics, including creating a basic web page, searching the web, evaluating web pages, documenting online sources, and so on. A crucial step in the development of the handouts was actually putting them to the test. We initially tested our materials with the internet writing consultants. This was, of course, a biased operation, because they were already somewhat in the know; even if the IWCs were learning a new technique or technology, the investment was already there. Although the IWCs were an already converted group, our authentic users—the students who came to the Writing Center for a session with an IWC—were often apathetic and frustrated. Most of the IWCs already believed that research and publishing on the web was an appropriate new focus in most classes and in the Writing Center. Students, however, would often come in with an assignment that required web publishing and their only interest was to "get it over with." The IWCs often resisted the directive teaching and tutoring approaches that the less-than-enthused students sometimes demanded, and the handouts often pointed to in their often linear, step-by-step instructions.

Regardless of the bias of this approach, we found that testing our methods and our handouts with the IWCs provided important direction. All of the IWCs were undergraduate students themselves, and thus wrote on the margins between tutor and student. They had been through many of the same courses as the undergraduates who frequented the Writing Center and, even if they had not taken the same courses, they had confronted the same situations. Often, IWCs would make comments such as "this isn't going to make sense to a first-year student taking an IAH (integrated arts and humanities) course" or "I think we need to break down these steps more. We're expecting too much jumping from point A to point Z here."

At the regular IWC meetings, we would meet as a group and, between eating pizza and sharing success and failure stories, would walk through the steps outlined in the handouts created by Writing Center staff and other IWCs. This approach was clearly threefold: First, IWCs were able to test the documents and better ready them for use with actual Writing Center clients. Second, IWCs were able to further their own understanding of the steps required to do one thing or another, or to think about a web writing or researching technique in another way. Finally, the IWCs were allowed to speculate about reactions students might have to certain assignments and approaches, and to develop consulting methods to negotiate those reactions.

Once we realized how successful this approach was to creating and revising documents, we decided to test the handouts with Writing Center clients themselves. IWCs would often note to clients that a handout or approach was new and still under development, and solicit feedback from the client. Feedback was already a built-in component of our consulting sessions (we asked all clients to complete a session evaluation form, which solicited primarily narrative comments, as shown in the list that follows this paragraph), so returning clients and IWCs were fairly comfortable giving and receiving direct feedback. We decided to have traditional writing clients and internet writing clients complete the same form, because we felt the questions fit both consulting groups. The demographic questions on the form included class level and ethnic/racial group questions that students did not have to answer, but the university required we ask so that both we and the university had a better idea of the student population we served. Additional questions we asked so that we had a better idea of our clientele included college (e.g., business, engineering, veterinary medicine), whether English was their first language, and whether this was their first visit to the Center. Narrative questions we asked students to respond to after a session was completed included the following:

- What did you bring to work on?
- What did you do during your meeting with the writing consultant?
- What did you find most useful in this conference?
- What did you learn about your writing that will be useful in future papers that you write?
- What did you learn or discover about your topic that you didn't know before?
- Will you return to the Center for help in the future? Why or why not?

One of the difficulties in requesting the feedback of clients of internet writing sessions was (and still may be) the difficulty in voicing one's critiques with such new processes. If a student has never authored a web page before and comes in to do so, it may be difficult to provide an immediate and critical reflection on the steps one follows and the support one receives in order to publish a web page. However, this difficulty did not make the feedback we received any less valuable. The broader the bandwidth of feedback, the more users represented (e.g., novice to advanced), the better it enabled us to refine our approaches and the questions we asked to solicit feedback from a group of students with widely varying interests and needs.

A larger-scale testing approach was undertaken when we offered to do web research and/or web publishing workshops for entire classes. Interested faculty volunteered their classes for such sessions and, afterward, distributed evaluation forms to students and completed an evaluation form themselves. This allowed us a larger group from which to solicit feedback, and a larger group often allowed for a more representative sample of the student body. These numbers better enabled us to refine our handouts and approaches. We worked closely with teachers of IAH courses (comparable to first-year composition). Thus, we worked with a group of students with whom the IWCs were already comfortable, and we were able to try our approaches in group situations before offering our services to the entire university community. We looked forward to taking that step, but weren't quite ready at this point. (Based on the climate at the university after the president's technology guarantee, we were pretty sure that the demand for our workshops would have been overwhelming.)

As we tested the handouts, we found ourselves concurrently reshaping our consulting approaches. For example, at our Writing Center, sessions lasted for 50 minutes. All sessions began at one of the tables in the Center, regardless of the focus of the session. The IWCs developed this approach because they found in test sessions that the machine would often interfere with the session's focus, which is the work the student and the IWC do collaboratively. We had learned that immediately sitting a student down in front of a computer and then attempting to talk about the focus of the session was disruptive and privileged the technology over the conversation that is such a key part of writing center work. This approach also allowed IWCs and students to create maps of the focus of the session before turning to the computer. Often, IWCs could be seen sitting with students and talking as the student drew circles and bubbles and squares on pieces of paper, accented by words and scribbles.

At the same time we were creating and testing our handouts and approaches, we discussed the developing Internet Writing Consultancy at the weekly graduate student meetings with the Writing Center directors. Here we mapped probable new approaches, discussing the fiscal, physical, and virtual realities of the ideas generated in the Center that week. At the Michigan State University Writing Center, graduate students were assigned projects. Sometimes the projects would overlap, but often these weekly meetings allowed us a space to share ideas regarding our projects with each other and to discuss the feasibility of certain approaches. Although our projects differed, we read and discussed common texts, sometimes focused on technology, such as Peter Lyman's (1995) "What Is Computer Literacy and What Is Its Place in Liberal Education" and Stephen Bernhardt's (1993) "The Shape of Text to Come: The Texture of Print on Screens."

Our questions included the following: Is it realistic for a graduate student to coordinate a team of Internet Writing Consultants? Could we reasonably expand our list of presentations (in high demand and scheduled throughout the semester) to include new internet-based presentations with different space, time, and room demands? How much time would be dedicated to internet writing consulting, so that consultants would still have enough time to work on traditional consulting and other projects?

These discussions often lent a practical angle to the processes developed and tested in the IWC meetings. The thought patterns and consulting practices of the IWCs were often both theoretically and practically rich. Brad, one of the IWCs, developed a variety of innovative approaches to internet writing consulting, including comparing learning HTML (hypertext markup language, the language used to create web pages) to learning a second language, arguing that HTML has its own grammar and structures that must be learned before a user/speaker can continue on to more advanced tasks.

Another component of our research practices included a formal survey, distributed to the IWCs. The survey consisted of two sections: one on traditional writing consulting, the other on internet writing consulting and solicited narrative responses. Another graduate student with strong ties to the Writing Center and I brainstormed possible questions and came up with a set that we felt fit our questions about hypertext in general and internet writing consulting specifically. We distributed the survey at one of the regular IWC meetings. The survey prompted a variety of interesting points regarding issues related to hypertext reading and writing; the discussion prompted by the survey continued on the IWC's electronic discussion list. Included below are responses to the question "What do you see as the goals of Internet Consulting? How do these goals (or do they) fit into the overarching goals of the Writing Center?"

Jenna: I really can't get into computer technology in general even when I see its exceptional uses and applications to things like writing. But as a consultant, I set that aside, and get involved in the creative process of creating a web page because I see that people really enjoy the creative involvement of putting some parts of their life together on the screen.

Troy: Fitting in with my goals of producing better writers, we must encourage and support the larger community of literacy—reading and writing. This is where Internet Consulting comes in; rather than expression only on paper, I as a consultant have to help people interpret the new literacy and discourse of computers…. Our role (and goal) then is to encourage and support this new discourse.

Responding to the question "What are your goals for a consulting session, and what techniques do you use in your consulting that you feel are helpful in achieving those goals?" IWCs noted:

Brad: To help my clients reach the next level of understanding about com- puters and writing. For now, that means skills, hopefully understanding "Internet aesthetics." For the future, understanding and explaining the po- tential of hypertext and Internet research.

Aimee: Concerning the technicalities of Internet Consulting, my goal is to not offer the plug and chug, step-by-step answers, but rather [to] lead clients to resources to offer lots of explanation so clients can apply technical Internet information to lots of different situations.

Jenna: I let them do all the work on the computer and explain to them ev- erything I can about how and why things work the way they do. I don't simply give directions, but I contextualize them so the client understands why they're doing things.

Strands we observed in the survey responses and the discussions that followed included the resistance of some IWCs. One noted that she did not really "get into" computers. Another noted that internet consulting sessions were often somewhat superficial, that a skills-based approach was often necessary. The surveys and follow-up discussions produced a reflective edge necessary to the circular approach our research methods took, involving constant questioning, constant evaluating, and constant revising of our handouts, our approaches, and ourselves as IWCs. If an IWC wasn't comfortable with a process, we certainly couldn't expect that person to adopt it. Instead, then, we rethought and revised, often as a group. We tried to get at the roots of our resistances, to break through some of our print-based biases. Sometimes, however, we had to abandon an approach because it just didn't "feel" right. This is a common experience for explorers in a new territory, but I would argue that even with new technologies, when something fits too well and feels too right, often we need to return to that technology with a more critical eye; chances are that some crucial aspect is being overlooked.

REFLECTIONS ON OUR RESEARCH PRACTICES

Looking back on our research process, I am able to draw several conclusions about our approaches. For one, although the intermingled and concurrent methods we chose seemed at the time to be random and sometimes messy, it's obvious that we followed three primary paths: when we tested our approaches and handouts with IWCs and Writing Center clients, we were engaging in usability testing (quite common in industry, especially the software industry, and useful in other domains). Usability testing involves engaging some sort of targeted, representative user group in trials of a document or procedure, then revising the document or procedure according the results of the trials. When the graduate students and staff met for our weekly meetings and discussed possibilities and practicalities, we were engaging in what I would call insider focus groups. Focus groups are usually facilitated but not overtly directed discussions that can include both insiders (as did ours) and/or outsiders. In our case, the acting directors of our Center facilitated our discussions. Finally, when we queried the IWCs regarding their thoughts on hypertext and how it did (or didn't) change reading and writing processes, we were engaging in surveying. Surveying involves a variety of techniques, from Likert-scale questions (e.g., ranking answers from "very important" to "not important") to narrative-response questions. Surveys are carefully prepared with some sort of test group already in mind.

Certainly, there are limitations to realizing your research process after the fact. However, in some regards our research practices matched the realm in which we were working. Writing centers are constantly evolving, dynamic places, and the internet is certainly an evolving, dynamic space. Without a research agenda defined before we engaged in our research, it was easier for us to engage in situated action (Suchman, 1987)—to shape our approaches to the moment-by-moment, day-to-day questions and concerns we faced. For some writing centers, the approach we took will not fit their administrative, financial, or pedagogical goals. Many centers will choose to take a different approach, whereby they adopt more formal research methods prior to engaging in the research that will eventually shape their practice. Other writing centers, however, may do quite well with an evolving research path much like ours. Crucial factors in what research path a writing center takes are the constraints and the freedoms that the writing center faces in its everyday practice. For example, a center with a small staff, two computers, limited software, and restricted access will probably choose to—in fact, have to—adopt a different approach to researching and testing possible practices. My advice is probably the same advice we very often offer our students: Know your possibilities. Explore what others before you have done. You may often feel isolated, but you're not alone. Engage in discussions on electronic discussion lists and at conferences. Question others about their practices (and limitations, and successes, and failures, etc.). Rigorous and well-defined research paths aren't always those that come from studying formal qualitative or quantitative methodologies, but instead are those that come from everyday practice.

A second conclusion is that there is no mistaking that we were in a privileged position. Although the university president had implemented the technology guarantee, and each unit and department was either directly or indirectly expected to play its part in fulfilling the guarantee, we had a good deal of autonomy in directing our computer-related efforts. Sadly, some of this autonomy stemmed from stereotypical assumptions about the writing center: that writing centers don't "do" technology, or, more broadly, that English Studies doesn't "do" technology. Regardless of the roots of the stereotypes, however, we were afforded a somewhat more leisurely path to technology. We weren't chased there; we twisted our own arms, pushed ourselves toward technology, and thus were able to choose our own path to develop our own local and critical practices with foresight rather than hindsight.

Third, as the Internet Writing Consultancy developed, the technologies involved often were submerged, underneath the discussions, the excitement, and the connections being made. This is not to say that we didn't have our share of terrifying technical moments—the day when a presentation had to be done by drawing HTML tags on the chalkboard because our laptop and data projector fizzled out; or the day a student fled the Writing Center frustrated and grumbling, leaving behind an IWC befuddled because the Computer Center changed a permissions setting for student web pages without widely announcing the change. In the eyes of the student, the IWC was inept and unable to help her with her web page. The IWC, unfortunately, had no way of knowing that a quick command that worked yesterday no longer functioned. However, quite often the technology was not the focus of our discussions. This realization alone is rather stunning in a society in which technologies are regularly assumed to be at the forefront of or the catalyst of change. Here, we found that the technologies themselves weren't as important as the context in which they were used. Cynthia Selfe might call this a "small potent gesture," a tiny but viable space we created for ourselves where we could see out from and beyond the technologies that were so enmeshed in our daily lives.

Finally, the initially opaque but later identifiable approaches described earlier provide an interesting vantage point from which to survey a historical moment in writing center work. Models for integrating technology into the writing center didn't yet exist (or weren't easily accessible), and rigorous research methods were harder to come by. Our development of the Internet Writing Consultancy occurred at a time when many writing centers were catapulted into—or catapulted themselves into—computer technology. Writing center-related MOOs and web sites began to spring up in earnest around the time we constructed our Internet Writing Consultancy, and e-mail tutoring was being adopted in many writing centers. Many of us weren't afforded a position from which we could develop, reflect on, and refine a research methodology. The changing structure of higher education (e.g., nontraditional students, distance learning) pushed many writing centers into technology before those writing centers were practically and theoretically ready to enter that territory.

Sometimes jumping in headfirst is a realistic way to negotiate new technologies and to provide a writing center with innovative new approaches. Without critical reflection—before, during, and after the course of the research—of our practices, however, it is difficult to fully understand those practices, to share our processes, and to preserve historical moments.

EXPANDING THE ROLES OF THE WRITING CENTER

As noted earlier, the writing center is an ideal place to address the literacy demands and practices of new technologies. We must encourage and practice an appropriate and critical theory of technology and writing, an approach that supports writing (and other literacy practices) "in a way that [does] not disrupt our practices, that [is] congruent with our particular theoretical and pedagogical stances" (Thomas, DeVoss, & Hara, 1998, 76). Computer technologies should not reshape the writing center or its goals but should instead create a different ecology in which the multiple and complex literacies students bring and are required to have may develop.

Notions of writing, of text, and of literacy took on richer, more complex meanings for us, meanings that intersect with notions of other literacies (e.g., computer literacies). These more sophisticated and complex meanings have changed and will continue to change notions of literacy and notions of the roles of writing centers. New goals of the writing center related to computer technologies and, specifically, to the web, but obviously not limited to, include the following:

1. *Supporting students as discussions extend beyond the walls of the classroom.* At Michigan State University, most first-year courses require the use of e-mail and also require students to post reading or discussion notes online via listservs or electronic discussion groups. Acclimating to a new discussion space, one that requires both basic typing and computer skills and the ability to negotiate multiple conversation demands and new interfaces, can be a daunting task for some students. We found ourselves working with students on reading and writing skills related to electronic discussion lists—often confusing spaces where a variety of people are posing questions and adding to a discussion not always threaded in a logical way. An excellent way for other writing centers to tackle this task might be to create an electronic discussion list for students interested in learning how to negotiate electronic discussion lists. Both students and writing center coaches could subscribe to the list and work out questions and challenges on the list itself.

2. *Enabling students to do effective and appropriate research.* For some classes, students were required to include both library and internet sources in their research papers. Most students were trained to negotiate the complex library system, but relatively few were comfortable searching and evaluating the web. Although most libraries now offer some training in web research and evaluation, writing centers can also provide such support, and help students at the crucial space where they must incorporate web resources into their written work.

Access to information and the ways of both print and hypertext often aren't made visible to students and, thus, the students don't realize the extensive review, publication, and cataloging processes of the texts that fill libraries. The role of the writing center here is to make such processes overt and address the new variables at play in electronic publishing. Legitimacy and value are to be found on the web, but different steps must be taken to find appropriate sources. And, certainly, this is not an isolated process; the skills students develop in researching at the library transfer to searching on the web, and vice versa.

3. *Helping students with new possibilities for publication.* With the web a focus of many courses and with many instructors requiring the authoring of hypertext documents, students have new rhetorical possibilities, intermixed with new questions regarding voice, authorship, design, and so on. Instructors often don't have the means or the time to address such key writing-related issues. A good way to approach such a task is to poll instructors to see which of them intends to require web publishing in their courses, and then offer workshops to the students in those classes.

This is a productive approach for several reasons, one of which is that often instructors are pressured within their departments to include web authoring in their courses, when they are unprepared to design and/or assess such assignments. Writing center involvement can occur at a variety of levels and aid both students and instructors. Also, writing centers save time and energy in several ways with this approach. First, coaches have an opportunity to meet with an entire group of students instead of one student at a time; thus, the writing center won't have to sacrifice too much of their traditional writing consulting time. Second, the coach or coaches leading the workshop can identify students at different levels of expertise in web publishing, students who can then work together during and after the workshop to support each other.

WHY THE WRITING CENTER?

Admittedly, most writing centers are strapped for resources and often for personnel. Writing centers are also often already overburdened places, bearing the responsibility of supporting student writing throughout departments, across majors, and within entire institutions. The writing center is, however, the ideal place to meet these new goals for a variety of reasons. We justified our move toward the Internet Writing Consultancy because of our model of peer interaction, whereby (ideally) authority and hierarchy are downplayed. Students are speaking, interacting, and working with someone they can identify as a peer—certainly a peer with some special knowledge, but a peer nonetheless. Peer–peer dynamics are currently difficult to find where computer technologies are concerned. When students at Michigan State University visit the Computer Center's help desk and speak with a consultant, often they find themselves submerged in technological jargon and an attitude of dismissal. They are almost always already required and expected to have a level of knowledge directly related to technology; the consultants in computing centers aren't often equipped to recognize and draw upon students' other literacies to make connections.

Writing center consultants know how to talk to people about writing. That is clearly the focus of a writing center. As we developed our internet writing approach, we were reminded of—and reminded ourselves of—our primary goal: That is, writing and writers are our focus. Not computers. Not new electronic media. Not the glitz and seduction of a new electronic tool. Writing and writers. The ability not only to address technological needs related to computer use, but also to address rhetorical and literacy needs related to writing makes writing center consultants well equipped to take on internet-related consulting.

The writing center is often a hub of institutional interactions. Few other offices or departments on a campus foster and facilitate the connections that writing centers do. Writing centers often have access to students from every discipline in an institution. The internet, likewise, spans disciplines and is not constrained by disciplinary territories or markers.

Traditional writing consulting and internet writing consulting sessions share many similar characteristics. Students often come to the writing center resistant toward writing. They have had bad experiences with writing, have had a lack of support, and/or haven't had access to the tools that would make writing more enjoyable or understandable. Likewise, many of them come to the writing center with a resistance toward computer technologies. Again, they have had bad experiences with computers, have had a lack of support, and/or haven't had access to the tools that would make computer-related writing and other related work more enjoyable or understandable.

Clearly, however, there are differences between traditional writing consulting and internet writing consulting. Traditional writing center theory privileges a hands-off approach, whereby the consultant or coach is not to write on the student's paper, is not to be directive, and is there primarily to provide support and give tips rather than to tell a student exactly how to do something. With internet writing consulting, sometimes it is necessary for a consultant to be directive. A student must click here or there, or must include this code for some element of the writing. However, as much as writing center theory privileges a nondirective approach, directiveness is *always* a part of internet writing consulting. As Mark, one of the IWCs, noted:

> When in regular consulting, it's realistic to take the approach that "I'm not an expert on writing, you also know a lot about writing, let's do the collaboration thing." However, with HTML/web stuff, let's be blunt: we have knowledge that our clients need, that they will not figure out on their own (at least initially). This I think lends itself to a more traditional transmission approach to consulting, more of a tutor approach. Is there a way to be effective and be a consultant? … I still remain a source of very definite information, such as tags. Do I tell them where to go to find it on their own? Yup.

Nichole, another IWC, continued by noting:

> My goals for Internet consulting are the same as writing consulting: let's do what the client wants.… It doesn't do me any good to say, "Click here; move this, type this and click again." My job is to guide and empower the client so that he/she learns something yet doesn't feel as though he/she has been lectured.

Because of the reasons mentioned earlier and others, writing centers must be prepared for change and to adapt approaches when integrating an internet writing consultancy.

Admittedly, sometimes there is less space for dialogue and responding in an internet consulting session. However, good consultants recognize this problem, negotiate these spaces, and make the dialogic and response-based spaces all the more fruitful. The mission statements and goals, the practice and the theory of writing centers need not be sacrificed to new technologies. Instead, a productive blend of critical approaches, appropriate theoretical stances, clear pedagogical goals, and measured thoughtfulness (Carino, 1998) is required to make for exciting and appropriate mergers of writing centers and computing technologies.

A SUCCESS STORY

One of the most memorable early sessions for one of the Internet Writing Consultants occurred when an international student came in. She was relatively unfamiliar with computing technology but was *expected* to know it. This is one of the most monumental pressures students faced: the expectation that they "knew" technology and thus the failure to see the need for support and instruction.

This student was required to create a web site for a course she was taking, and she was distraught. She did not know where to begin. She and her IWC, Mark, sat down at a table and after several minutes of discussion (which included Mark's addressing the fact that the technology should never get in the way of her excitement and creativity), she had drawn out several elaborate pages on paper. One had a background of the flag of her native country and had the names of the national newspapers of that country written across it. Another had a background of stars and moons and had squares with stick figures in them, representing the pictures of her family that she wanted to publish as part of her project.

Eventually, the two moved to a machine and began working there. They wove their way through the web, finding pictures that she felt best represented her sketches. She wrote some code and watched her sketches unfold in full color on the screen. By the time the session ended, two of the pages she sketched were created and published and much of her anxiety about the technology was resolved.

This story makes the new genre of consulting seem very easy to enact; success, however, did not come easily. The success the IWC experienced here in this session makes invisible the layers of complexity we faced—the failures, the tiny victories, the research, the work, the institutional barricades, the floundering, the important relationships we formed, and so on—in developing the Internet Writing Consultancy to the point where success stories like this became realities.

QUESTIONS FOR FUTURE RESEARCH

Certainly, our research questions transformed as our research practices and our internet consulting approaches evolved. Questions we still ponder and that other writing centers might consider in adapting their practices to new media and new online spaces include the following:

- What are the strengths of organic, unfolding research agendas? What are the weaknesses of the sorts of research approaches described here?

- Is a writing center doing too much by attempting to address issues related to internet research and web page publication? Is it a writing center's responsibility to teach the computer skills often required before rhetorical writing-related issues can be addressed?

- What practices are we reproducing in internet writing consulting? Are we sculpting individuals to better perform within a system that should instead be changed?

- What sorts of literacies are we supporting in developing and maintaining an Internet writing consultancy: functional literacy (a "real-world" oriented, more vocational than critical literacy) or expressive literacy (a student-autonomy supporting practice; see Grimm, 1996)?
- How can we shape our internet writing consultancies to address multiple literacies rather than privileging a dominant one?
- How can a writing center find and/or train consultants for an internet writing consultancy? This chapter outlines one approach, but it is certainly not transferrable to all writing centers.
- Who should coordinate an internet writing consultancy? Graduate students are clearly sources of innovative and interesting work, but the turnover for graduate students, especially students working toward their master's degrees, is very high. Writing center staff, on the other hand, are already overwhelmed by administrative and teaching tasks.
- How can writing centers better support faculty to include internet-based discussions and assignments in their classrooms?
- What future research can we do in writing centers to better understand how students read and write hypertexts? How they negotiate online discussion forums?
- In what ways does internet writing consulting change the traditional practices of writing centers and of writing consulting?
- How can internet writing consultancies be better assessed? Postsession student comments enabled us to see immediate responses, but how can longitudinal observation and dialogue be conducted to assess long-term results and impact on student writing both hypertextual and traditional?

CONCLUSION

Writing centers are often dynamic realms, realms in which students, faculty, and staff transform themselves, their writing, and their other literate practices. Jane Nelson and Cynthia Wambeam (1995) warn writing center directors and staff, arguing that when writing centers fail to "actively participate in development and use of computers for writing, they risk not only marginalization and limitations on resources, they allow people who are not experts in writing to make important decisions about writing technologies" (online).

We must address Carino's (1998) challenge. It is crucial for the writing center to develop pedagogy to respond to the changes that technology generates. However, we must not stand idly by while computing technologies emerge and take stronger and stronger roles in shaping our institutions. Instead, as writing center directors and staff, we must engage these technologies to emerge with a better understanding of their benefits and problems. We must also engage in dialogue with other sites within institutions that take a crucial role in shaping and using technologies. Another key area of such better, more critical technological development is interaction with the companies that produce the software and hardware used in educational institutions today. As Nelson and Wambeam (1995) argue, "writing centers should become campus leaders in development and use of computers for writing" (online). With a focus on expanding literacy skills and an eye toward the critical yet innovative use of computing technologies, writing centers can situate themselves as core institutions for the better use of technologies and the development of the literacy skills of our clients.

REFERENCES

Bernhardt, S. A. (1993). The shape of texts to come: The texture of print on screens. *College Composition and Communication, 44*(2), 151–175.

Blythe, S. (1998). Toward Usable OWLs: Incorporating Usability Methods into Writing Center Research. In E. H. Hobson (Ed.), *Wiring the writing center* (pp. 103–118). Logan: Utah State University Press.

Bolter, J. D. (1991). *Writing space: The computer, hypertext, and the history of writing*. Hillsdale, NJ: Lawrence Erlbaum Associates.

Carino, P. (1998). Computers in the writing center: A cautionary history. In E. H. Hobson (Ed.), *Wiring the writing center* (171–193). Logan: Utah State University Press.

Grimm, N. M. (1996). Rearticulating the work of the writing center. *College Composition and Communication, 47*(4), 523–548.

Joyce, M. (1995). *Of two minds: Hypertext pedagogy and poetics*. Ann Arbor: University of Michigan Press.

Landow, G. P. (Ed.). (1994). *Hyper/text/theory*. Baltimore: Johns Hopkins University Press.

Lanham, R. A. (1993). *The electronic word: Democracy, technology, and the arts*. Chicago: University of Chicago Press.

Lyman, P. (1995, Summer). What is computer literacy and what is its place in liberal education? *Liberal Education*, 5–15.

Nelson, J., & Wambeam, C. A. (1995). Moving computers into the writing center: The path to least resistance. *Computers and Composition 12*(2), 135–143.

Suchman, L. (1987). *Plans and situated actions: The problem of human/machine communication*. Cambridge, England: Cambridge University Press.

Thomas, S., DeVoss, D., & Hara, M. (1998). Toward a critical theory of technology and writing. *The Writing Center Journal, 19*(1), 73–86.

III

*Writing Centers as Sites
of Inquiry Into Practice*

Chapter 11

Seeing Practice Through Their Eyes: Reflection as Teacher

Kathleen Blake Yancey
Clemson University

Early in my doctoral program, I attended a lecture about teaching: Was good teaching mostly a gift, or was it acquired, the speaker asked. Anxiously, I awaited the answer, hoping that good teaching could be acquired, because "acquired" offers a kind of hope that "gift" does not. At the end of the lecture, I could breathe again: it's acquired. *<Sigh>*
   Which, of course, begs the real *question:* However is good teaching acquired or developed? Or for that matter, good tutoring? *I hadn't actually planned to take this question up when I recently taught our practicum in tutoring writing. Not that it isn't an interesting question; not that I don't think about it often. But I hadn't planned on acquiring the gift myself just now, and I certainly hadn't planned on acquiring it from the students I was supposed to be teaching.*

***

That fall I taught UNC Charlotte's Tutoring Practicum for 11 graduate students, 6 undergraduates, and 1 student who couldn't decide which she was. After about 6 weeks of "developmental" readings and activities, the students begin to tutor for 3 hours weekly in our Writing Resources Center (the WRC), which serves all our students, but whose major clients include a gracious plenty of ESL students and first-year writers.
   In many ways, our three-credit tutoring course was unremarkable: It looks like many others across the country. We used Muriel Harris' (1986)

189

Teaching One-to-One; we read Steve North's (1984) "The Idea of a Writing Center"; we did mock tutorials; we heard from our own guest lecturer—on different learning styles and ways to accommodate those. We talked in class about what was working and what wasn't. We read Kinkead and Harris' (1988) *Writing Centers in Context* to see how the UNC Charlotte model of Writing Center compared to others, and what the trade-offs were. We identified ways of assessing our own practice, and we talked about the big picture: how what we were seeing connected to curriculum and classrooms and writing and teaching and learning and back to tutoring.

But included in this course—everywhere, throughout, and in multiple forms—was reflection, which, borrowing from Donald Schon (1995), I had defined as

> Recording practice,
> Reviewing it,
> Understanding it, and
> Then learning from and applying it elsewhere.

Through reflective observation of and review of practice, Schon claims, we become the "causal inquirer." Causal inquiry, he says, is the systematic examination of practice and about the only kind possible given the nature of our work—given, that is, that it's work with human beings. Such work, according to Schon, prohibits the use of technical rigorous scientific methodology that is appropriate to things, not people. At the same time, in work with human beings, cause and effect do need to be established in order that this social work accomplish its (humane) aims. Given its nature, such work is complex and ongoing. Often the cause and effect are being hypothesized even as the work occurs. This inquirer, then:

> investigates puzzling phenomena in order to figure out what to do about them, and when she takes action in order to fix what a causal story says has gone wrong or capitalize on what it says has gone right, she subjects the story to a critically important test. In organizational practice, therefore, the very same actions tend to function at the same time as exploratory, intervention, and hypothesis-testing experiments. (87)

A tutor-as-causal-inquirer, in other words, intends to intervene helpfully with students. To do that, the tutor must ascertain in various ways what purposes might be served in that tutorial and in other possible tutorials—through interaction with the student both verbally and nonverbally, through review of various kinds of texts and sometimes responses to texts, through teacher referrals, and so on. Acting on his or her understanding of this situation, the tutor intervenes—by asking the student for context or guidance or goals, by suggesting strategies that tutor and student try out, or by reviewing subject-verb agreement. At the same time that he or she is hypothesizing what might work, the tutor is also implementing a plan based on that emerging hypothesis. This, then, is Schon's *reflection-in-action,* a reflection that aids the tutorial as it helps determine both the shape and substance of it.

There is also a second variety of reflection, what I've elsewhere called *constructive reflection* (Yancey, 1998) and what Schon calls *reflective transfer:* the process by which a single tutoring event and/or several tutoring events are reviewed and understood as a part of practice *theorized.* Causal inquiry, Schon says, typically centers on a particular situation in a single organization, and "when it is successful, it yields not covering laws but prototypical models of causal patterns that may guide inquiry in other … situations—prototypes that depend, for their validity, on modification and testing in "the next situation," "Reflective transfer" seems to me a good label for this kind of generalization" (97).

Given the concept of practice theorized, I also used *theory* and *practice* as another, complementary way to frame the intellectual work of the course: the theory of the Writing Center directors that we see in Harris (1986) and North (1984), the practice that students acquire; alternatively, the theory that suggests how writers learn, the tutoring practice that rewrites that theory. Three linked frames, then: reflection, practice, theory. And multiple occasions and genres in which to discourse upon any and all three of them:

- *Reflective letters* every other week, in which tutors comment on anything that seems germane to them (e.g., readings, tutorials, their own experience as writers); I write back a letter to the class
- *E-mails* (on a closed list server) every other week where we talk about ethics in writing center practice, about ways to assess our work, about WCENTER and what can be learned there
- *Logs* where students record what they have done in tutorials and comment on them in mode ranging from speculative to evaluative,
- *Finger exercises* in class, focused on progressive definitions of the word tutor, on ways tutoring dis/connects to teaching, and so on
- *Formal writing assignments* that build on the reflective activities (in particular, one that was a case study of a student)
- *Portfolios* that include a final, cumulative reflective text.

The structures of these places for reflection vary, as does the timing; seen collectively, these forms provide multiple contexts that themselves encourage insight, both individually and together. Said differently, they provide multiple frames through which to understand the same experience, and it is often, as Arthur Koestler (1975) reminds us, through the crossing of such frames that insight is generated. As important is the diversity of genre. The letters, for instance, are unstructured; they favor the writer who prefers the open page and a personal approach. Other textual places, like the log, are highly structured. The intent of the texts in the aggregate is to encourage both familiar and unfamiliar ways of seeing and to put those ways of seeing into dialogue with each other so as to produce insight—knowledge.

When I asked the tutors to keep their logs, I thought of them in rather obvious ways—as a place to keep track of what the tutors were doing and to interpret and/or to assess that practice. Simple enough. But looking back at this place for reflections—in this, *my reflective log-of-sorts*—I see it somewhat differently now. The log includes two components: first, a place where tutors record what had gone on—where they would get to *know their practice;* and second, a place where they *reflect on this practice, make sense of it.* In the reporting function, I think now, I created a place for tutor-as-agent; in the reflective function, a place for tutor-as-learner.

It's a twin identity, tutoring: helping others while learning oneself. Put another way, working through both these frames concurrently—reporting and reflecting—what did the tutors learn? To take their own sense of what a tutor is, to add that to what the theory of the course told them, and to combine those with their experience to create their own theorized practice. Try again: Speaking rhetorically, such writing, such reflection is an act of invention, or perhaps several acts: *inventing practice, in the course of which the tutors* invent themselves.

***

Sometimes, especially at the beginning of the term, the logs didn't look, nor did they sound, like reflective practice. They didn't sound like tutoring; even when they linked theory to practice, it wasn't in a way we'd characterize as insightful. But they provided a starting place, and they gave us all an opportunity to read practice.

> *Yuen Fun Tang—She is an L2 student and a Finance major. She brought in a paper on the company Best Buy. She wanted to work on grammar. Her paper was organized into a set form. So we worked on LOCs [Lower Order Concerns]. She had a problem with subject-verb agreement. She also had no idea how to even start a Work Cited page. We worked on both of these.*
>
> *Natsuko Nagaoka—She is my referral student [i.e., required by the instructor to meet with the tutor for four sessions]. She brought in a paper from her Film Criticism class. It was a paper on film noir and how it shows up in Casablanca. She brought in a half of a page on what film noir was. I had her to list some examples from the movie that fit the film noir definition. Then we tried to incorporate them into her paper.*
>
> *Christine Evans—She is an Engineering major. Here again, I was asked just to check grammar. This was her second time to the WRC. A tutor checked the first half of her paper for grammar errors. She told me her paper was due in an hour and a half, so*

we only had time to look at LOCS. Her paper was horrible. It was full of sub-ject-verb-agreement errors and verb tense errors.

    What I Learned—Now I see what North was talking about in his article. Everyone seems to think the WRC is a fix-it center. They think they can just bring their papers in and we will correct their grammar errors for them. I have not had a student yet, who came on his or her own, and who wanted to talk about anything else besides grammar. What annoys me is that most of these students believe if they turn in an error-free paper, they will make an "A." That's not the way it usually happens.

The tutor here seems increasingly frustrated: She wants to work on writing; she's being asked to work on editing; and she responds as negatively to what she perceives as the students' attitudes as to what it is that is asked of her: *Everyone seems to think the WRC is a fix-it center.* At the same time, however, the tutor has accomplished a good beginning. She clearly sees each student as an individual: That counts. She also reads the students *as a set* and links that set to what she has read in North's piece, so she is making the kinds (if not the specific) connections that go into good practice: That counts. Not least, she brings her own understanding of how writing works in college into her interpretation: Error-free papers, she says, are not necessarily A papers, since *That is not the way it usually happens.* There is a lot here to respond to favorably, and I do, marking in yellow highlighter observations that I think the tutor might pursue. I don't do more than this; I don't want to script the tutor more than I already will, given that I'm the teacher of the practicum (and they aren't). At the same time, I want to give some response, to identify what I think works—suggestively—so that the tutor may make use of it, or not.

    As the term progresses, many of the tutors write longer records, interpret more fully, begin to design the "writing-centered" curriculum that North calls for.

    Shani is one of my referrals [i.e., assigned to the WRC by the classroom instructor]. To-day, she and I threw around some ideas for her policy paper. She has chosen television censorship as her topic, and I tried to get her to narrow the spectrum just a little (cable, regular network, daytime, nighttime, etc.). Her claim is that television censorship should be more lenient. I played devil's advocate, forcing her to anticipate some of the ar-guments against her. She really understood just how broad the topic could be, once I gave her some opposing viewpoints. We clustered a bit, and she developed a focus and some good starting points. She will be back next Wednesday, the 30th, to read her first draft with me prior to turning it into Professor XXXX.

In this record, we see the process represented as well as the problems addressed. We see a use of language that characterizes good practice: The tutor and student *clustered, developed a focus*, and will produce *a first draft*. Even the idea of first draft suggests that others will follow.

    The record is then followed by the reflection:

Shani is very soft-spoken, but she's very bright. Our goal for the semester is developing her organizational skills. She tends to go all over the place in her papers. She's getting really good at clustering, though, so I'm really proud of her. Her hard work is beginning to show in her writing. If I had to do anything differently, I think that I would have asked her to brainstorm on her own for about ten minutes before we jumped into clustering together. It's not that I feel that I led her along; I just think that she may have benefited from a critique of her initial written conception of her argument. I suppose that the outcome was the same, but although she had control of clustering (they were her ideas), I think that she may have felt as if she had a bit more control if she had developed a supposed starting point by herself.

Here, in the reflection, we see the tutor framing the tutorial in larger, multiple ways. She sees the single episode as part of something continuing, so that this session makes sense to the extent that it fulfills the larger goal. Or should I say goals? One is textual and strategic: developing *her organizational skills.* But another is linked to the writer's sense of confidence: *I just think that she may have benefited from a critique of her initial written conception of her argument.* In other words, here the tutor is analyzing and assessing her own tutorial, and beginning to think that using the same method—allowing the student *control* and then inviting analysis and assessment and critique—might help the student in the same way that it is helping her. This log, of course, embodies what I want to see: a particular student engaged in useful work with a knowledgeable and appreciative tutor.

Earlier, I mentioned the word *recursive,* a word that is commonplace in the literature on composing processes, one that also connects to reflection. As the structure of the log suggests, reflection is often recursive; in reflection, we revisit practice, reinterpret, make new sense of. But the tutors completed the log, typically, in a single setting, so most of the tutors reflected immediately, which seems almost a contradiction in terms. Reflection seems to entail the notion of time, time afterward, time recursive.

That's what the reflective letters seemed to provide, in addition to the open textual space. Often tutors would return to a session or set of sessions and make new sense of them—later. Remember Natsuko Nagaoka? She's the ESL student who had the assignment on *Casablanca* as an instance of film noir. All we really learned in the log was that the tutor tried to help with Natsuko's invention problem. A month later, Alisha chose to revisit this session in a reflective letter, and the story she tells is more detailed, more complex, more theoretical—made possible, by the form of the letter, the incremental experience, and the time intervening.

"It is almost over; I have one more student to see before I end my first day of tutoring." This is exactly what I was saying to myself on my first day of tutoring. I had finished two tutoring sessions that day, and I was waiting for my last one, Natsuko Nagaoka. The name alone was enough to send me into shock. I was told that she was a Fluency First student [an ESL student in a class for those with limited English proficiency], and that was all I knew about her. When I finally met her, I thought she seemed harmless enough. She did not look like the type that would laugh at everything I suggested. I tried the "get

to know you" thing at the beginning of the session, but she was not interested. I asked her how she was doing; she said fine and handed me her paper. She wanted to get straight to work. After all, wasn't that why she was there? She pulled out a paper with a half a page of writing on it. Her assignment was to compare and contrast two movies she had seen in her Film Criticism class. Fighting off the urge to cry, I continued reading her paper. I could find nothing in the paper about the two movies. I suggested she make a list of similarities and differences in the two movies. I spent the entire fifty minutes trying to understand what the two movies were about and how they were similar. She was very vague and did not remember much about the movies; if she did remember she was not willing to describe them to me. We went through the paper, and I made suggestions on using more detail and examples. After the session ended, I wanted to scream. I felt so confident after the first two sessions, and then my head was pounding after Natsuko left.

Ah, so that's what happened that first day.

In this letter, Alisha's longest, she describes what she has learned in the four sessions since then: about Natsuko as a person; about Japanese education (e.g., *In Japan the teacher does* all the talking in the classroom, and the students only listen. I asked her which method she *preferred, and she answered, "Japan");* about how Natsuko's personality connects to her writing and writing difficulties; and about how this makes a certain kind of sense, given Natsuko's background and experience:

> *She does not have much to say; therefore, she does not have much to write. She makes her papers very short and very simple. She leaves out important details. For example, she wrote a paper on comparing two movies, and she did not include the names of the two movies. When I asked her about them, she said her professor knows which two she is talking about. I explained to her that he teaches other classes whose students may have to write a paper on two other movies. The names of the two movies are an important detail that should not be left out of her paper. Now I have a better understanding of why she leaves out these important details. She feels like she is stating the obvious lots of times, because it is obvious to her. However, most of the time it is obvious only to her.*

Given enough time, both the student and the tutor look very different indeed.

✳✳✳

I've subtitled this chapter "Reflection as Teacher," which to me means doubly. As is no doubt self-evident, I expected that tutors, through reflection, would learn more about their practice, would learn to theorize it, would begin developing a tutoring identity. Surprisingly (or not?), *by using the same processes, I am finding myself learning about how tutors learn to tutor.*

In some ways, this reflective learning process is captured in the phrase "read the data," the data being what we are experiencing and all the representations we have of that. The tutors have many experiences and representations:

The actual session.
Their interactions with the students.
Multiple and developing texts.
Discussions with peers (in class, online, and in the WRC).
(Sometimes) feedback from the instructor.

I have my observations and my interactions, too, but in some ways most important, I have *multiple documents that collectively teach me —in their own words—how tutors learn to become tutors.*

I read the materials of one tutor, then of another. Soon I am learning about all of them—from their letters, their e-mails, their logs, their classroom discourse, and their inventions. Then I need to do what I've asked the tutors to do: *Read the data. I* need to see them as individuals, yes, but also as a class (how does this group of tutors learn), and as possible representatives of something larger, of a process (or processes) by which students become tutors. From the data, I look for particularities, for difference, for patterns: I theorize.

Such theorizing isn't at odds with practice; it's complementary to it—through it practice is enhanced, and from that enhanced practice we theorize anew. As Bobbie Silk explains,

> *Theory is simply the interpretation of experience for the purpose of better understanding and more effective interaction with the world. When theory doesn't improve practice, we modify or discard it, or we limit the application of the theory to those situations where it does work. Theory is a way to re-see a situation in order to give us inspiration to find other ways to deal with it. Copernicus' theory that the earth revolved around the sun (rather than vice versa) was the re-seeing of the earth and the heavens. Einstein's theory of relativity permitted scientists to predict and plan for the exigencies of space travel. In a situation closer to our own interests, the problem-solving theories of Gestalt psychology permitted the development of process theory in writing instruction. Good theory is practical.*

What, then, do I see when I read the tutors' data? And what theory do I construct to make sense of it? I see that:

- *Sometimes new tutors arrive in a writing center with no sense of what a tutor is, but that just as often they have a rather minimal behavioral definition that itself may bear scant resemblance to accepted practice.* Evoking whatever tacit understanding exists provides perhaps the first starting place for developing the identity of a tutor: you can't really get there, except from here.

  At the beginning of the semester, when I first started my journey as a tutor, I thought of myself as just that, a "tutor." To me, the word tutor *was just a generic word that encompassed all people who worked with others. I saw nothing special about being a tutor, because I saw tutors as being robots. They would come off a factory line looking the same, acting the same, and approaching student problems in the same way. I assumed that there would be some kind of tutor's manual that would tell me what I was supposed to do in each and every situation. I thought that a tutor must have all the answers to every question that could be asked in a session, and since I knew I had hardly any of the answers, I felt inadequate and scared at the prospect of becoming a "tutor." I was bogged down by all the information that was being thrown at me in such a short amount of time. Harris and North intimidated me. There was so much to be done in a fifty-minute period that I felt there was no way I could accomplish all of these tasks and work with a student at the same time.*

Asking tutors to revisit their notion of tutor provides a means for understanding their own growth.

- *Consistently keeping a log of recording and reflecting fosters tutorial agency and learning.* Recording helps tutors remember what they did, makes it real, and gives them a representation of what happened that is subject to interpretation and evaluation. It also encourages a habit of mind: of monitoring one's own practice, of believing that the tutor can assess practice and enhance it, and can theorize.

- *Focusing in a sustained way on a single student, which is what the first formal writing assignment called for, asks for a different, more comprehensive, yet complementary kind of analysis and understanding and theorizing.* This assignment pulls from the logs, and often from the letters, so we see in the formal paper an increased complexity and coherence. In the paper, the tutor is to represent the student in multiple contexts—personal, institutional, cultural, classroom, tutorial—in much the same way that the tutor represents his or her own practice. The assignment itself is authentic in that it calls for real learning, about which the tutor—not the practicum instructor—has the most expertise.

- *The multiple times and structures of the reflection invite a framing and a recursiveness that is hospitable to a practice-based theory.* The final reflection in the portfolio asks for a kind of cumulative overview; in it, tutors are asked to address just five words: *tutor, Tutor, practice, theory, and you.* These words provided frames through which to understand experience, and they also seemed to act as a kind of heuristic that the tutors recursively applied. Through putting the words they had used all term in dialectic and dialogue with each other, the tutors were able to articulate further their own theory and their own practice.

Now that my time in the WRC as a tutor has ended, I do not see myself as a tutor; I see myself as a "Tutor." I know now what I should have realized all along. I am my own person with my own distinct style and personality; so therefore, I am not a robot that has come off the assembly line with all of the information I need to become a tutor. I am an individual who is different from all other Tutors in the WRC. I have a style that work best for me, and there is not a book anywhere that can tell me what this style is or should be. I am a Tutor, who knows the theory behind the writing conference and is confident enough to take this knowledge and weave my own individualism into it.

These, then, are some of the patterns that I make from the data that the tutors have provided me. More than any test score, more than a grade, more than even a single observation or two, they tell the story of how tutors learn to tutor.

What I've shared so far is, of course, only part of the story. *If it's only part of the story.* What's missing—even when this practicum "works"? And what of the tutors who in completing the forms were unable to develop the substance, that is, what of the tutors who really never became tutors, or who didn't develop as we'd hoped? How do these missing pieces—these gaps in my story—complicate it? Reading the data means reading presence and absence; successes and failures.

In particular, I want to talk about absence, and in two ways: in the sense of what I've come to call the big picture problem; and in the sense that reading the data has prompted many questions for me. Thinking about both these issues will complicate and enrich whatever theory I've developed so far.

Responding to the portfolios for these tutors, I found myself repeating the same point:

> *Your theory works best at the micro-level. Your weekly logs are outstanding examples of this as you seek to interpret what happened, and you're not afraid to see the negative, articulate it, and consider it. Don't lose this.*
>
> *As you move to the bigger picture, you lose some of the acuity that works for you in the micro. I think that's a function of lack of practice.*

Or, as one tutor put it herself:

> *As I read over my logs, I realized that a major problem that I had was with the students who were stuck on brainstorming. The answer to this problem? Anticipation. I did not anticipate their next assignment, so I did not discuss goals with them. For example, I should have asked them to have a rough draft for the next session, by first brainstorming at home. Writing my first paper made me realize this level of the problem, yet it was not until today that I realized the next higher level of my problem .... This semester I focused more narrowly, on the individual student, and didn't consider how to apply my experiences with individuals to the teaching of masses.*

The tutors did well on the micro-level, where they were asked, encouraged, helped to learn; where that learning—made visible in letters and logs and reflections—was read and responded to. But I really did not ask them to work toward the big picture: my fault, not theirs. So, now, how do I help tutors do this? By what assignments? What structures? Placed where in the course? With what kinds of dialogue and perhaps collaboration? Good questions.

Reading the data, observing patterns, can permit some stories; it can obscure others. For instance, I've talked about the tutors as a kind of collective, but in fact they could be classified in a number of ways that might be relevant to their development. For instance, do the graduate students and the undergraduates learn about tutoring in the same ways? How would I seek to find this out? Or if systematic differences distinguish these populations, perhaps they derive from other factors: prior experience, age, motivation for tutoring, personality type, and preferred learning style, to name but a few that come to mind almost immediately. In other words, what I've shared thus far describes the group as a collective, but it might be useful—we might do a better job helping tutors *become* tutors—if we could make some finer distinctions and design the curriculum to accommodate those, much as reflection itself has been constructed pluralistically.

Finally, my story has some absent tutors: those for whom tutoring really didn't work, or more often, those for whom development was stunted. Who are these students? It could be, in the case of failures, that they were not intended to work with other students: I'm more than prepared to accept this. Not everyone can teach; not everyone can tutor. (And, if truth be told, I had one of those this term.[1]) Often, the principal problem is a relationship one: The tutor cannot see him or herself in the student, so that no relationship between tutor and student can evolve, and without a relationship no learning takes place.

But some other tutors—good tutors—didn't develop in the way I'd expected, and I have the feeling that if I knew more about how tutors develop, I too could have *anticipated,* and thus, intervened helpfully. An example: a young man, returning student, self-identified as a (creative) writer. About halfway through the term, he found himself changing in ways

---

[1]Too often we talk about what works, but seeing what does not work is every bit as instructive, and is in fact necessary if we are to develop an adequate theory of tutor development. In the case in question, the tutor seemed not able to identify with the students at all, either in practice or in theory. In practice, she was angry at what she perceived as errors; in theory, she related the learning of the class to her development rather than (also) being able to see how the lessons could be used to help others. Thus, for instance, when the guest lecturer helped us understand different learning styles, this tutor's application was exclusively to herself as a particular kind of learner; how such information might be used to help the students she was tutoring was not considered. This self-orientation was typical throughout the term: I began to think of it as "Stuck in self."

Having observed this same phenomenon in students in methods classes for middle and secondary school, I'm beginning to think that for some students, this is a necessary part of the process, but for others, it's a sign that teaching/tutoring isn't perhaps a wise choice for them or their prospective students. See my (1997) "Teacher Portfolios: Lessons in Resistance, Readiness, and Reflection," In K. Yancey and I. Weiser (Eds.), *Situating Portfolios: Four Perspective* (246-265). Logan, UT: Utah State University Press.

he didn't like: *Where did that warm, trusting, sensitive, concerned tutor disappear to during the semester?* Looking back over the term, in his final reflection, he hypothesizes what he thinks went wrong:

> My personality probably plays a large part. I don't like failure, in any form. I don't like admitting something is not a success, In short, I took the tutoring process much too personally.... My doubts are: If I pursue teaching, or even working in a writing center, will I be able to get the "separation" necessary to be successful? Or will I be consumed by it all?

Although short, this is a rich passage. For one thing, the tutor is perceptive: I agree that he took the tutoring too personally. But the separation metaphor speaks of other issues—identification and overidentification. On the one level, given that the student's success or lack thereof is not his, he needs to *separate* himself from that. But I think that on a more personal level, he read too much of himself into many of his students, so that he found it difficult to see them as *other*. For instance, he tended to work with students he saw as similar to him, as he says in discussing the subject of his case study paper: *My reason for selecting Christy as the topic for my paper is one of familiarity. Her environment and background are essentially the same as mine were the first time I attended college.* There is a logic to his enthusiasm, but his tendency was then to see her as a replication of him. When she wasn't as motivated or as disciplined as he, he was disappointed. So the separation here works multiply.

And I see a bigger picture: tutors do need to see themselves—identify with—the students with whom they work; this is the humanity that is, ultimately, our common text. But we also have to be able to separate, to see and appreciate the *other* in our students; that difference is what enables us to bring to them what *they* need. Now that I understand this duality of identity and separation/difference as a part of the process of becoming a tutor, I include it in class as a specific exercise: how are you like your students, yes, but how are they unlike you, and how can you value those differences?

***

It's only fair to ask, "What did I learn from this reflective rendering of the course?" I had hoped that including reflection in the tutoring practicum would help students develop a habit of seeing and thinking and talking about practice that is theoretical: their documents suggest that reflection does indeed produce this effect. More specifically, their reflective texts also show what we could define as *a set of stages or perspectives* that developing tutors experience, chief among them these three:

> Identifying with their students,
> Separating from them,

Seeing students as developing writers whose needs might be anticipated.

How uniform or diverse or generalizable these stages are is yet to be determined—but can be so determined if we continue to work with students, if we continue to make practice visible, if we continue to use practice to talk back to theory. Or: What I hadn't understood was how much these reflective texts can teach us about how tutors learn.

***

Although this story has not ended, it plays out thematically in diverse ways—it's a story about this class; about these tutors' reflections and about how they learned from them; about how I also learned from these reflections about a process that is not very well understood: How do we learn to tutor?

If we continue to ask our students, they will teach us.

REFERENCES

Harris, M. (1986). *Teaching one-to-one: The writing conference.* Urbana, IL: National Council of Teachers of English.

Kinkead, J. & Harris, J. (1988). *Writing centers in context.* Urbana, IL: National Council of Teachers of English.

Koestler, A. (1975). *The act of creation.* New York: Dell.

North, S. (1984). The idea of a writing center. *College English, 46,* 433–446.

Schon, D. (1995). Causality and causal inference in the study of organizations. In R. Goodman & W. Fisher (Eds.), *Rethinking knowledge: Reflections across the disciplines* (69–103). Albany: State University of New York Press.

Silk, Bobbie. " Re: theory and practice (pragmatics)," WCENTER, 1-22-97; available email bsil@keller.clarke.edu.

Yancey, K. (1997). Teacher portfolios: Lessons in resistance, readiness, and reflections. In K. Yancey & I. Weiser (Eds.), *Situating portfolios: Four perspectives* (pp. 245–265). Logan: Utah State University Press.

Yancey, K. (1998). *Reflection in the writing classroom.* Logan: Utah State University Press.

Chapter 12

The Return of the Suppressed:
Tutoring Stories
in a Transitional Space

Nancy Welch
University of Vermont

I

What peer tutor and tutee do together is not write or edit, or least of all proofread. What they do together is converse.

> —Kenneth Bruffee, "Peer Tutoring
> and the 'Conversation of Mankind'"

I think I've had many sessions where that conversation doesn't happen.

> —Maggie, interview, Spring 1997

To grasp these two relations . . . requires a kind of transitional space, which can encompass the paradoxes that arise when we are aware that two or more competing and convincing perspectives apply to the same phenomenon.

> —Jessica Benjamin,
> *Like Subjects, Love Objects* (1995)

At the end of the fall semester, I asked Maggie, a writing center tutor, to tell me the story of her first semester tutoring. Maggie replied, "[O]bviously

203

what I've learned and what I've continued to learn is it's a collaborative process and that what's the most important thing . . . is the conversation between the tutee and tutor . . . . It's a relationship where two people are dependent on each other."

I also asked Maggie to tell me the story of moments from her tutoring that don't fit with this tale. She replied:

> I think I've had many sessions where that conversation doesn't happen . . . where someone comes in and says, "This is my paper. Tell me what I did wrong, and I'm going to sit back and relax while you mark it along the way," and I've had some really difficult tutees who don't want to participate at all, who just want to get their forms signed and get out of there as fast as possible. You get stuck in those situations.

Maggie's two stories interest me particularly because of the difference in how each story is told. In the first, she uses a third-person, detached narrative voice to sketch "two people," and to tell what takes place between these two people just enough to shore up the lesson of collaboration that starts the tale. This story is by now for Maggie and the other new tutors a familiar one that needs little elaboration beyond its key words of *collaboration, conversation, relationship.* It's the story of tutoring they've learned in their first-semester tutoring class through reading essays such as Kenneth Bruffee's (1984) "Peer Tutoring and the 'Conversation of Mankind'" and Stephen North's (1984) "The Idea of a Writing Center." It's a story they've also composed through end-of-semester articles they wrote for possible publication in *The Writing Lab Newsletter* or *The Dangling Modifier*, Maggie writing a short article on using open-ended questions to facilitate conversation. This "official" story of what should take place in the writing center is one that nearly all the tutors told me in response to my "Tell me the story of your first semester in the writing center" prompt, and they likewise employed the third-person, detached narrative approach that simultaneously invokes and distances the teller from this tale.

Thus it's striking that in response to my second prompt, Maggie switches to a more intimate, involved first-person voice: "I think I've had many sessions where that conversation doesn't happen"; "I've had really difficult tutees who don't want to participate at all." Distance between teller and tale shrinks, and distance between tale and listener also shrinks as Maggie switches her narrative approach a third time. Shifting at the end to second-person, she invites listeners to consider how they've experienced this "suppressed" story of tutoring too: "You get stuck in those situations."

A strong temptation in writing center research, composition research, and beyond might be to call Maggie's first story the "theory" or "wish," and her second story "practice" or "reality." Such a temptation leads to flat pronouncements about an unbridgeable divide between theory and practice; it sets up writing center practitioners to choose between two limiting options.

We can either rescue the first, official story by eliminating any conditions that make the second, suppressed story possible, or we can champion the second story as exemplary of the unrepresentable, untheorizable nature of tutoring while repudiating the first story as mere "theory-hope."[1] If we accept this choice between rescue or repudiation, however, we can't consider that Maggie doesn't actually offer these two accounts in opposition. Instead she offers, side by side, two stories, two narrative constructions. She constructs characters. She constructs point of view. Both of her stories are also rhetorical constructs. Through constructing characters, constructing point of view, Maggie also creates two convincing arguments about tutoring, her second story not transparent reality but a countertheory: "This conversation doesn't happen *when* tutees are difficult." More, both stories, both arguments have for Maggie persuasive claims. Though the second account does appear to arise less from class readings and more from tutorial experience, Maggie stressed throughout this initial interview that her first account is one she also believes, has experienced from time to time in the writing center, would like to experience more often . . . but isn't sure how.

In a recent article, Elizabeth Boquet (1999) likewise begins with two stories from her campus writing center, and she wonders which story —the story of the tutee who is "questioned, drawn out . . . valued and encouraged" or the story of the tutee whose work is "dropped off" and "cleaned up" in the tutorial-as-laundromat —is the real story of this center (464). At the start, her article seems poised to repeat the theory-versus-practice, rescue-or-repudiate divide: One story must win out over the other. By the article's end, however, Boquet has sketched another possible response: a search beyond the limits of both stories, a search for the excess. She argues for paying attention to those moments when writing center practice *exceeds* the institutional laundromat space to which it's been assigned, and also for paying attention to those moments when writing center practice *exceeds* its stated philosophy of nurturing writing through conversation between peers. Ultimately she argues for telling an excess of stories about writing center work, not to correct those stories and not to uncritically celebrate them either, but rather to examine and learn from their excesses.

-----

[1]Recently, Steve North urged a *rescue* of earlier writing center ideals through eliminating all conditions that disrupt those ideals. To ensure that all tutees in a writing center are "really motivated to write" (North, 1984, 443) and are not merely motivated to "finish writing" and have this writing "win them a good grade" (North, 1994, 10), he calls on writing centers in the most recent essay to create a "tighter orbit" —as his campus writing center did by preferring students enrolled in the English major's writing track. In contrast, Eric Hobson (1994) *repudiates*, rather than seeks North's closer match with, prior theories. Hobson argues that to seek correspondence between theory and practice is to participate in a "seamless, Enlightenment-defined vision of theory" (1). Rather than argue for what a post-Enlightenment understanding of theorizing might involve, he rejects theory entirely in the name of a practicality that "*accepts* the contradiction between theory and practice. . ." (8, my emphasis).

In this chapter, I want to pick up on this idea of excessive writing center stories. Following the work of Maggie and her classmates during the second semester of their year-long tutor-preparation class in 1996-1997, I'll explore how official stories of tutoring lose some of their officialness and how suppressed stories gain in visibility and in knowledge-making potential when both are examined *as stories* —stories whose narrative devices, manifest claims, latent contradictions, and unwritten surpluses all bear investigation. To Boquet's call for the writing and telling of an excess of stories about writing center work, I'd also like to add this argument: that any single story we tell about a writing center contains an excess, a surplus, something under-narrated or suppressed, not quite controlled, not fully in service to the story's guiding rhetorical claim. Though our stories of writing centers *do* attempt to contain and control their narrative elements, making those elements serve a particular claim —"Writing centers promote learning through conversation"; "That conversation doesn't happen" —there is in any story something that simply does not fit and something that, if pursued, might get Maggie, and the rest of us, "unstuck."[2] This chapter, then, is about reflective research through reflecting on the stories we daily tell in writing centers, especially by reflecting on the rubs —and potential for dialogue —between suppressed and official tutoring tales. This chapter is also about engaging tutors in the process of investigating their stories from the writing center, countering the sense of a great divide between what we're reading in the tutor preparation class and what these tutors are experiencing day to day, countering the belief that there's writing center "research," on the one hand and "what really goes on" on the other. Before I turn to the tutors in Maggie's class, though, I want to look at a story from a more recent tutor-preparation class that dramatizes what I mean when I say that any single story contains a surplus of meaning and when I offer the examination of a story's excesses as a model for reflective research.

II

In a way the session was somewhat intense; I don't think he had any great passion . . . .

—Jesse, tutoring journal, spring 1999

---

[2]I take these ideas about excess and surplus from both Bakhtinian narrative theorist Gary Saul Morson (1994), who argues that any story contains its "sideshadows," signs of another story that might have been and still might be, and psychoanalytic-feminist theorists such as Jessica Benjamin (1995) and Joan Copjec (1989). Copjec, for example, writes that no single theoretical construction can ever mirror back fully and completely the desires of a self, because desire is created by multiple, competing constructions plus an "inch of nature" that exceeds linguistic understanding. For Morson, Benjamin, and Copjec, there is always excess, surplus, a persistent Otherness that no one story can capture and contain. Because Mikhail Bakhtin was resolutely opposed to Freudian psychoanalytic theory, it's fascinating, I think, to note that in the excess of Bakhtinian dialogism and in the excess of post-Freudian feminist psychoanalysis there is this overlap, this unexpected and unacknowledged connection between the two.

It is easy enough to give up one side of the polarity in order to oscillate toward the other side. What is difficult to attain is a notion of difference, of being unlike, without giving up a sense of commonality, of being a "like" human being.

—Jessica Benjamin, *Like Subjects, Love Objects* (1995)

Recently Jesse, a junior history and English major and first-year writing tutor, brought the following journal entry (which I've condensed) to his tutor-preparation class,[3] a class that, like Maggie's 2 years earlier, focuses on the telling and investigation of tutoring stories. Jesse introduced the entry before reading it out loud by saying, "I let the tutee set the agenda but I'm not sure this is always the right thing to do" and "Maybe I'm just lethargic on Friday afternoons and that makes the tutee lethargic too." He read:

> Another question is the matter of approaching a paper the way the student wants to, as in my last session with my first ESL student. Jae-Nam was keen to work on a sentence at a time, and so we did, although I found as I went through his paper [a proposal for starting a small business] that there was a certain lack of substance. I think I didn't want to address content too much (neither did he) because it seemed subordinate to the importance of making his sentences at least grammatically correct. He thought the best approach was to go over it a sentence at a time. So that's what we did. *At one point he told me a story about a restaurant which had been all set up but had been there waiting to open for a long time because the owner had forgotten to order glasses, and Jae-Nam was saying how complicated it was to remember all of the different things you needed to start a business.* In a way the session was somewhat intense; I don't think he had any great passion for learning how to write proper English, but rather seeing that it was correct so he could hand it in. (journal entry, spring 1999, my emphasis)

In this journal entry—one I admire for its detail, complexity, and work to give voice to a suppressed tutoring tale, a session that wasn't an obvious "success"—Jesse offers a series of manifest arguments:

Jae-Nam lacks passion.
Jae-Nam sets the agenda to work on correctness.
Jae-Nam doesn't realize, as Jesse does, that his paper lacks substance.

---

[3]This chapter draws primarily on the work of students in a spring 1997 tutor-preparation class at the University of Vermont, supplemented by the work of students in the spring 1999 class. I team-taught the spring 1997 class with Kerry Litchfield and Michelle Fay, and as a participant-observer I attended the Spring 1999 class, team-taught by Sue Dinitz and Jean Kiedaisch. In both semesters I drew on microethnographic and teacher-research practices—keeping an observation notebook during class meetings, collecting journals and tutorial log notes, and interviewing four or five of the tutors from each class. At the tutors' request, I use their actual first names in this chapter and I quote them with their permission. I have, however, fictionalized the name of the tutee appearing in Jesse's tutoring story.

The same entry, though, also contains elements that exceed and even contradict the manifest arguments:

> *The session was somewhat intense.*
> *Jesse—along with Jae-Nam? instead of Jae-Nam?—sets the agenda to work on correctness.*
> *Jae-Nam, in telling of the restaurant that couldn't open, wants to work on substance.*

Like Maggie, whose two stories offer competing perspectives on what it means to tutor, Jesse offers within a single journal entry two competing views of this session and at least two responses to the question of who has set the agenda. Especially in Jae-Nam's anecdote of the restaurant (which I've italicized to highlight its surprisingness, its seeming out-of-placeness) there is excess, surplus, and, I believe, a "potential" or "transitional" space. The anecdote opens up a transitional space in which Jesse and Jae-Nam could discuss their *shared* view that what they both want for this business plan is more than the editing they've been doing. In this transitional space, too, Jae-Nam might appear to Jesse as someone other, someone more than the "ESL student" whose writerly concerns must be "subordinate to" the writing of "proper English."

A potential or transitional space—terms I take from the school of post-Freudian psychoanalysis called *object-relations theory*—exists in the negotiation between desired and sanctioned meanings, between the "me" and the "not-me," between what one initially thought and what one is starting to recognize now. Within a transitional space, individuals can take a tradition or an ideal such as "The tutee should always set the agenda" and negotiate its meaning: "Sometimes a tutee states one agenda but then suggests another . . . Sometimes the tutor directs what happens without realizing the tutee is asking for something else." Within a transitional space, individuals can also revisit and question initial constructions of a situation: "I was seeing this tutee only as 'ESL' or only as 'practicality-minded business major' but now as I look back on the story I've told about this session, I wonder . . . ."

It's through creating transitional spaces for questioning, negotiating, and playing with meaning, D. W. Winnicott (1971) writes, that individuals become active participants in their realities and address the obstacles, differences, and contradictions they encounter with a sense of zest rather than dismay. In a transitional space, we can consider, as feminist object-relations theorist Jessica Benjamin (1995) writes, how competing, convincing perspectives can arise from the same situation. Importantly, within such a space, we can examine the differences of those perspectives with interest, even fascination, and a belief in our ability and authority to rewrite prior perspectives found to be incomplete, not always or entirely true. Within a transitional space, the divide between official and suppressed stories of tutoring break down as all become transitional, available for questioning and play. Within this space, all stories are open to the questions, "But what else might this story be saying? What's an overlooked detail here that needs to be brought into play?" It's a space that takes seriously Jesse's highlighted argument about his session with Jae-Nam, yet takes all the misfit details seriously too.

Through object-relations theory (an excessive rather than reductive field of psychoanalytic theory). I'll be reading the story of Maggie's tutor-preparation class. By highlighting object-relations theory I don't mean to suggest that this is the only frame for reading writing center stories. Instead, it's one possible context that helps me move from "I *want to reflect* on what's happened here" to "Here's *how I can begin*." Object-relations theory is one example of theoretical approaches joining reflection *and action* that I'm particularly attracted to (Bakhtinian narrative theory is an obvious other) especially as its key words of *excess, potential, transitional,* and *play* remind me, always to keep my own reading in transition, in play, in search of the excesses that don't neatly cohere. These key words tell me that at this chapter's end, I need to come back to Jesse's story about tutoring Jae-Nam—because there's more to this story, a not-yet-narrated surplus that make my claims in this chapter transitional too.

III

The way we worked in class, in groups and all together, it *was* a collaborative process . . .

—Maggie, interview, spring 1997

It got so we just go around and tell . . . gripe stories about our tutoring.

—Elizabeth, interview, spring 1997

[L]ater integrations should neither seamlessly subsume nor replace earlier positions but rather refigure them.

—Jessica Benjamin, *Like Subjects, Love Objects* (1995)

Twelve students, with majors primarily in the humanities, made up the 1996-1997 tutor-preparation class. During the class's first semester, which was taught by the writing center's director, the tutors read articles about writing centers plus chapters from Meyer and Smith's *The Practical Tutor* (1987). Because most of these tutors had never taken a writing class, this first semester also immersed them in practices of drafting, revising, and editing in a range of genres including an autobiographical essay, weekly journals about their tutoring sessions, and a short article developed from the journals. In other words, the tutors not only read the official stories of tutoring as collaboration and writing as a process, but also experienced these ideas through the class. "The way we worked in class," Maggie said at the end of this semester, "in groups and all together, it *was* a collaborative process. It wasn't just me trying to get ahead and excel" (Maggie's emphasis). Here, I think, Maggie calls into question my distinctions between "official" story and "suppressed"; she tells me that the articles she read, the practices she experienced in class didn't merely represent official, authoritative discourse imposed from without. These articles and practices were also, in Bakhtinian terms, internally persuasive, suggesting possible worlds that Maggie and the other tutors believed could be made real and, indeed, had experienced as real.

By the first semester's end, however, tutors also spoke of frustration at a growing gap between the tutoring stories they had read—what one tutor, Elizabeth, called the "great" stories of tutoring—and those they were increasingly telling—what Elizabeth called the "gripe" stories of tutoring. Elizabeth explained in an interview after that first semester, that most of the time was devoted to discussing readings and working on writing projects with 5 or 10 minutes at the end for discussing their latest tutorials. "Everyone would say a problem,"she said, "but . . . I think we never made that extra step to get to the analysis of the story."

Here we might conclude that Elizabeth and the other tutors are telling an innocence-to-experience story as the first blush of enthusiasm and idealism gives way to increasing disenchantment, as tutors look back and call these initial heady beliefs about tutoring "wishful" and "naive." Such a conclusion—one that's underwritten by Freudian ideas of development—is one I want to resist because I believe that the Freudian developmental narrative is flawed, even spurious. According to this narrative, so pervasive in our stories of teaching and learning, we start with no awareness of difference, existing in the bliss of complete identification—a complete identification, for instance, with the idea of tutoring as animated conversation between equals. Then, as difference becomes increasingly apparent, we respond with fear, upset, a growing alienation between our increasingly separate, distinct selves and our initial, identificatory loves. Finally, we reach (so this story, which is the Oedipal story, goes) what's taken in classical Freudian theory as the penultimate stage in human development: a post-Oedipal identity that has, once and for all, repudiated pre-Oedipal attachments. Early identificatory loves are judged illusory, childish, and naive; the "great" stories of tutoring are replaced by "gripe" stories; the belief that "what [tutor and tutee] do together is converse" is replaced by "that conversation doesn't happen." Such is the Freudian story.

In contrast with classical Freudian theory, feminist object-relations theorists such as Jessica Benjamin consider a much different story of human development: one in which there is no final stage of separation, differentiation, and repudiation of all prior attachments but rather a complex, on-going interaction between self and other, sameness and difference, claims and counters. Extending the work of child psychologist D. W. Winnicott, feminist object-relations theorists focus on the creation of a "shared reality" in which an individual can recognize others as "*both* part of the self *and* as an equivalent but different center of existence" (Benjamin, 1995, 41, my emphasis). According to Benjamin, difference isn't a later, more mature stage that supplants the earlier, naive stage of identification; rather, difference speaks back to and refigures our identifications. Difference asks us to appreciate the complexities of context, to take pleasure in particulars, and to do so *in conversation* (not in "one-must-win-out" competition) with our prior ideas and ideals. Here, separation isn't a final achievement but rather a stage we continually pass through to as we learn to recognize another's reality, as we learn to form with another person a "shared reality" that attends to difference, that believes in commonality too (Benjamin, 1995, 41).

The object-relations story of learning and development is messy and excessive as it strives to hold likeness and otherness in relationship, as it responds to otherness not with stand-offish fear but with zest, involvement, and even joy. After all, Benjamin (1995) writes, mere imitation—the mirroring of a prior ideal, the telling of "great story" after "great story"—is never so satisfactory as "complex interaction". Complex interaction, I think, is what Elizabeth is calling for too when she looks at the stories she and her fellow tutors were telling at the end of the first semester. She doesn't say, "The 'gripe' stories are the reality." She doesn't ask, "How do we make it so we have only 'great' stories to tell?" Instead, she calls for another step: for analysis of all the stories being told.

IV

What a wonderful experience it was. Maggie and I really gave our somewhat lost tutees a very good example of the possibilities and how to dissect a piece of poetry. The collaboration was invigorating.

—Dan, tutoring journal, spring 1997

The self engaged in identification takes the other as a fantasy object, not as an equivalent center of being . . .

—Jessica Benjamin, *Like Subjects, Love Object* (1995)

What happens if the great session I'm writing about turns out not to be so hot after all?

—Dan, in class, spring 1997

It's here that we began the second semester, with official stories and suppressed, with great stories and gripe, and with the need to take an extra step toward analysis in the space of a classroom that makes all stories transitional. First, though, we needed to work at drafting fuller narratives since most tutors came to class with journal entries that packed a week's worth of tutoring into single paragraphs, the paragraphs typically featuring We as each story's protagonist: *we* talked about . . . *we* tried . . . we considered . . . *we* concluded. . . . This collective perspective is one effect, I think, of the discourse of collaboration: the tutor and tutee quickly merge into an undifferentiated one even though, as Elizabeth pointed out in a class discussion about this collective perspective, "It's never really what 'we' did." The tutors also brought to class stories that highlighted their evaluations of a session— "I had a great session on Tuesday morning" or "This tutee was completely unmotivated"—while submerging or omitting entirely the details. "It's difficult," Elizabeth said in a year-end interview, "to tell what you did without your reaction to it. . . . you write, 'This is what we did *because of this*,' not 'This is what the situation was *and then* this is what we did" (Elizabeth's emphases).

In class (which was team-taught by me, a graduate teaching assistant, and a third-year tutor), we asked the tutors to rewrite passages from their tutoring journals without using "we," or to expand on a brief journal account through the multiple perspectives of, for example, Peter Elbow's (1981) loop-writing steps. This work of rewriting and expanding through multiple perspectives—of attending to difference, of bringing competing perspectives to bear on a single story—was in itself unsettling. One tutor, Dan, brought to class a journal entry about a "wonderful" session in which he and Maggie led three female students from an introductory poetry class in a discussion of a sonnet—these "somewhat lost" tutees, as Dan wrote in his initial entry, coming to "see various possibilities" and "build on their own interpretive ideas." When he reached the "dialogue" loop-writing step, Dan began to tell a much different story:

> *Maggie*: What do you think the poem's about?
> *Tutee #2*: An author and his canvas.
> *Dan*: Really? I was thinking it was about a dream.
> *Tutee #2*: Really?
> *Us*: Yeah, fantasy, imagination, dream, whatever you want to call it.

At this point, Dan stopped writing, looked up, and said, "What happens if the great session I'm writing about turns out not to be so hot after all?"

A standard feature in tutor-preparation classes is this writing out and reflecting on fuller tutoring narratives. Typically, though, what would happen next is a critique of Dan's session and then a rewrite. Typically, the goal of the rewrite would be the creation of a fictional tutorial dialogue that turns this not-so-hot session into a great one, that makes this session reflect (which is very different from interact with) a prior ideal. In quick rewriting, however, all complications would be erased, the step of analysis that Elizabeth called for skipped right over. In fact, I think it's because Dan's story doesn't match the official stories of collaboration that it has much to teach and much it can call on us to analyze.

Dan—an older student who manages a small-town trailer park and who has returned to school after serving in the military and working as a truck driver and bookkeeper, among other jobs, has taken a stance in this session that he did understand to be collaborative, even inviting. He heard his interpretation as a first raw reaction to a sonnet he'd never read before, and in class he said he was surprised that the tutees accepted his statements instead of reacting against them. Bold statements spark reaction, counter-statements, new ideas: This is the understanding of conversation through which Dan had read and understood Bruffee's (1984) "Peer Tutoring and 'The Conversation of the Mankind'" during the first semester, and this is the idea of conversation that he values over the conformity and complacency he experienced in the military. More, latent in Dan's initial story of the session is another idea about tutoring that needs to be drawn out and discussed, not excised and hushed up: the "Moses" idea of the tutor who leads his "somewhat lost tutees" into the promised land of discovery and understanding.[4] If Dan simply rewrote this session to eliminate any sense of difference and re-assert a complete identification with one official idea of collaboration, the tutees would still be cast, I think, as the session's "fantasy objects," represented as passive and compliant in whatever kind of tutoring narrative they're placed within. And if Dan simply rewrote this session to replace assertive statements with open-ended questions, to tone down the representation of lost students and Moses-tutor, we would miss everything this story asks us to consider: how conversational practice is informed by gender, by class, by the discourse communities we're coming from or working against; how masculinity can be an exercise of power in a tutorial and how social class — the seemingly open-ended questions that mark middle-class pedagogical discourse — can also be an exercise of power or else a problematic stance of complacent "neutrality." As Dan's journal entry and in-class writing suggests, the emerging problems of these tutoring stories were interesting, engaging, and instructive, and our next step wasn't to correct these stories but to converse with them.[5]

---

[4]See Jane Gallop (1988) for an examination of the ideas of teaching and authority represented in Moses/lost children narratives.

[5]I'm indebted to Mary Ann Cain (1995) for this idea of conversing with stories, as distinct from correcting a story or seeking to control its contradictions.

For example, at Maggie's request, the class read and discussed a story she'd composed during the loop-writing exercise about a tutorial with a business student. In response to the "First thoughts" loop-writing prompt, Maggie wrote: "Huge was the first word that came into my head. . . . Everything about him was strong and overbearing for someone my size—even his five-page business paper. . . . Maybe he thought because of his varsity hockey jacket that he deserved special attention and treatment—and as disappointing as it was—I gave it to him." In response to other loop-writing prompts such as "scene" and "dialogue," Maggie added additional details to this initial story of tutoring-turned-sexual-victimization: that the tutee's instructor had promised five bonus points to anyone who got her or his paper (a start-up plan for a small business) "checked out" at the writing center; that as the tutee told Maggie to "Go ahead and get started" proofreading, he also told her about his plans to start his own business as soon as he got through school, which he viewed as a "complete waste of time."

All these details were a part of the story that the tutors looked at together in the next class, our discussion preceded by writing from the prompt "Describe, without labeling the tutee, what his understanding of the writing center seems to be and what relationship he's trying to set up with the writing center tutor. What might have created his understanding of the writing center? How might this tutee's actions make sense?" In response, some tutors considered that yes, this story does suggest an intimidating man who has cast his tutor as subordinate, order-taking female, and they tried out psychological explanations: "Maybe his aggressiveness covers up his insecurity about his writing." Another tutor, Joanna, felt the word *aggressiveness* too quickly labeled this tutee since, she pointed out, his instructor set him up to view the tutors as secretaries whose work would get him five bonus points. "Maybe he's a go-getter," Maggie offered. "He knows what he wants, and the writing center is a step in the right direction for him." Still others countered the growing sense that a secretarial aid is all this student desired; they pointed to the strange gap between the tutee's story of starting his own business and his view of school, including the business plan assignment, as a "complete waste of time." "Maybe it's because he doesn't think school is the 'real' world," Dan said. Maggie, returning to her feeling of being in the tutorial, observed, "How this guy treated me was certainly real."

Though much of this class focused on reading, not quickly revising, in this session the tutors did want to know how not to get stuck in such situations. I also wanted options for Maggie beyond "as disappointing as it was—I gave it to him." Near the class's end, we considered, "Given your reading of this session, how might you proceed?" Some tutors, highlighting the student's possible view of tutoring as secretarial help, imagined starting with a conversation about what tutoring means. Others drafted versions of this tutorial in which the tutor and tutee discuss the strange, interesting gap between his future plans and present assignment. A few tutors, challenging the idea that tutor and tutee are the only characters in this story, wrote about the need to ask the course instructor to meet with the writing center tutors to discuss his goals, their goals, and the problem of bonus points. Each story they wrote pointed toward a possible future. Each story also arose from a reading of the initial situation. As tutors shared their imagined stories of this session, they also listened to and responded to each other's different constructions, none of these constructions emerging as the single right way to interpret and proceed.

V

Development thus requires not a unilinear trajectory away from the overinclusive [idyllic] position but the ability to return without losing the knowledge of difference.

—Jessica Benjamin, *Like Subjects, Love Objects* (1995)

This in itself has forced me to look very closely at the way that power and relationships are established and how quickly collaboration can fall apart.

—Elizabeth, journal, spring 1997

I don't mean to suggest that in the end these tutors learned that writing center practice is untheorizable, entirely relative, or as a good colleague of mine recently put it, "something you just can't generalize." In end-of-the-semester interviews, tutors suggested that the opposite may be true: This work of writing out, interpreting, complicating, and rewriting stories of tutoring engaged them in the difficult, ongoing work of theorizing, the difficult, ongoing work of revisiting the generalizations we constantly, necessarily make. As Joanna said in an end-of-semester interview, she was sharply aware of how often she judged tutees as "unmotivated" or "uninterested"— generalizations she formed if a tutee kept glancing at the clock or shrugged when she asked, "What do you want to work on?" In the transitional space of the class, however, Joanna opened up these generalizations about tutees by examining the rest of the story—by examining the conditions that had brought that student to the writing center in the first place—and, maybe especially, by acknowledging how little of the whole story she actually knew. She explained: "You've got to try to interpret different reasons for what [a tutee] is saying and what might have been going on. . . . You can say it *seemed* he didn't want to be there because he was fidgeting or kept looking at the clock, but you can't say he was a bad student or an uninterested student because you don't know what happened right before he came in."

For Joanna and Maggie, this seemingly small move—from saying "This was an uninterested student" to "This student is fidgeting and looking at the clock. Why might that be?"—was crucial as both had voiced all semester discomfort with the authority to name and judge fellow students as uninterested, unmotivated, difficult. This seemingly small move also has the power, I think, to alter, without suppressing, the argument with which Maggie began the semester: from "That conversation often doesn't happen because these difficult tutees don't want to participate" to "That conversation often doesn't happen. I have these tutees who don't want to participate. What's going on? Why would this not wanting to participate make sense?"

In asking these questions, these tutors aren't moving away from the ideas of the writing center they had read, discussed, and wanted to believe in their first semester's class. Rather, I think they are returning, again and again, to those ideas, to those earliest identifications, but with differences and complications and with an increasing belief in their abilities to refigure and revise. Near the end of the second semester, the tutors also looked more and more at the writing center's role in the breakdowns of collaboration, the writing center's role in difficulties that can't simply be assigned to "difficult tutees." Joanna asked the class, for instance, to reconsider how they fill out "log notes," descriptions of tutorials that, if the student requests it, can be sent to a course instructor. For most of the year, Joanna explained, she had filled out log notes, according to the writing center's standard procedure, at the end of sessions while tutees were packing up to go. Recently, though, she had begun asking tutees to write the description of the session—to continue rather than abruptly cut off that sense of peer relationship, and also so she could see and converse with the tutee's understanding of the session. "I think it helps in making it more of a collaborative process," Joanna said. "Not like with a doctor where they came in and left, and I write them up." Here Joanna has examined a division: between the ideal of collaborative process and the not-at-all-collaborative power she's been assigned to wield as she wrote descriptions of tutorials to send to a tutee's instructor. And she addresses that division, brings the procedure for completing log notes into transition, changes the story of how these log notes are done.

In a final interview, Dan also made this move of bringing an earlier story into transition. Early in the semester, he'd described a tutee who said that he wanted to be a writer, then became silent, even sullen, as Dan tried to work with him. He'd concluded with a derisive laugh: "And he *says* he wants to be a writer!" In the interview, though, he returned to that story from a different direction: "The student who wanted to be a writer, I said to him, Look, here's how to make your paper better and I immediately put him in a hierarchy where I was saying, "Look, I'm the writer, not you." Dan continued:

Come to find out—I found out toward the end of the session because I actually resorted to just bullshitting with him . . . —come to find out what he really wanted to be doing was writing for something like *Sports Illustrated* . . . What he liked was the way they were able to write sports statistics in ways that were exciting to read. If I'd found this out at the beginning, I could have woven that in . . . something to build on that came from him . . .

Dan revisits a story that initially argued, "What an impossible tutee. He doesn't even know what being a writer means"; he considers his possible role in this student's shift from involved to detached; he reclaims the possibilities for collaboration but with an added understanding of the hierarchies that must be negotiated, hierarchies that prevent a tutorial from simply, easily being a conversation among peers.

Any story holds within it a silence, a suppression, a contradiction, another story that could be told out of conversation with that silence, that contradiction. The story of the tutee who didn't know how to be a writer contains within it the story of the tutor who positioned this tutee as anything but a writer; and the story of the tutor who positioned the tutee as anything but a writer contains within it the possible story of tutor and tutee meeting as writers who find something to build on together. This possible story that Dan suggests at the end likewise suggests a silence, a suppression, a further fascinating contradiction when he refers to talking with this tutee as "bullshitting." Talking, he suggests, isn't knowledge building, isn't central to a tutorial. Talking is "bullshitting" to be pursued only in desperation and as a last resort. Such an idea of talking does have official weight in our culture, and yet it has little or no mention at all in our official tutoring tales. Here, then, is another suppression, another story that needs to be examined, needs first to be told.

VI

Whatever breakdowns in recognition occur, as they inevitably do, the primary intersubjective condition . . . is that of "experiencing the dizziness *together.*"

—Jessica Benjamin, *Like Subjects, Love Objects* (1995)

I'm half wondering if I should even ask them what they want . . .

—Katie, class discussion, spring 1999

When I first drafted this chapter, I ended with Dan's story from the last section. Paradoxically, Dan's excessive stories-within-a-story seemed a good way to provide this chapter with a tidy finish, sum up my argument, and close the discussion. But there's always more to any story than what's narrated, an excess that can't be contained. Dan, now a graduate teaching fellow, continues to grapple with hierarchies and relationships. He revels in this institutional position he never dreamed he'd hold; he loves it when his students call him "Professor" and doesn't always want to correct them. He wants to be a professor and also recognizes that there's a part of this desire that's at odds with what and how he desires to teach. Jessica Benjamin (1995) stresses that there is no penultimate stage in learning and development. There is no moment when we can say, "I've got it now" but instead a constant need to bring our stories—our institutional positions into transition—and to examine where and how we recognize each other as anything but peers.

Another excess that can't be contained: Early in this chapter I introduced Jesse's journal entry about his tutorial with Jae-Nam and its competing, contradictory claims about lethargy and intensity, and about limited and expansive agendas. Left out, however, was the class discussion that followed Jesse's reading, a discussion in which his classmates focused on his highlighted arguments, not at all on the moments of excess:

> *Katie*: I had a session similar to this. . . . She wanted to look at commas, so I felt sort of insecure about saying, "We should look at more than commas."
>
> *Sue*: Was that an ESL student?
>
> *Katie*: No, but the issue was the same.
>
> *Liz*: It doesn't seem to me like the problem in [Jesse's] session was a language barrier but lethargy, like the tutee didn't care.
>
> *Emma*: I think he sounded like a classic businessman.
>
> *Drew*: Totally. Exactly. As far as doing what the tutee wanted to do, I'd point out the major problems anyway . . . .
>
> *Katie*: I'm half wondering if I should even ask them what they want because then I feel like I'm going against what they're asking for.

This conversation makes a lot of sense to me. By picking up and agreeing with his term *lethargy*, the other tutors showed their support for Jesse. By regarding his story as offering one message, by attending to what coheres and by ignoring what does not, they were reading and responding in the ways we are typically educated to read and respond to stories. Later, one of the tutors, Liz, explained that in any story tutors tell of difficult sessions, the tendency is to blame the student: "It's either that or blame ourselves." One person must be to blame, one story must win out. As I end this chapter, turning back and forth between Maggie's class in 1997 and the new tutors I'm meeting with now, between stories viewed as opening up competing, convincing perspectives and stories made to serve single claims, I want to keep the tensions of this class conversation in play. Although this spring's class has moved on from that conversation and its contained reading of stories in all kinds of important and complicated ways, I want to end with that conversation because it's a good reminder that along with an excess of writing center stories, we also need excessive ways of reading those stories—if we're to hear all the questions they may raise. For example:

How can attending to the contradictions of a story be seen as a way of supporting a tutor like Jesse?

In drawing out suppressed stories—not to correct them—but to converse with them, can we discover options beyond "Tell a story that blames the student" or "Tell a story that blames the tutor?"

Is it possible to recognize how a tutee like Jae-Nam differed from the "eager wrestler-of-texts" (North, 1994) presented to these tutors in their first-semester's reading, yet still recognize him as a writer, a person of purpose and desire?

What if the central issue in this session *is* that designation of "ESL student"—not as a "language barrier" but as a barrier to imagining the range of concerns, interests, and abilities this tutee brings?

And especially, is it possible to question, contextualize, complicate, and expand the official stories of collaboration and peer relationship, but without oscillating to the opposite side, without ceasing to wonder what this other wants, and without giving up on the idea that when tutor and tutee sit down there's a chance for "experiencing the dizziness together"?

REFERENCES

Benjamin, J. (1995). *Like subjects, love objects: Essays on recognition and sexual difference.* New Haven, CT: Yale University Press.

Bouquet, E. H. (1999). "Our little secret": A history of writing centers, pre- to post-open admissions. *College Composition and Communication, 50*, 463–482.

Bruffee, K.A. (1984). Peer tutoring and the "conversation of mankind." In G. A. Olson (Ed.), *Writing centers: Theory and administration* (pp. 3–15). Urbana, IL: National Council of Teachers of English.

Cain, M. A. (1995). *Revisioning writers' talk: Gender and culture in acts of composing.* Albany: State University of New York Press.

Copjec, J. (1989). Cutting up. In T. Brennan (Ed.), *Between feminism and psychoanalysis* (pp. 227–246). London: Routledge.

Elbow, P. (1981). *Writing with Power.* New York: Oxford.

Elbow, P. & Belanoff, P. (1999). *A Community of writers.* Burr Ridge, Il: McGraw-Hill.

Hobson, E. (1994). Writing center practice often counters its theory: So what? In J. Mullin & R. Wallace (Eds.), *Intersections: Theory-practice in the writing center* (1–10). Urbana, IL: National Council of Teachers of English.

Meyer, E. & Smith, L. Z. (1987). *The practical tutor.* New York: Oxford University Press.

Morson, G. S. (1994). *Narrative and freedom: The shadows of time*. New Haven, CT: Yale
    University Press.
North, S. (1984). The idea of a writing center. *College English, 46,* 433–446.
North, S. (1994). Revisiting "The idea of a writing center." *The Writing Center Journal,
    15,* 7–19.
Winnicott, D. W. (1971). *Playing and reality*. London: Tavistock.

Chapter 13

The Subject is Literacy: General Education and the Dialectics of Power and Resistance in the Writing Center

Judith Rodby
California State University—Chico

American educators, and university professors in particular, have a long history of anxiety about who students are, who students should be, and who students become because of their college education; in current times, conservatives such as Allan Bloom, E. D. Hirsch, Dinesh Da Sousa, and progressive educators such as Stanley Aronowitz and Henry Giroux debate over who students should be. Among the issues raised in these culture wars are the ways students use language and literacy. Even liberal educators want students to become subjects of their disciplines' discourse, without eliminating the languages and language uses they have brought from home. For example, departments of English want students to be interested in language and literature. If and when students appear disinterested, faculty are disappointed and even angry. Conflict over discursive subjectivity occurs not only between faculty and students but among faculty as well. Faculty may position themselves as hostile to the objectives of other fields of study, and in particular, they may resist ways of using language and literacy, which differ from what they perceive as their own disciplinary values. These differences of values about language and literacy are an integral part of the intellectual, ideological, and social milieu in

221

composition programs, Writing Across the Disciplines programs, and Writing Centers.

At our Writing Center we have struggled with these conflicts as we run small tutoring groups that support writing in a variety of general education (GE) courses: collaborative groups in political science, revision groups in sociology and human sexuality, portfolio groups for world literature classes, critique writing groups for theater classes, and so on. This work has been difficult, fraught with problems and misunderstandings that result in professors, students, and tutors expressing their frustration over writing assignments, writing requirements, and the operations of the Writing Center itself. Most simply, these misunderstandings arise when faculty give writing assignments that students and their tutors see as conflicting with the values and ideologies the students bring to the course. However, because both faculty and students' subjectivity (s) are mediated by the discourse of the discipline and the place of student writing in that discipline, the conflicts are not always simply faculty versus students; both faculty and student may be positioned in a variety of subjectivities that they both may resist and continuously transform.

This study sets out first to interpret a series of misunderstandings between a student and a tutor as their interactions were mediated by the discourse of a writing assignment. This chapter is not intended as a critique of the assignment, of academic writing in general, or of writing in any specific academic discipline. Rather, I hope to develop a framework that can be used to interpret tutor and student misunderstandings in working with writing assignments. In particular, this framework can be used to examine how subjectivity and power play out as faculty assign writing, students write and revise, and tutors coach. In a later section of this chapter, I will discuss the dilemmas presented by researching a situation in which many of the participants are also teaching. I will also discuss the role that critical theory has played in this work and its potential role for writing center research. First, however, I will briefly discuss the terms *subject* and *subjectivity*.

SUBJECTS AND SUBJECTIVITY

The "subject" might be thought of as a construct, which opposes the idea of the "individual." Conceptually, an "individual" embodies a free, self-determining, and undivided consciousness. In opposition the subject abides in and is constructed through relations to language, ideology, and institutions such as schooling. We are many subjects; subjectivity is always partial and our subjectivities seldom cohere. In everyday life, we live in and through institutions, discourses, and ideologies. These interactions and relationships comprise our subjectivity or subjectivities. In these relationships we become subjects. We occupy a multiplicity of subject positions.

The work of Louis Althusser (1971) is useful in thinking through the relationship of ideology to the "subject." Althusser distinguishes between ideology-in-general and specific ideologies. Ideology-in-general has no history; it is a permanent, inescapable feature of all society; it is what provides any and all cohesion to social formations and ensures their continuance. A specific ideology has particular institutions, apparatuses, historical forms, and subjective effects. Althusser argues that human beings are "interpellated" or called on as subjects for a specific ideological formation or apparatus; interpellation occurs by means of a process "which can be imagined along the lines of the most commonplace everyday police (or other) hailing: 'Hey, you there!'" (174). When the person turns to respond to this call, the individual becomes a subject of this discourse by recognizing his or her relationship to the authority of the police. In everyday life subjects are interpellated into being (as subjects) through specific social discourses, which are not necessarily available to consciousness.

I would agree with critics of Althusser who argue that his model of subjectivity is finally too simple. He does not account for the fact that interpellation can fail and is never complete; a social discourse may hail a subjectivity that human beings successfully resist. The individual can refuse to acknowledge the authority of the police and keep walking so that he or she is not a subject of this discourse. And in real life humans are hailed by multiple discourses, which are in conflict with or are even contradictory to each other. Regularly humans live through overlapping subject positions. However, even though Althusser's own work ignored the problem of resistance to discursive interpellation, his later interpreters use his insights into the ways in which discourse(s) functions so that they can then both acknowledge and explain resistance. The notion of interpellation is a crucial tool in explaining the sources and strategies of resistance. Furthermore, as critical theorist Paul Smith (1988) argues, beyond resistance itself is agency: "What is produced by ideological interpellation is contradiction, and through a recognition of the contradictory and dialectical elements of subjectivity it may be possible to think a concept of the agent" (37). By using Althusser, I can not only analyze the problems of the tutoring sessions but also recognize possible solutions to these problems, because I can conceive of agency alongside resistance.

Herein I will discuss the subjectivities interpellated and resisted through the discourses involved in a set of writing assignments and tutoring sessions that occurred in connection with a course counting for general education credit. Throughout, I deliberately use Althusser's terminology of *interpellation* to emphasize that the student's, tutor's, and faculty's responses to writing are effects of discursive formations. Althusser's insights about ideology and subjectivity are crucial here—and I agree with Smith (1988), who argues that "the concept of interpellation is an indispensable tool for describing the way in which the 'subject' is brought into place by specific ideological and discursive formations" (21). The terms *interpellate and subject position(s)* used throughout the article are reminders that writing and response to writing are effects of ideology's calling (through discourse). This is a very different stance from one that assumes that students have "personal" interests, histories, or psychologies, that stand outside of ideological formations producing discourse and responses to discourse.

UNIVERSITY DISCOURSES, THE WRITING CENTER, AND THE DEPARTMENT OF ENGLISH

As mentioned earlier, the Writing Center regularly works with large numbers of students from a single course, especially when instructors of GE courses feel that their students are not meeting their expectations for writing. When students from courses that are termed GE and tutors from the English department meet in the Writing Center, they are interpellated by many discourses and subjectivities. The Writing Center is at least partially constructed by the discourses of the English department. It is physically housed down the hall from the English department office, located alongside the English department classrooms and faculty offices. The students working in the Writing Center are trained via an English department course, taught by a compositionist from the department, and 90% are English majors or graduate students, with a few students who intend to teach K–12 (kindergarten–high school).

Writing Center tutors by and large define themselves as English majors and are saturated with the values of their English department literary studies. In tutoring, they become engaged in conflicts between the construction of literacy in courses officially designated GE, and the ideas about literacy promoted in literary studies in the department of English. Discussions in the course on tutoring (in which all Writing Center tutors participate) reveal that some of the English department tutors are leery of the textual practices and values of other disciplines. Many would privilege narrative or poetic qualities in texts. They deeply desire all texts to be beautiful and are disdainful of texts and assignments from other departments, and of academic writing in general.

In actual tutoring sessions, then, students and tutors are hailed by multiple and often conflicting subjectivities of the discourses of the English department, the Writing Center, and the discipline of any given course itself. To illustrate, I will discuss a particular tutoring session in which a student worked on an assignment for a GE course in recreation. While the tutor and the student were both frustrated by the session, neither was aware of the complexity of the subjectivities they were being called into as they tried to work together.

DISCOURSES OF THE TUTORING SESSIONS

An instructor from the department of recreation and parks management had called and asked if she could send to the Writing Center some students who were having a very difficult time with the writing assignments for her course. Soon the tutors reported that they were having problems in their sessions with recreation students, especially those dealing with a particular assignment. The tutors complained that the students did not understand the assignments even though the assignments were very explicit about what the students were to write about and how they were to write it. I examined one assignment and could see that it was very detailed, almost algorithmic in its specificity, but even after talking to the tutors I was not sure why they were having problems, so I made arrangements to sit in on a tutoring session.

In the session I observed, a young man came to the Writing Center to get help with a draft of an assignment. The instructor had given him a failing grade and had written on the bottom that he needed to go the Writing Center and get help with revision. The student was Mexican-American and bilingual. He came from a small town near the university, an area heavily populated with migrant agricultural workers. Although he had never worked in the fields himself, his parents labored in the almond and walnut orchards. The tutor was a senior English major who wanted to write a novel and was very excited about Natalie Goldberg's book of free writing exercises called *Wild Mind*.

The assignment that the student had come in to work on asked the students to "[discuss] your personal definition of leisure" and then to "identify two outstanding personal leisure experiences. Describe them, explaining why they were beneficial and memorable for you." The students were to discuss "which of the various theories of leisure can be related to [their] experiences, and finally to conclude by restating [their] personal definition." Attached to the paper was a grading sheet in which the points for the paper were broken down to correspond to each part of the paper.

The student appeared nervous, not looking at me or the tutor as the tutor introduced herself and explained that I was there to help because the recreation assignments were difficult for many students. The student opened the session by telling the tutor that he thought he had accomplished the task called for by the assignment. The tutor asked him to read his paper so he began reading: "Leisure is free time, no work and no school. Time you can choose about." The instructor had given him one point (out of five) for this section and had written "can you explain more" and "compare to the theory in the book" in the margin. The tutor asked the student if he understood the comments, and he said no. Pointing to his definition, he said, "This is leisure; why use the book?" In the same paragraph, following the sentence "time you can choose about," he had written about spending time at his grandmother's house as an "outstanding experience." Then he wrote about his grandmother's death, saying that this experience was not "outstanding." His grandmother's death completely eliminated his ability to spend leisure time with her in her home, he explained. The tutor seemed stymied and asked, "What do you think the teacher is after here?" pointing to the teacher's marginal note, which read "what was your experience?" The student first said, "I don't know." Then he intoned very deliberately, "She wants to know my experience" as if repeating a chant. For the first time he looked up and into the face of the tutor, asking about the teacher's motives: "What does she want? What does she wanna know this stuff for? What does she want me to do here?"

In response, the tutor attempted to explain "what the teacher wants." She said that the teacher didn't mean for him to write about a person; "a person can't be leisure time." The tutor told the student that he needed to write about an activity, a leisure *activity*. The student again stared at the paper. The tutor tried again to explain. She said that the teacher wouldn't accept his grandmother as an outstanding leisure experience. He stared at the tutor, silent for what seemed to be an interminable length of time. Then he changed the subject, asking her questions about when the paper was due and whether the instructor would change his grade if he wrote it again. After the tutor's explanation, he asked in an exasperated tone, "But what do I have to do?" And the tutor answered by quoting from the assignment: "You have to revise the paper so that you give a 'clear statement of your definition of leisure and two outstanding personal leisure experiences' and then finish it with the rest of the assignment." The student replied curtly, "But I already did that."

The tutor tried again to explain what the instructor wanted by pointing at the assignment, reading it and paraphrasing it. She gave examples. She and her fiancé had gone on a picnic recently and seen many wildflowers. That afternoon, she asserted, was an "outstanding leisure experience." The student stared at the paper. At one point he reasserted compliance with the assignment: "But I did that" became his litany. Then, he asked to take a break and left the Writing Center for a minute or two.

While he was gone, the tutor told me she was going to be "positive" with him. When he returned, the tutor changed her tactics. She said she was tired of trying to convince him to write this "dumb assignment their way." She pointed to the word creative in the assignment instructions and told the student that she believed he was quite creative. She said, "Writing is essentially a creative activity," and then she talked about her own writing goals and her creative aspirations. She said that he could be creative in his response to the assignment. Maybe he could write a *story* about what *activity* he had done at his grandmother's house. In a mocking tone, he said that he didn't have *activities* at his grandmother's.

Then, rather abruptly, the tutor said that she understood the student's point: "Yeah I guess your grandmother could be leisure. I guess I don't know what she [the instructor] wants either. Let's work on fixing the spelling and stuff." The tutoring session continued for another ten minutes with the tutor attempting to get the student to work with her on the errors in the paper. She would ask him where he thought the error was in a sentence. The errors had been coded with the numbers on a handout. He said he didn't know where the error was and the tutor tried to explain. She fixed a few sentences—mostly punctuation and spelling. She walked him to the desk and signed him up for another appointment.

After the session the tutor put her head down on the desk and made a noise of frustration. "I didn't know what to do," she said. "He didn't understand anything about leisure."

DISCOURSES AND SUBJECTIVITIES

All discourse calls its participants to be its subjects. To greater and lesser degrees interlocutors affiliate themselves with ideology (s) and social roles implicit in the discourses in which they participate. In schooling, the demands of discourse are especially obvious. Writing assignments call students to be subjects of schooling —students are to turn assignments in "on time," and do them exactly to the specifications set out by the professor; students are called, in other words, to be subordinate subjects in the discourse of writing assignments. However, writing assignments also call students to be subjects not just of schooling but also of particular disciplines. At best, history assignments ask students to think and write about the world and its events as historians do, for example. Of course, students are not always compliant subjects of these discourses. Students may resist the call to subordinate themselves to schooling. They also may resist the ideology(s) implicit in some assignments or the disciplines they are studying.

While some students regularly experience conflicts with the subjectivities hailed by academic disciplines, the Writing Center tutors reported that many students were troubled by the recreation assignment. The assignment discussed earlier called on the students to identify themselves and their lives with an image of their experience projected from the discourse of recreation; they are asked to become subjects of the discipline of recreation. This is to be expected. But while assignments may be resisted because they were calling students into discursive positions (or subjectivities) that they might not have inhabited prior or that were subordinating, student resistance to the recreation assignment may have been exacerbated by the students' finding the very notion of a *theory* of leisure paradoxical. They tried to resolve this contradiction by attributing nefarious, dominating impulses to the assignment and even the course itself.

This particular assignment was very explicit in its directions about both the form and the content of the students' writing, and this explicitness contributed to some students experiencing the course and the writing assignments as if the discipline of recreation were attempting to actually control their personal lives and subjectivities. The tutors discussed their experiences with this assignment and concluded that most of the recreation students they worked with knew that they were to write themselves as subjects whose lives fit with the textbook's theories of leisure and thus found it ironic that they were also told to "begin your paper by discussing your personal definition of leisure." The writing assignments themselves became the locus of student and tutor *resistance,* not only to the recreation course but also to the power the university and its general education requirements had over their identities. One student was reported as saying that "this assignment goes too far—we have to write not what we think but what we do—that's too far. What I do is not [the professor's] business."

The specific tutoring session described in the last section can be understood as a series of interpellations, often conflicting and contradictory; because neither the tutor nor the student was any interpellation complete or stable. Both student and tutor revised their subject positions ongoingly as the discourse mediated their subjectivities. As the student resisted discursive interpellation, the tutor changed discourses and subject positions accordingly. She moved from Writing Center tutor to budding novelist and reader of literature to undergraduate student. These discourses were not merely effects of the assignment, they were brought about by the relations among discourses as the session progressed. Dialectically, the tutor asserted discursive power and the student resisted. Each discourse was brought into being in conjunction with the other.

Throughout the session, the tutor represents institutional power as the discourse of Writing Centers interpellates her tutor subjectivity. She accepts the position of the good tutor who will, at least tacitly, support a professor's right to give assignments to which students are to respond. The discourse in the tutoring session maintains the professor's authority. The tutor demonstrates that she knows what a good tutor says and does; she is not judgmental about the assignment or the discourse generated as a result of it. Also she does not tell the student what to do, but rather she tries to engage him in making decisions about the text himself.

The student resists her efforts, however. He will not be subordinated to the demands of this assignment. The student's resistance presents itself as a contradiction for the tutor, because her subjection as a tutor is defined in dialectical relation to his as a student. She must change discourses. She continues to be a Writing Center tutor, engaging in working with a student on an assignment, but she acknowledges that she has a life that involves picnics and poems with her fiancée. She maintains her affiliation with the power of the university discourse by taking her own recreation, her picnics with her fiancée, and making them and herself the subject of the assignment. Even though she subordinates herself to the assignment, ironically this position (as a tutor) enables her to continue to assert power over the student position.

This move does not yield a compliant subject either, however. The tutor must gain the student's recognition of, if not engagement in, the discourse to maintain her subject position affiliated with the power and ideology of the university. Her position is dialectically related to his. She finds another discourse that will not sever her links with the university but will nonetheless affiliate her with the student's resistance. She draws on an appropriation of the discourse of the field of creative writing and asserts that the assignment is "dumb" and that [the professors of recreation "want students to write like cookie cutters." She evokes creativity as a subject to be (rather than the organized, ever-so-rational planner of leisure time), and she attempts to convince the student that he should understand the assignment as a call to be creative. At this point in the session, she is no longer aligned with the assignment and its institutional goals, but the student still resists.

Finally, her subject position changed again, in part, because the tutor herself comes to the tutoring session with a history of subject positions as a *student*. In an interview she related that "the only thing he was interested in was getting a better grade and in meeting the revision deadline." As a student, she herself has struggled for good grades and tried to figure out "what the professor wants." This student discourse often declares that the professor has one right answer, which is unknowable, arbitrary, and chimerical. And so the tutor eventually asserts, "I don't know what the professor wants either," in seeming contradiction to the discourse of the past 30 minutes. This subjectivity will momentarily align her with the student until she repositions herself yet again. Affiliating herself (once again) with the university, she implies that she *does* know that the professor wants a clean text and that maybe she can help the student with these demands. This allows her to maintain her affiliation with the discourse of Writing Centers. At least she can tutor him at *something*,

We can readily see that the student is resistant to the assignment, the tutoring session, and all of the tutor's suggestions. He did not even try to enter the discourse of the recreation course. He would not put the assignment or any of its requirements in his own words. When asked what the teacher wanted, he quoted her exact words in a voice mocking the teacher, emphasizing his separation from these words, this assignment, and its demands of him. He did not use words from the textbook or other sources when he did define leisure, and he did not and would not define the things that he did at his grandmother's house as "activities." He even removed himself from the physical context of the discourse by asking to take a break and leaving the Writing Center. When the tutor switches to discussing the punctuation and spelling errors the student has made, she tries to persuade him to write on his paper but he sits with his arms folded and does not touch the paper. She becomes impatient, grabs the paper, and begins writing down the changes herself.

The student has refused to be interpellated by most of the discourses operating in this scene—those of the tutor, the assignment, the recreation course, the textbook, or finally, academic discourse in general. His resistance was in part an effect of the assignment that hails or calls the student to be a theorist of recreation, and it was an effect of the tutor's subjectivities as well. The student was not accustomed to talking about his family's activities in the arena of school. He could not envision the subject called for by the recreation course, and he was suspicious of the motives of the professor and the assignment in which she solicited the details of his grandmother's house where he "hangs out, eating, talking, and watching Spanish TV." Unwittingly, the tutor increased the student's discomfort as she switched discourses, revealing details of her personal life and extolling the virtues of creativity. Initially, he had mocked the assignment discourse and even the professor's response to his draft, but as the tutor tried to entice him into discussing his home and his grandmother, he seemed defenseless. He just stared at her as she talked about her boyfriend, and eventually he got up and left "to take a break in the hall."

The tutor's changing tactics increased the student's resistance. He became more distant and removed from the conversation, not even replying to her direct questions, locking his arms in front of him and pushing his chair back from the table as the session progressed. He was unfamiliar with the English department discourses, which the tutor invoked, and he refused her hailing him as a mock friend with whom she shared her experiences during the weekend. His absolute resistance is not surprising—each tutor move preserved the power hierarchy established at the beginning of the session as well as her affiliations with the university and subordinated him to the assignment.

Undoubtedly, the discourses of which he as a Mexican-American in California, a son of a farm worker, and a grandson of "illegal" immigrants had become a subject had made him deeply suspicious of and cynical about the ideology implicit in the discourse of the assignment. His relations to "free time" were ideological. He said in the very first minutes of the tutoring session that free time means "no work." He comes from a farm worker culture in which "work" (picking and canning) is not remotely related to what one does in one's free time. The relations between work and leisure are ideological and seem to him obvious and natural. "Why use the book?" he asked. Yet the assignment appears to ask him to blur the boundaries, to turn free time into a commodity, into the confusion of means and ends typical of late 20th-century capitalism. No wonder he resists.

WORKING WITH THE CONFLICTS OF DISCOURSES

What to do? This situation with many discourses at play was exceedingly complicated. The tutoring sessions themselves were sites of dialectical contradictions. As student and tutor struggled in identifying with and resisting the sites of institutional power, the conflicts were ideological; yet none of the participants was conscious of the ideological forces at work. This tutoring session and its dialectic whirl could not be fixed by simply providing the tutor with more or different tutoring "strategies." To progress, both the tutor and the student would need to be able to step out of the dialectic of power and resistance evidenced in their discourse. The tutor clearly needed to understand more about the discursive field in which this assignment played a part.

As it was, the tutor's perspective was fairly narrow. She thought that the assignment was at fault because it was too restrictive and didn't allow the student to be creative. However, the problem resided not with the assignment per se; all assignments call students into discourses with which they are more or less familiar. She had no sense of what the faculty's goals were or what they thought about literacy and its uses in GE.

It would have been useful for her to understand just how the faculty thought about literacy, writing assignments, and the relationship of GE courses to the discipline itself. As I realized this need, the project gradually turned from tutor training to Writing Center research, and I interviewed the faculty. Both recreation professors I talked with appeared to believe that the GE writing requirement is good for their students, and they were trying to carry out this responsibility in the best way possible for students to learn and succeed in their course. The professor who had designed and written the assignment discussed earlier told me that writing was used in this GE course to assist student comprehension of the materials, the theories about "how people use free time to make decisions for lifelong learning." The goal of the course was for "students to develop a personal theory of leisure." "It's not a course about should and should not," he said emphatically. But he did want students to be subjects of recreation; he wanted them to "use research and apply the material, the concepts, to their lives." Another professor said that the goal of the class was to develop skills—"to identify problems such as stress." This instructor maintained that writing should enable problem "realization, conclusion, and solution.

Both professors acknowledged that the students had a hard time meeting their expectations. One said that generally the students' understanding of content and their ability to write the assignments went hand and hand. "Mostly when students fail," he said, "they don't answer what was asked; they don't follow the assignment guidelines." He was emphatic about the fact that the assignments were very explicit so as to help students succeed; the assignments told the students exactly what to do, what things to put in their papers and where to put them. He said he really didn't understand why the students didn't follow the guidelines.

Another faculty member thought that many students couldn't "follow a thought" and had "abundant grammar problems." She had told students to use a handbook and had prepared a handout on error: "Some just can't write; they misspell common words and mix up sentences," The assignments require sources, but "asking them to use references overwhelms them. They will stick a reference right in the middle of a paragraph. They don't know how to state their opinion and back it up with references." She said she used to get angry; now she was just frustrated because she's not an English teacher and doesn't know what to do.

She also talked about the difficulties students have with the assignments themselves. She said that for some of them the problem was attitude: "They are just lazy." She said students feel that the "writing requirements in Rec 18 are unfair. Students have the attitude that a class in leisure is supposed to be easy." Because of these problems, she occasionally modified the assignment sequence, abandoning the "personal theory of leisure" paper that had given so many students so much trouble. She has asked instead for her students to write about stress management and fitness, and she said, "I give them more choices in how they write the ethnic activity paper." In reflecting about the assignments in general and the students" specific problems in writing, she rather tentatively ventured that "sometimes I think the directions are too much. Would more freedom change the students' response?"

METHODOLOGY: GOOD TUTORING
AND GOOD RESEARCH

In pondering my response to her questions, I become aware of several dilemmas. My interview with this professor made clear that in much composition research there can be no clear-cut distinctions among the activities of doing research, of writing about research, and of pedagogy—that is, of consciously changing a situation, in this case during and because of the research. I had contacted and interviewed this professor because I wanted to work with the tutors to understand more about what was happening in their tutoring sessions. However, in the process of working with the tutors and interviewing the faculty, I began writing this chapter (first written for a conference). So, when the professor asked me for an opinion about changing the assignment, I was not sure whether I should reply as a researcher, a Writing Center Director, a compositionist consulting informally as in writing across the disciplines, or . . . ? I had not informed the professors that I had begun to write about the recreation assignment problems, and as a result I was uncertain about what role was appropriate in responding to that particular professor's question and whether I should now, suddenly, inform her that I was writing a chapter related to this.

I realized that with each option I had posed for myself, I had (as had the tutor) asserted my power to claim, shape, and define the discourse. Then I began to wonder what this project would have looked like if, from the beginning, I had imagined the faculty, the tutors, and the students to be partners in an investigation about what writing is and what writing could and should be in GE courses. Belatedly I found myself in agreement with Thomas Newkirk (1996), who argues that a classroom-based research project should, in some sense, be undertaken as a collaboration between the researcher and teacher. In particular, I was struck by Newkirk's insight that "the researcher should grant the teacher (and when relevant, her students) the opportunity to respond to interpretations of problematical situations. When, ..., those being studied have access to the researcher's emerging questions and interpretations, there is an opportunity to offer counter interpretations or provide mitigating information" (p.?). For me, the salient word was *emerging*. When this work did evolve into "research," I could not discuss the project and my interpretations with the student and the tutor because the semester had ended and they had left the university. I had tapes of the sessions and notes from conversations with the tutor. I could (and did) tell the professors what I was thinking after the fact, as I was writing about them and their students. But I was uneasy about having formulated questions about their work (e.g. Is this a bad assignment?) and having posed the questions to the professors indirectly (e.g. Are you happy with student response to this assignment?), and about having reached conclusions, even tentative ones, without including my research "subjects" in formulating the conclusions.

There was also the issue of what Newkirk calls the "bad news" about the way the assignments were working for some students. As Newkirk poignantly points out, "Because we present ourselves as completely well-meaning, we find ourselves in moral difficulty when we write bad news in our final rendering. Even though the negative might be balanced by the positive, and even though we have carefully disguised the identity of the person we render, we (and the subject) feel as if a trust has been betrayed" (3). In writing this chapter, I have attempted to mitigate my worries of betraying all parties involved by revising this text with their interests in mind. I have been concerned, for example, about whether the tutor would agree with my interpretation of her actions and whether she would mind my writing about her picnics with her fiancée (my making her private life the subject of composition research, in other words).

Second, I realized that to analyze the tutoring and the research relations themselves, I needed to employ theoretical tools that could account for power relations and dialectics in discourse. In the tutoring we had done at the time, we had tried to mitigate or even ignore completely the dynamics of power, subjectivity, and resistance, to no avail. We could not ignore these issues. While critical theorist Althusser works well to elucidate the impasse reached by the tutor and student and the ways in which the recreation assignment was functioning, his vocabulary is foreign to many in composition and so presents a challenge of deciding how much of his terminology and apparatus to include and how much to translate into other, more familiar terms. In spite of any difficulties Althusser may pose, the insights gleaned from using him are invaluable, and as noted previously, they extend to my work with faculty from other disciplines and the writing of this article.

Having faced these problems in writing this article, I have initiated a broader-based research project involving conversations about writing assignments with many faculty who teach general education courses. My goals and perspectives have changed as I undertake this work—my goal is not to inform them about the power dialectics in their writing assignments, but instead for us to develop a common vocabulary to talk about writing assignments and to share our differing perspectives. I can see how valuable it would be to extend such a project, for students and faculty to hear each other's perspectives on literacy and language with the Writing Center functioning to make this articulation of links possible. These efforts could also result in student awareness of the multiplicities of literacy and its social contexts, and in this light perhaps students would find themselves less often the leery subjects of literacy.

REFERENCES

Althusser, L. (1971). *Lenin and philosophy*. New York: Monthly Review Press.

Newkirk, T. (1996). Seduction and betrayal in qualitative research. In P Mortensen & G. E. Kirsch (Eds.), *Ethics and representation in qualitative studies of literacy* (pp. 3–16). Urbana, IL: NCTE.

Smith, P. (1988). *Discerning the subject*. Minneapolis: University of Minnesota Press.

Chapter 14

Why Feminists Make Better Tutors: Gender and Disciplinary Expertise in a Curriculum-Based Tutoring Program

Jean Marie Lutes
Manhattan College

Experiment to me
Is every one I meet ...

> —Emily Dickinson, #1073

I tend to be really skeptical about research and how it relates to reality.

> —Anita, undergraduate writing fellow, interview, spring 1999

This chapter considers the Undergraduate Writing Fellows Program, a curriculum-based peer tutoring initiative at the University of Wisconsin, as an "experiment" in crossings: crossing disciplines, crossing lines between generalist and discipline-specific tutoring, and, most critically, crossing feminist and writing center pedagogies. Although the program discussed here was not designed specifically to promote analysis of gender, it *was* intended to encourage undergraduates to see themselves as active participants in an academic community devoted to critical inquiry of all types. As such, it offers an opportunity to examine what happens when

235

student tutors enter into unusual positions of intellectual authority, when they obtain an "insider's" view of what professors want in specific assignments and then collaborate with student writers to help them complete assignments more effectively. Unlike tutors who work in a writing center, the writing fellows must mediate directly between student writers and the professors who (quite literally) embody disciplinary knowledge in the classroom. Thus, I turned to the writing fellows themselves to provide the relation whose existence Anita is so quick to doubt — the link between my research and their reality, and, less obviously, the link between *my* reality (what I thought was true about the program) and *their* research (what they reported to be true in their written analyses of tutoring).

A familiar question drives this study: How can educators create opportunities for transformation within the institutional structures of the university? Because my research subject was a tutoring program I helped to design and implement,[1] this question was especially acute for me. What follows, then, is as much an act of retrospection as a research project, incorporating my memories of the program's inception with a study of its current shape. This "look back" evolved not only from the predictable recognition that everything did not work out as I had expected, but also from my desire to integrate my roles as feminist literary critic, writing teacher, and administrator. If, as feminists have convincingly demonstrated, disciplinary knowledge within academic institutions is often perceived in gendered terms, how do students who tutor across disciplines negotiate those terms? Examining how gender is embedded in the Writing fellows' cross-disciplinary tutoring strategies, I found that a better understanding of feminist ways of knowing may, in fact, facilitate successful tutoring across disciplines. In other words, the gendered definitions of knowledge that surface in cross-disciplinary tutoring encounters can interfere with the collaborative model most writing centers advocate.

Curriculum-based tutoring programs like the writing fellows initiative are inevitably caught between contradictory impulses: while they preach active, collaborative learning, they also promise to socialize students into disciplinary ways of knowing that are rarely up for negotiation. Yet I saw the Fellows as promising research subjects in part because I imagined that their unique position would give them special incentive to reflect critically on writing practices in different disciplines. Given the program's interdisciplinary nature and the supportive atmosphere it sought to cultivate, I expected that critical reflections would emerge from the undergraduate tutors' attempts to help their peers succeed in different disciplines—and from their empathy for their peers' struggles. What I found reinforced my belief in the potential for such

---

[1]Initially, the Writing Center director at UW—Madison hired me as a project assistant to help research and propose the program. When we secured funding for a pilot program, I served as assistant director for its first year.

reflection and students' ability to achieve it. However, the writing fellows' discussions of their own tutoring also suggested that they lacked a framework for negotiating disciplinary differences from a critical perspective and, not surprisingly, that they tended to reproduce gendered notions about disciplinary knowledge. If they did take a more critical approach to knowledge production, that approach was grounded in experiences outside the program itself—such as having taken Women's Studies courses.

Several composition scholars have noted similarities in the transformative goals of composition programs and women's studies, gay and lesbian studies, ethnic studies, and labor studies. Building on that observation, feminist analyses have suggested that composition programs are less radical than they could—and should—be.[2] Writing Across the Curriculum (WAC) programs have been especially susceptible to this charge. As Harriet Malinowitz (1998) observes, WAC is capable of "subverting faculty and institutional cultures" (293) by promoting cross-disciplinary exchange and challenging traditional hierarchies between and among faculty and students. Malinowitz insists, however, that WAC programs can be transformative only when they take risks akin to those taken by other nontraditional programs such as Women's Studies.[3]

In another call for risk-taking, Nancy Grimm (1996) argues that writing centers can make academic institutions more democratic, but only if writing center workers see themselves as part of "knowledge-producing units" (539) and "move out of the awkward triangulation between student and teacher, where they are expected not to change what students learn but to get students to conform to institutional expectations and values" (530). Only then, Grimm suggests, will writing centers fulfill their liberatory potential, by becoming places "where knowledge about the conflicts among literacies can be generated and shared" (530). To skeptics who ask if it is fair to expect the undergraduates who often staff writing centers to meet such

---

[2]To cite just a few examples of such critiques: Jarratt (1991) urges teachers of writing to develop "a pedagogy designed to confront and explore the uneven power relations" that result from gender, race, and class differences (115). Gunner (1993) calls for a restructuring of the values of the university so that composition, with its emphasis on nurturing and social consciousness, is on the top. Bizzell (1998) argues that educators need to make "ideological avowals" that articulate an alternative vision, rather than continuing the "pedagogical bad faith" of pretending, for example, that we are just teaching our students about differences (385). Reynolds (1998) makes a related argument when she rejects the "service-course ideology," suggesting instead that composition programs should offer students "more and greater means of resistance" to traditional genres, and, ultimately, "rethink radically the forms of writing we find acceptable" (77).

[3]Malinowitz (1998) offers a thoughtful critique of WAC's liberatory potential, comparing the more conventional aims of writing-in-the-disciplines advocates and with the more politically radical goals of the writing-to-learn approach. Bazerman (1992) defends the transformative potential of writing-in-the disciplines, while Kirscht, Levine, and Reiff. (1994) argue that both subsets of WAC offer opportunities for positive change. For an excessively optimistic assessment of WAC's impact on the academy, see Fulwiler (1991).

ambitious goals, Grimm argues that students are often eager and capable of taking up such tasks, given the opportunity: "The naïve and childlike subjectivity we have constructed for them is the chief barrier to their participation in theoretical discussions and institutional change" (546).

The writing fellows program, as I understood it, seemed capable of lifting that barrier and giving students just the kind of opportunity Grimm imagines. A brief outline should illustrate why. Adapting our program from the model developed at Brown University,[4] we devised a rigorous selection and training process for the undergraduate tutors, called Writing Fellows. A primary goal is to foster an interdisciplinary community of undergraduates who can explore writing as an object of intellectual inquiry while helping their peers achieve success as writers. To that end, the training seminar requires extensive self-reflexive writing assignments; the first major paper is a literacy autobiography.[5] Typically, the reading list includes a variety of recent scholarly articles on collaborative learning, revision processes, the politics of peer tutoring, and strategies for effective commenting and conferencing.[6]

Each writing fellow, under the guidance of a professor who has chosen to participate, works closely with 15 to 20 students enrolled in a writing-intensive course. After consulting with the professor about the expectations and goals for specific assignments, the fellows write comments on drafts and hold conferences with students to discuss how to improve papers before they are submitted to the professor for a grade. (All students enrolled in the course, *not* just those identified as in need of extra assistance, must participate. Thus, the fellows reach out beyond the self-selected students who visit the writing center.) The program is cross-disciplinary; fellows are recruited from a wide range of majors and assigned to courses in a variety of disciplines. While the program sends fellows directly into the "awkward triangulation between student and teacher" that Grimm wants writing center workers to escape, it also seeks to reconfigure that space. Through individual and group sessions, faculty participants are coached about how to design appropriate assignments and how to work effectively

---

[4]See Haring-Smith (1992) and Soven (1993)

[5]See Fox (1999), especially 22-36, for details on how literacy autobiographies can promote critical reflection on academic writing practices in a first-year composition course. Unfortunately, the many needs served by the Writing fellows seminar (introducing students to a variety of tutoring strategies and giving them practice in conferencing and commenting, to name just two) preclude undertaking the semester-long study of academic literacy that Fox describes. However, the Writing fellows' research paper options include investigating writing in a particular discipline—another one of the methods that Fox advocates to accomplish the paradoxical goal of preparing students to succeed in the academy while also enabling a re-evaluation of academic standards for success.

[6]For the semester of my study, for example, the assigned reading included K.A. Bruffee's "Peer Tutoring and the Conversation of Mankind,"(1984). M. Harris' "Talking in the Middle: Why Writers Need Writing Tutors" (1995) N. Sommers' "Responding to Student Writing" and P. Lassner's The Politics of Peer Tutoring" (1987).

with writing fellows (and, by extension, how to work effectively with student writers in general). Faculty also receive a handbook with detailed guidelines about the program's philosophy and the fellows' role as peer tutors. At the same time, the fellows are encouraged to see themselves not simply as faculty helpers, but as advocates and negotiators on behalf of their peers and their own developing philosophies about writing.

As we designed and implemented the fellows program, we developed ambitious goals—and equally ambitious rhetoric—for it. The publicity and recruitment brochure explains that the program "places undergraduates in positions of intellectual leadership and forges teaching partnerships between professors and students." It also promises that writing fellows "join a diverse group committed to integrating intellectual inquiry with service to the university; they take on leadership roles while honing their own skills as readers and writers." In planning meetings, brainstorming sessions, and pep talks, the rhetoric that my colleagues and I adopted was sometimes even grander: we spoke of "changing the culture" of the university, empowering undergraduates, challenging traditional modes of education and re-aligning traditional axes of power. I believed then (and still do) that because of the new space it creates for undergraduate peer tutors within the institutional system, the fellows program creates unique opportunities for transformation and empowerment in a university setting that is too often alienating to many different kinds of students.

But as I sought to bring my interests in feminist pedagogy and composition together through an analysis of the fellows' voices, I was confronted with something that should have been obvious from the beginning: that what I viewed as the program's source of subversive power must also be understood as a conservative force. To begin with, the fellows themselves are successful students, so they appear to have little to gain by challenging a system that is already rewarding them. And the program pairs fellows with faculty whose own work is shaped by disciplinary conventions and who are seeking assistance in teaching those conventions. By inserting peer tutors into the institutional system, by linking fellows directly to professors teaching specific courses, the program stakes its success on maintaining some of the very disciplinary boundaries I once imagined it might challenge. It also subjects fellows to faculty oversight in a way that "regular" writing center tutors rarely face, since when grading time arrives, the professors receive not only the revised papers from their students, but also the earlier drafts with the fellows' comments. Thus the program complicates the peer relationship between fellows and students; when fellows comment on drafts, they inevitably write not only for their immediate audience (the student writers), but also for their future audience (the professor).

In short, the experiences of the writing fellows highlight a question with which writing centers have always had to grapple: How can we sustain and promote constructive critique of writing practices in colleges and universities, while still serving the needs of students and faculty within those institutions? To ask the question in this way, however, is to assume that cultivating a critical approach to writing practices *necessarily* conflicts with the goal of helping the student who is struggling to master disciplinary conventions required by a particular paper assignment. Without minimizing the potential for such conflict, I want to challenge its universality. Ultimately, my analysis suggests that *not* encouraging peer writing tutors to evaluate how disciplinary boundaries shape knowledge—and, more precisely, how gender influences their perceptions of disciplinary differences—shortchanges both the peer tutors and the students they are trying so earnestly to help. If we do not want our students to become cross-disciplinary tourists, visiting new fields of knowledge without engaging them on a critical level, we must provide them with better travel guides, by making them critical readers not only of student drafts but of gender and disciplinary conventions as well.

IN SEARCH OF FEMINIST KNOWLEDGE: MULTIPLE PERSPECTIVES ON EXPERIENCE

The reflections that follow draw on four primary sources: my experience in helping to create and implement the program and my many informal conversations with the writing fellows; papers written by the fellows in their training seminar; student evaluations of the fellows; and, finally, follow-up phone interviews with fellows whose experience in crossing disciplines made them stand out in some way, either because they faced special challenges or because they came from disciplinary backgrounds that were underrepresented in the program as a whole. The first data source (my personal experience) obviously stems from the time I was involved directly in the tutoring program. However, the written assignments from the training seminar were collected after I was no longer physically present or directly involved, and the follow-up interviews were conducted long distance. Thus, I approached the written assignments and interviews with something closer to an outsider's perspective. Nevertheless, despite that distance, I communicated frequently with the current administrators of the program, and I presented an early version of this chapter as part of a conference panel comprised of writing fellows. Given my continuing connection to the program and its students, my perspective is closer to the teacher-researcher model than not.[7] The results—based on my experience in a single university setting over a limited period of time (2 years' close association with the program and 10 months' observing it from a distance)—are suggestive rather than conclusive; I offer them in the hope of pinpointing issues that warrant closer study.

---

[7]See Ray (1992) for an excellent discussion of how teacher-research challenges the positivist paradigm.

Because poststructuralist feminist scholarship shaped this inquiry in form and content, a brief discussion of this critical backdrop anchors the discussion that follows. My first assumption, simply put, is that gender matters in the world of the peer writing tutor. Gender influences not only how tutors and tutees interact, but also their understanding of what constitutes an academic discipline and what it means to cross disciplines as a writing tutor. The rich outpouring of feminist research in composition studies has gone far toward illuminating the many ways that gender influences writing center work, from working conditions within a feminized profession to interactions between tutors and writers.[8] Equally important, feminist scholars have reevaluated how "research" is defined.[9] In her book on principles of feminist research, Gesa E. Kirsch (1999) carefully explains her definition of "better research":

> When I speak about better research, I want to be clear that I am not suggesting that we aim at discovering singular truths, or that we describe these truths in a singular voice. Instead, we should attempt to reveal, as much as possible, the conflicting points of view emergent in our data. This might include information from multiple perspectives that makes us feel uncomfortable, that portrays realities we may dislike, or that reveals our fears or biases. (13-14)

I sought to meet at least some of Kirsch's standards in this study, by highlighting the conflicting points of view emergent in the writing fellows' voices. Because of my commitment to—even my fondness for—the program and the students who constitute my object of inquiry, I had to negotiate between my desire to critically evaluate the program and my desire to offer evidence of its many triumphs. My own subjectivity as researcher, then, has been conflicted throughout, shaped by my conviction in the writing fellows' potential as agents of change, my sensitivity to the often-delicate institutional position of new writing programs, and my lingering reluctance to criticize my own work and that of my colleagues.

While this conflicted subjectivity made it more difficult, at times, to draw conclusions (especially negative ones) based on my findings, it also enriched my study by forcing me to consider implications of my arguments more seriously than I would have in other circumstances. Knowing that newly selected writing fellows may read these words some day in a future training seminar, I have tried to hold myself accountable not only to the

---

[8]See, for example, Enos' study of women in the profession (1996) and Dixon's analysis of a young man and young woman learning to write successfully within the academy (1997). For a brief critical survey of feminism's impact on composition, see Ritchie and Boardman (1999) Flynn (1995).

[9]See, for example, Sullivan (1992) and Flynn (1991). Flynn's suggestion that feminist composition research should "encourage connectedness between researcher and subject and that invite transformation of the subject rather than detached analysis" (150) is especially relevant to my study.

professional voices of composition scholars, but also to the voices of the many talented and dedicated undergraduates who choose to be tutors. Achieving a detached, "objective" perspective as a researcher was neither possible nor desirable in this project. As Kirsch's definition of "better research" quoted previously suggests, feminists have sought to assert themselves as authentic producers of knowledge while revealing the limitations of *any* singular truth and refusing to claim a subject position that transcends socially constructed boundaries. This principle has shaped critical approaches to "experience" as a category of analysis. Laura Brady (1998) articulates that approach succintly when she writes, "Personal experience is one interpretation of an event, shaped by a subject's positioning and type of agency; it should invite discussion and analysis of the conditions that construct both the event and the narrative" (40).

REACHING OUT ACROSS DISCIPLINES:
GENDERED ASSUMPTIONS IN ACTION

To launch an analysis of experience-as-interpretation such as Brady suggests, I consider the writing fellows' reports of their own experiences, using a combination of interviews and papers that they wrote at the conclusion of a required seminar on tutoring writing across the curriculum.[10] In the final paper, the central task, according to the seminar assignment sheet, was the following: "Drawing from your experience fellowing and from some course readings, write a five-to-six page paper in which you answer these questions: How would you describe yourself as a writing tutor? What are your most important goals as you fellow? And what strategies do you use to achieve these goals? Why these goals and strategies?"

The resulting essays are, in an intellectual sense, the culmination of each student's first semester as a tutor. The assignment asked "What kind of tutor are you?" and then required the students to answer this question by integrating their own experiences with theoretical models. The resulting papers, of course, cannot be read as transparent or unmediated proof of what kinds of tutors the fellows had become; as a graded assignment with a specific context and parameters, each paper inevitably reflected the writer's perception of the course instructor's "ideal tutor." This is not to say that the fellows' essays are inauthentic. Quite the opposite—they are frequently heartfelt, searching, and even confessional. However, they demand to be read as constructions of subjectivity, or, more precisely, constructions of self-as-writing fellow within a specific institutional structure. As Giroux and Freire (1988) have noted, the school experiences that constitute political identities and subjectivities are "always contradictory and represent an

---

[10]As noted earlier, I collected these essays long distance; I did not teach the seminar for which they were written.

ongoing struggle between social forms that limit and enable individual capacities" (x). The writing fellows' reports of their experience represent that ongoing struggle.

On first reading, the "What kind of tutor are you?" essays did not appear to have much to say about gender *or* about the construction of disciplinary knowledge, much less about any relationship between the two. The assignment did not ask the students (nine women and five men) to highlight gender as an issue, and none of them did.[11] In addition, very few essays mentioned field-specific conventions or even referred to the actual content of student drafts at all. However, in the rare moments when the writing fellows chose to mention course content or disciplinary conventions as a formative factor in their tutoring styles, gender was always *also* identified as a critical issue. This convergence illustrates the gendered assumptions that operate, usually unacknowledged and unnamed, within conceptions of different disciplines, shaping not only how students perceive field-specific knowledge but also how writing tutors reach out to students across disciplines.

Jill, a junior majoring in English Education,[12] deals more directly than any other writing fellow with the problem of tutoring students from different disciplines. Her essay stands alone in recognizing, in an explicit way, fundamental differences in ways of producing knowledge. It also contains an exchange that poses a radical challenge to the peer tutoring program itself—the kind of challenge that I had imagined I might see more of in the Fellows' essays. In this exchange, Jill is forced to defend her decision to be a peer tutor when a friend accuses her of helping an oppressive academy to stifle students' creative voices. She quotes this friend directly in her essay: "You're a sell out, and worse, you are going to be shoving this stuff down other people's throats, encouraging them to look at writing the same way you do, the same way your professors do!" When Jill defends her role as a peer tutor, she takes a traditional approach, insisting that she will foster her peers' creativity by giving them a expanded repertoire of writing strategies: "The more a person knows about the standards of writing ... the more creative freedom he or she possesses." Yet Jill fails to address her friend's more fundamental challenge: *does* she look at writing the same way her professors do? If she says she does, then she

---

[11]In this particular semester, the seminar reading list included two feminist essays, a selection from Rubin (1993) and a chapter on gender and conferencing in Black (1998). Neither essay discussed gendered notions of disciplinary knowledge in any detail. Only one essay named an explicitly gendered tutoring strategy: In it, a male writing fellow argued that Rubin's "maternal paradigm" best described his tutoring role, which centered on developing "personal relationships" with his tutees. The essays uniformly used gender-inclusive language—even to the point of grammatical error: a singular student's paper was often called "their."

[12]The names of the writing fellows have been changed, as have the names of students who appear in their essays.

must explain and defend the professorial approach. If she says she doesn't, then she must explain why she thinks it's worthwhile to help her peers to please those professors. Jill, understandably perhaps, avoids either task.

Meanwhile, the deeper issue behind the challenge—why *do* professors write the way they do?—remains unarticulated. Jill's failure to engage this question seriously may suggest that she simply used her obstreperous friend as a straw man (the paper identifies him as male). Yet, especially given the absence of such challenges in the other tutors' essays, Jill's choice to raise this issue at all struck me as impressive: She recognized the political implications of peer tutoring more directly than anyone else. By far the most common anxiety the writing fellows mentioned in their papers was fear about living up to the "ideal tutor" described in their composition studies readings—*not* concern about the possibility that they had become complicit in a system that discouraged resistant modes of writing and enforced unnecessarily rigid conventions. Thus, Jill's willingness to include such a harsh judgment of peer tutoring in her essay can be read as a promising sign of a developing critical awareness.

This critical awareness, however, dropped out of Jill's discussion of her own tutoring work. Like the other tutors, Jill accepts the task of teaching a particular discursive practice and does not question that practice in a substantive way. At the same time, because Jill characterizes academic majors in concrete terms, she lays bare some gendered assumptions that could hamper any peer tutoring (curriculum-based or not). Despite Jill's incipient critique of institutional ways of knowing, elsewhere in her essay I found evidence suggesting that her tutoring had suffered because of unarticulated assumptions about gender and disciplinary differences. Indeed, Jill's paper contained the most aggressively gendered portrayals of tutoring in this group of papers, particularly as she describes how she adapted her tutoring strategies to work with two students majoring in different fields. These descriptions attest to her creativity and commitment, but they also reflect the blindnesses that result when disciplinary knowledge is viewed—uncritically—through a gendered lens.

Jill was assigned to a literature class in which students had to write analytical essays with thesis statements, so Jill focused primarily on helping students develop and support strong statements of argument. She asked the students to answer seven questions (via e-mail) to help her understand and respond to their learning styles.[13] To demonstrate how her learning style survey worked, she discusses two students in depth. Her first example

---

[13]The questions, according to Jill's paper, were: "What's your major, and if there is a reason, why did you choose it? Do you have any extracurricular activities? Do you see yourself as a good reader? Do you see yourself as good at math or science? Do you see yourself as a good listener? Do you write lists, or do you write things on tiny slips of paper all over the place yet somehow manage to keep track of them? Do you use a daily planner? What is/was your favorite class taken either here or at a different school?"

is Eliza, who wrote back "saying she was a Com Arts [Communication Arts] major, who loved chatting over email, saw herself as a good reader, average at math and science, and an excellent listener." She "doesn't write lists but uses a daily planner" and her favorite class was "Com Arts 370, Conflict Resolution." Jill concludes that Eliza likes to talk things through, and she adapts her tutoring strategy to accommodate Eliza's learning style by listening, affirming, and frequently asking content questions:

> In conference I realized she really didn't know what she was arguing. . . . She talked through the main points she wanted to argue while I wrote them down. When she was finished, I took the list she had made and turned it into an example thesis, modeling how one point followed the other . . . we worked through another example thesis statement using the same strategy. . . . Finally, Eliza took the two examples . . . and worked them into a thesis statement that was effective, deep, and expressed exactly what she wanted to say. . . . Through that dialogue Eliza was able to articulate her thought process and prove to herself she now understood a new way of putting a thesis together. Eliza first imitated the model I gave her, then applied the model in a new, creative way.

Although one can't help suspecting that this conference is a little too neatly wrapped up, the description suggests that Jill worked successfully with Eliza.

The second student Jill describes responded to her learning style survey very differently. Charlie, Jill tells us, was a mechanical engineering major who "did not feel he read well, thought his strength was in math and science, wrote things down in very exact lists, and chose calculus as his favorite class." Charlie's response lead Jill to several conclusions about his field and his ways of thinking: "Right away, I surmised, Charlie liked structure, Charlie understood structure. His favorite class being calculus, I also assumed he liked to solve things in linear formulas and functions, unlike Eliza's roundabout way of coming to a conclusion. For Charlie, my approach became more directive than with Eliza; I encouraged Charlie to imitate me in more ways than I did with Eliza. That is what Charlie is used to, seeing how a problem is solved, then imitating the process over and over." Jill mistakenly lumps all math and scientific thinking into one mode of follow-the-formula, and adapts her tutoring accordingly, by giving Charlie "formulas" to organize his paper.

Although Jill recounts a successful conference with Charlie, her own description of that conference is telling. It suggests that her comfort with Eliza's "roundabout" way of thinking led to a successful conference, while her (unspoken) discomfort with Charlie's "linear" way of thinking did not. In the conference narrative quoted earlier, Eliza occupies the subject position in many of Jill's sentences: Eliza *takes, works, writes, articulates,* and *applies.* Charlie, in contrast, appears only as the recipient of advice (as the direct object but never the subject) in the conference description: "I gave Charlie word choices," "I rerouted a sentence or two," "I gave him a couple formulas;" "I gave him examples." In Jill's well-intentioned attempt to adapt to Charlie's way of thinking, she appears to have silenced him entirely. This may not be true; Charlie may have spoken frequently. But Jill does not represent him as an active conference participant.

The disciplinary differences that separate Eliza and Charlie in Jill's account are gendered in distressing ways. Eliza is portrayed as a stereotypically female communicator and thinker: she likes to chat, she values negotiation, she reasons in a nonlinear ("roundabout") way, and she sees herself as only "average" at math and science. Charlie, on the other hand, appears as the masculinized counterpoint to Eliza: He excels at math and science, he likes crisp and predictable ways of thinking, and he seems to crave "structure" and "formulas." That Jill reproduces unexamined notions about gender seems almost to go without saying here. Certainly, she deserves credit for seeking to understand and minister to what she perceived as Charlie's differences. However, her attempts to do so were hindered, in part, by the fault lines of gender that run unexamined beneath her conference descriptions. What Jill describes as disciplinary differences are, in fact, determined as much by gender as by academic field.

Jill's essay shows the persistence of stereotyped notions of male/female ways of thinking and supports the work of composition scholars who have argued that practicing an ethic of collaboration is not necessarily liberatory.[14] Equally important, Jill's essay demonstrates that gendered assumptions about disciplinary differences—particularly in the sciences—can interfere with admirable attempts to move beyond the comfortably narrow and familiar. Without a critical awareness of how knowledge is produced and an appreciation for the conflicts *within* fields (not just between them), student tutors' assumptions about disciplines—their own and others'—can inhibit their tutoring.

The story of Charlie's apparent silencing indicates how closely intertwined ideas about gender and field-specific ways of knowing can become. When challenged to engage peers who may have very different ways of thinking, tutors may compensate for their unfamiliarity by falling back on all-too-familiar assumptions and stereotypes. Advocating a collaborative approach is not enough; collaboration is only available to the student the tutor perceives as able to collaborate. Jill apparently assumes that Charlie will not participate in a collaborative exchange, so she goes out of her way to insure that he doesn't have to. Perhaps Jill incorrectly assumes that mathematical and scientific thinking is hostile to collaboration; perhaps she feels too alienated from Charlie's perspective to create

---

[14]In an important critique of feminists' tendency to assume that collaborative learning is politically transformative, Ashton-Jones (1995) points out that supporters of collaborative models have underestimated the gender hierarchies involved in acts of communication. Citing several studies of communication between the sexes, Ashton-Jones demonstrates that collaborative groups often reproduce the very gender structures that feminist educators hope to challenge.

opportunities for his voice to be heard. Whatever the reason, her conference descriptions suggest that a critical vocabulary about gender may have enabled Jill to evaluate her own tutoring strategies more effectively.

By identifying and analyzing stories such as Jill's, student tutors can expand their repertoires to accommodate a wider range of writers across disciplines. Although the writing fellows training seminar promotes critical self-reflection already, it could do more to encourage students to reconsider their own tutoring practices using gender as a critical category. Creating opportunities for such analysis outside the necessarily evaluative structure of a formal essay, through informal small-group discussions in class or perhaps even through informal sharing of journal entries among peers, could promote authentic self-questioning and yield provocative results. The singularity of Jill's discussion (Jill's was one of very few essays that addressed discipline-specific ways of knowing *at all*) indicates that analyzing disciplinary knowledge was far from a priority for the student tutors. Yet Jill's own tutoring descriptions also suggest that perhaps it should be a priority—that such analysis does not simply supplement effective tutoring, but enables it in the first place.

INSIDE WOMEN'S STUDIES:
COLLABORATION IN A SCIENCE COURSE

In the conference described previously, Jill assumes that Charlie the engineering major would not (or could not) engage in the same form of collaborative exchange as Eliza the communication arts major. This case illustrates how profoundly a conference can be shaped by a tutor's assessment of a peer's attitude toward collaboration. That attitude—and the tutor's assessment of it—is influenced by a variety of factors, including the way a course is set up, remarks made by professors in class, and prevailing attitudes toward collaboration in specific fields or departments. The experiences of two writing fellows assigned to a Women's Studies course on biology and gender offer a more in-depth look at how a feminist emphasis on collaboration can shape the self-perceptions and strategies of student tutors. When I say "feminist emphasis on collaboration," I mean to suggest a model of collaboration that takes a self-conscious approach to differences among collaborators. As the case discussed earlier demonstrated, collaborative efforts do not necessarily achieve feminist goals. Given the many studies showing that gender inequalities persist in mixed-gender communications,[15] I suspect that some of the successes I discuss below can be attributed to the same-sex nature of the collaborations; both the writing fellows and all of the students were female. Without suggesting that such success is easy to achieve, I want to detail the perspectives of these writing fellows—who worked with student writers in a

---

[15]See Ashton-Jones (1995).

challenging, even intimidating, course—to highlight the potential for productive interaction between Women's Studies and WAC programs.

In the "What Kind of Tutor Are You?" essays, only one writing fellow claimed that her disciplinary specialty had directly influenced her tutoring strategies and philosophy. Anita—a junior Women's Studies and social work major assigned to a Women's Studies course taught by a botany professor—identified herself as part of the disciplinary community of Women's Studies and used that identification to define her role. "Being a peer tutor in my own discipline," she wrote, allowed her to develop successful collaborative relationships with her peers. "Given what I have experienced from professors and TAs [teaching assistants] within the Women's Studies program, instruction that takes a non-directive approach is usually the most effective in getting Women's Studies students to learn." When I asked Anita to elaborate on this connection in a follow-up interview, she stressed two aspects of Women's Studies that helped her succeed as a writing fellow: an ethic of collaboration and a skepticism toward established authorities.

> The conversations I seemed to have with women were able to mirror the type of conversations they have in class, the type of language used, the way ideas are presented. It's a whole dialogue that goes on within a Women's Studies classroom that's a little different than other classrooms. Women's Studies as a discipline comes from the idea that being feminist means being collaborative. To me anyway, to be feminist you're supposed to be engaging in a dialogue, not directing people. . . . I feel like when I'm in a writing conference, I want to make it clear that I'm not trying to be an expert. . . . I see myself as someone who has more knowledge and practice. . . . as opposed to being an expert.

Anita finds that her experiences in her Women's Studies major reinforce and in fact dovetail nicely with the collaborative model that is so central to writing fellows training. Her resistance to the term *expert* is, in many ways, a statement of the party line for the peer writing tutor, who does not share the institutional authority of a professor or teaching assistant, and must find less "top-down" ways to discuss writing with students. Yet Anita's resistance to the "expert" stems not just from her desire to connect with student writers as a peer, but also from her identity as a feminist, and from her own understanding of "feminist knowledge." Her resistance to the expert model, then, is both a tutoring strategy and an acquired skepticism, learned through her Women's Studies major. It suggests that for her, being a writing fellow has helped to create a space of self-reflection, intellectual authority, and critical distance from at least some academic forms of authority. By her own account, this approach served Anita well in a difficult tutoring situation, since many of the students were intimidated by the scientific subject matter of the course itself: "Very few had ever taken a 'real' science class like chemistry or genetics or astronomy. They were fearful going into it, like, 'I haven't done this since high school' . . . 'I've gotten out of it this far.'" For Anita, using mostly nondirective tutoring strategies—asking questions, listening, encouraging her peers to set the agenda for conferences—integrated the theory and practice of *both* Women's Studies and the writing fellows program.

The student evaluations of Anita's performance affirm her success.[16] Asked to rate the helpfulness of their interactions with their writing fellow on a scale of 1 ("not helpful at all") to 5 ("extremely helpful"), the 17 students Anita tutored in the biology and gender course gave her an average of 3.4, placing her somewhere between "helpful" and "very helpful." This is an especially strong rating, given that the students in this course were juniors and seniors, who typically give the writing fellows lower "helpfulness" scores than first- and second-year students. In response to the question, "What, in particular, did you find especially helpful about the conferences?" many wrote comments that valued Anita's collaborative ethic, such as "Engaging in a dialogue about my writing helped clarify things," and "It was a way for me to 'talk out' my next step, which gave me an even clearer picture of what I needed to do." Such remarks, in valuing "talk" and the process of working out ideas with a sympathetic listener, echo Anita's perception of the conferences.

Of course, Anita has wholeheartedly embraced at least one form of academic authority: Women's Studies. Indeed, one might argue that Anita's tutoring assignment has not required her to do much "crossing" of disciplines at all; after all, she's a Women's Studies major working with students in a Women's Studies course. It would be misleading to romanticize Anita's feminist version of being a writing fellow; she is not a radical on the academic fringes, reshaping knowledge through sweeping changes. Rather, she is a student of an interdisciplinary field that is defined by collective endeavor. Because Women's Studies seeks to operate within the academy while also resisting some traditional academic hierarchies, it values and even nurtures such resistance in its students.

But how would a writing fellow without an interdisciplinary Women's Studies orientation fare in the same situation? The experience of Anita's tutoring partner, the other writing fellow assigned to the biology and gender course, suggests that the Women's Studies context was supportive even for a tutor without a feminist background. Helen, a senior English and journalism major who had never taken a Women's Studies course, said in an interview that she found her task to be "tricky" on several levels: "I was working with students who weren't familiar with science, and I myself am not very familiar with science overall. . . . The majority of the students were social science and humanities majors, so this was really difficult for them. . . .

---

[16]The two-page evaluation forms—distributed each semester to students in every course that is assigned writing fellows—are completed anonymously and returned to the writing fellows program by course professors.

I was operating out of discipline, and they were operating out of discipline."
While Helen may have agreed in principle with Anita's rejection of the
"expert" label, in this particular case she felt so far from *expert* that she
didn't need to spend any time rejecting such authority.

Given her disorienting sense of being "out of discipline," Helen paid even
more attention than usual to the professor's expectations for assignments.
When one assignment required critical analysis of a scientific argument, Helen
said many students critiqued the argument in sociopolitical terms, rather than
grappling with the scientific concepts involved as the professor wanted them to
do. "What they were supposed to do with this assignment was to show how one
writer's argument wasn't scientifically valid. The teacher didn't want
political-type reasoning." In this case, Helen had to find a way to shift students'
analyses away from the "political-type reasoning" that they presumably had
grown accustomed to using in other (non-science) Women's Studies courses.[17]
To negotiate between her own uncertainties and her realization that many
students needed to substantially revise their first drafts, Helen resorted to a
more directive version of the let-them-talk strategy: "I learned a lot about how
you can help people expand on their arguments, about talking things through.
One of the tactics I tried to use was just to get people to talk about it, and when
they said something close to what I thought [the professor] wanted, I'd say,
'Oh, say more about that.'" While this tactic reveals the controlling force of the
professor's goals even in the professor's absence, it also reflects a necessary
compromise between enabling student writers to develop individual voices
and helping them to meet the demands of particular assignments. And it
shows that Helen, like Anita, successfully defined a role for herself as a
collaborator without occupying a position of expert authority.[18]

Helen and Anita received equally positive evaluations from their
peers.[19] When asked to explain what they found especially helpful about
conferences, Helen's peers wrote similar comments to Anita's; they found
value in "talking" with her about writing.[20] Not surprisingly, Helen's lack of
disciplinary-specific knowledge did come up in the evaluations. In Helen's
case, five students reported that more knowledge of the subject matter

---

[17]Helen's description reflects the importance of discipline-specific modes of thinking, even
in a women's studies course; the professor did not want "political-type reasoning."

[18]In fact, according to Helen's account, the very limited level of field-specific knowledge
that she did develop—after the professor told the writing fellows exactly what the students
were supposed to write in the assignment—made her task more difficult, not less: "The fact
that I 'knew the answer' made it even more complicated. . . . At first I thought it would make it
easier, but once I knew the end point, it was hard to figure out how to help them get there."

[19]Helen's "overall helpfulness" rating from the 17 students who completed evaluation
forms was 3.5 (one decimal point better than Anita's 3.4).

[20]In Helen's evaluations, students wrote that they especially valued "Time to think through
how to make a better paper and bounce ideas off of a peer"; "The ability to talk out awkward
parts"; "The chance to talk about their comments and to ask someone questions—it really was
instrumental in allowing me to talk ideas out"; and "Having another opinion, and talking
about the ideas—trying to explain the point often helps you understand it more."

would have been more helpful; in Anita's case, three students reported the same. These numbers, however, were not substantially different from evaluations of writing fellows from other (nonscience) courses. Especially given the high level of anxiety about the scientific subject matter reported by the biology and gender students, these results are a strong endorsement of the fellows' success as "nonexpert" collaborators.

To say that Anita's perspective on tutoring was shaped, at least in part, by her major in women's studies—or that Helen's success in negotiating an unfamiliar discipline was aided by the collaborative atmosphere fostered by Women's Studies—does not diminish their achievements as tutors. However, it does demonstrate the power of the various "ways of knowing" that we teach our students, implicitly and explicitly. It also suggests that Women's Studies brought something extremely valuable to their experiences as peer tutors. Thus we must ask: Should curriculum-based peer tutoring programs be providing that "something" for the *other* peer tutors—the majority of peer tutors, I daresay—who do *not* tutor within interdisciplinary programs that operate in resistant modes? Is this even possible? If so, how?

Developing explicit links with not only women's studies but also ethnic studies, labor studies, and gay and lesbian studies would be a first step for programs like the writing fellows. Those links might include making special efforts to assign fellows to courses in interdisciplinary programs with activist agendas; inviting faculty who teach in these programs—and students who major or minor in them—to make presentations during the first-semester training seminars or ongoing training sessions; and establishing regular communication channels with administrators in these programs (through informal office visits, phone calls, and e-mail exchanges, or more formal committee or task force meetings). However, this is only a step. We also need to find ways to foster and reward student reflections on why professors write they way they do—for all fields, not just for those that foreground their politics.

Malinowitz's (1998) skeptical analysis of the transformative potential of WAC programs reminds us that the academy as it now exists does not foster or reward such reflections. Although Malinowitz agrees in principle that WAC can encourage students to evaluate and critique forms of knowledge, she points out that most of the time, WAC does not do so: "In the absence of such a critical framework, students are easily beguiled by the mystique of dominant knowledge systems" (293). And, Malinowitz adds right away, challenging dominant knowledge systems is often worthwhile only for students whom the current system excludes in dramatic ways. Her critique bears directly on the writing fellows program: How radical, after all, can a peer tutoring program be?

Because Malinowitz sees no way to reconcile the essentially conservative goals of a writing-in-the-disciplines approach with transformative goals of a writing-to-learn approach, she argues that WAC programs must articulate their desire for change openly or stop pretending to try. Yet I would suggest that the writing fellows occupy a middle ground that Malowitz's critique does not take into account. Curriculum-based peer tutors exist in a paradoxical place where their success in helping their peers succeed in discipline-specific writing is itself a form of subversion, in a place where their estimation of their own value as tutors and collaborators depends on a subversion of traditional sources of authority. My final case relates the experiences of a very successful writing fellow to chart the dimensions of that paradoxical middle ground.

BEING A "REAL" WRITING FELLOW:
IS IT A "PSYCHIC THING"?

Most writing fellows—who do *not* tutor in interdisciplinary courses or in programs with activist agendas—are likely to encounter stronger resistance to the non-expert model that Anita and Helen employed in tutoring the biology and gender students. Institutional structures may discourage students from valuing collaborative work even when they excel at it, because possessing individual expertise is viewed as more impressive, as more of an intellectual accomplishment. This dynamic can shape not only student tutors' interactions with their peers, but also tutors' understanding of their own skills and successes. While Anita's feminist articulation of her work as a tutor, quoted earlier, confidently asserts her own value as a nonexpert collaborator, her perspective is not necessarily representative of the student tutors. The self-perception of another successful writing fellow—from a very different disciplinary background—offers a different view.

As Helen's "tricky" situation reminded us, for writing fellows assigned to courses in unfamiliar disciplines, centered on unfamiliar subject matter, listening to and learning from their peers becomes less of a goal than a necessity. Because the program is dominated by students from the humanities and social sciences (despite continuing efforts to attract students from the sciences), the limited number of writing fellows who are science majors play a special role. In addition to being a minority among their peers in the training seminar, the science majors are more likely to be assigned to courses in unfamiliar subjects. For them, participating in the program entails even more discipline-crossing than usual. Rajit, a senior majoring in molecular biology and zoology, acknowledged that he felt his difference keenly. "For me, I felt like an oddball in this group [of writing fellows]," he said in an interview. "But I'm glad I'm an oddball because they look up to me. I think a lot of people are surprised at how successful I can be as a writing fellow."[21] While Rajit's positive spin on his own alienation may be more indicative of his ebullient personality than anything else, his

---

[21]Although Rajit's reference to feeling like an "oddball" was based on his status as a science major, his status as one of very few students of color in the writing fellows Program gives his comment special resonance. An ongoing commitment to recruiting applicants not only from diverse majors but also from diverse ethnic backgrounds is absolutely necessary for peer tutoring programs to promote the kind of critical engagement across disciplines that I am advocating.

reflections on tutoring across disciplines are instructive. His comments reinforce the familiar point that disjunctions between a peer tutor's background and the course content can enable effective tutoring, while also emphasizing the inaccuracies of gendered stereotypes such as the Eliza—Charlie dichotomy (as becomes apparent later, Rajit, a male student of the sciences, is obviously comfortable talking in a "roundabout" way).

More interestingly, Rajit's perspective bears traces of a gendered subtext that devalues talk and lionizes text. In other words, the critical skills of questioning and listening to writers are *under*valued, while the (also critical) skills of analyzing a specific text and focusing on the written words on a particular draft are *over*valued. In the tutor-as-text-analyst model, peer tutors draw authority from specialized knowledge and expertise, while in the questioner/listener model, tutors abandon that expertise in favor of a student-centered approach. For Rajit, despite his impressive success in working collaboratively, "real" work as a writing fellow began when he occupied something closer to the position of expert. In the absence of a context such as Women's Studies, which values collaboration highly, the exercise of expert authority can trump questioning-and-listening skills far too readily.

Rajit spoke from experience tutoring student writers both inside and outside his discipline. In his first semester as a fellow, he worked with juniors and seniors in a geography course, while in his second semester, he worked with seniors and graduate students in a conservation biology course. When I asked Rajit to compare these experiences, he suggested that being familiar with the discipline actually *kept* him from being connected to the students:

> I think I'm a little more distant from my students [in conservation biology] because I feel like I can rely on them covering the material and presenting it adequately. That prevents me from getting to know them really well. Last semester [in geography], the material wasn't mine. I had to approach them [the geography students] really carefully. It was more of a psychic thing, to see how what their thought processes were, pay attention to how they think. I became closer to those students. . . Instead of directing questions about the paper, I directed questions about their knowledge. I just set the paper aside and said, "Let's just talk with this." This semester [in conservation biology] I would jump right into the paper and spend all our time on it.

In this description of his tutoring strategy, Rajit positioned the geography students as the experts, turning to them as authorities, and relying on them to explain things to him. His simple statement, "I just set the paper aside and said, 'Let's just talk with this,'" carries the promise of a transformative moment, in which students are encouraged to see writing as just one aspect of an ongoing process of creative and critical thinking.

Yet despite Rajit's intense connection to the geography students (who, incidentally, gave him some of the best evaluations of any fellow that semester), he did not see that tutoring work as equal to the work he did with biology students. In the biology course, he said, "I feel like I've been a real writing fellow." When I pressed him to explain, noting that from his own description, it sounded as if he had conducted extremely productive conferences with the geography students, he elaborated: "I'm tackling more writing issues this semester... I'm applying more of what I learned in the [writing fellows] seminar. Last semester, my teaching or tutoring was based on the knowledge I had acquired prior to becoming a writing fellow." Certainly, Rajit's already-existing skills (such as listening) had helped him succeed as a fellow in the geography course. Yet he made a similar assertion about his tutoring in biology, when he explained, "I have the background knowledge, so I have an idea of what they're trying to present." Somehow, using *that* discipline-specific "background" did not diminish his status as a "real" writing fellow, but using the other "background" (his ability to foster collaboration) did. While a predictable learning curve could account for some of Rajit's experience (he gained confidence in his second semester as a fellow, so he felt more like a "real" tutor when he was helping the biology students), the ease with which he discounted his collaborative skills is distressing.

Rajit's account suggests that even a male student who excels as a questioning-and-listening tutor may dismiss his achievement, in part because of societal norms that inaccurately categorize collaborative skills as traditional—and nonintellectual—women's work. When Rajit describes listening and paying attention to how students think as "more of a psychic thing," he obscures the authentic intellectual challenges involved in understanding other writers' thought processes. In his description, the symbolic capital of disciplinary-specific knowledge holds, while the notion of expertise in collaborating across disciplines collapses into an easily dismissed "psychic thing." Although Rajit's work with the geography students can be interpreted as a sign of his successful development as a writing fellow (by implementing the collaborative model introduced in the training seminar), he did not see it that way: he felt less confident, in fact, that he was actually doing any work at all. Adapting the fellows seminar to include some of the tutor-training strategies that Nancy Welch suggested (chap. 12., this volume)—to encourage tutors to re-narrate their own tutoring accounts and thus make visible the "excess of stories" and the untidy details suppressed by most official stories of writing center work—may have helped Rajit to identify and rethink his assumptions.

"GETTING A HAND IN": MULTIPLE POSSIBILITIES

In keeping with Kirsch's call for "better research," I have sought to present some of the multiple realities of the writing fellows program, arguing for the co-existence of entrenched gender stereotypes with new opportunities for critical thinking about discipline-specific knowledge. These realities suggest the need for more research on how peer tutors perceive gender and disciplinary differences and how they react to such differences, as well as on the ways the generalist (nonexpert) tutor model is feminized and hence undervalued, even by the students who succeed within that model. In the meantime, we must foster more explicit discussions about how gender influences tutoring strategies, asking our students to consider not only how gender differences shape interpersonal interactions, but also how their own gendered assumptions may be influencing their understanding of disciplinary differences. In retrospect, I can see that in order to meet my expectation that the writing fellows act as agents of change, the program would have to articulate that expectation more explicitly and involve students much more directly in discussions about what kind of change they want to bring about and why.

Like all boundary-crossing enterprises, curriculum-based peer tutoring programs will always be fraught with contradictions. This tension-filled position is not their failing, but their strength. This is especially true when such programs can foster a community of peer tutors who can act and react *together*, pondering those contradictions and deciding how (or whether) to resolve those tensions. Michael, a junior majoring in English language and linguistics, summed up his first year as a writing fellow by invoking the power of community within the larger world of a research university:

> I feel really proud of our class of writing fellows because I think we've all really done a service to undergrads in letting them know they can get involved. Other students realize there are ways to get a hand into the academic parts of the university. . . . Because the faculty respects the program, we have an opportunity to be critical in the process. . . . The way that we act as a community and look at things as a community, it puts us on the same level [as faculty]. Our students' input to us filters up—so we can kind of act as a liaison, as opposed to them going to the prof and saying, "I don't like this part of the assignment," we can say, "Fourteen students didn't understand this part of the assignment. Could you clarify this or ask this question more directly?" Sometimes I feel like a union representative.

The subtext of Michael's optimism is an acknowledgment of just how difficult it can be for students to "get a hand into the academic parts of the university." His use of a term often applied to alienated manual laborers—hand—and his reference to feeling "like a union representative" reflects his awareness of the tremendous power gap between faculty and students. While Michael doesn't suggest that programs such as the writing fellows program eliminate that power differential, he does believe that they can mitigate it, by opening up space for dialogue and exchange. Keeping that space open, enlarging it—or, perhaps, simply finding ways to avoid closing it down—should be a priority for all educators.[22]

---

[22]Increasingly, compositionists are calling upon their colleagues to promote this kind of dialogue and exchange not only within academic institutions, but outside of them as well. See Mortensen (1998) and Petersen (1998).

ACKNOWLEDGMENTS

Special thanks are due to the writing fellows who shared their writing and time with me, and to Bradley T. Hughes, director of the Writing Center, the Writing Across the Curriculum Program, and the Writing Fellows Program at UW—Madison. This chapter would have been impossible without Brad's assistance and encouragement. I would also like to thank Emily Hall, associate director of the Writing Fellows Program, who provided key information about the program, and Alice Gillam, whose thoughtful, detailed feedback shaped this chapter in its final stages.

REFERENCES

Ashton-Jones, E. (1995). Collaboration, conversation, and the politics of gender. In L. W. Phelps & J. Emig (Eds.), *Feminine principles and women's experience in American composition and rhetoric* (pp. 5–26). Pittsburgh: University of Pittsburgh Press.

Bazerman, C. (1992). From cultural criticism to disciplinary participation: Living with powerful words. In A. Herrington & C. Moran (Eds.), *writing, teaching, and learning in the disciplines* (pp. 61–68). New York: Modern Language Association.

Bizzell, P. (1998). Beyond antifoundationalism to rhetorical authority: Problems defining "cultural literacy." In M. Bernard-Donals & R.R. Glejzer (Eds.), *Rhetoric in an antifoundational world: Language, culture, and pedagogy* (pp. 371–388). New Haven, CT: Yale University Press.

Black, L. J. (1998). *Between talk and teaching: Reconsidering the writing conference.* Logan: Utah State University Press.

Brady, L. (1998). The reproduction of othering. In S. C. Jarratt & L. Worsham (Eds.), *Feminism and composition studies: In other words* (pp. 21–44). New York: Modern Language Association.

Bruffee, K. A. (1984). Peer tutoring and the "conversation of manking." In G. A. Olson (Ed.), *Writing centers: Theory and administration* (pp. 3–15). Urbana, IL: National Council of Teachers of English.

Dixon, K. (1997). *Making relationships: Gender in the forming of an academic community.* New York: Peter Lang.

Enos, T. (1996). *Gender roles and faculty lives in rhetoric and composition.* Carbondale: Southern Illinois University Press.

Flynn, E. A. (1991). Composition studies from a feminist perspective. In R. Bullock & J. Trimbur (Eds.), *The politics of writing instruction: Postsecondary* (pp. 137–154). Portsmouth, NH: Boynton/Cook.

Flynn, E. A. (1995). Review: feminist theories/feminist composition. *College English, 57,* 201–212.

Fox, S. L. (1999). Inviting students to join the literacy conversation: Toward a collaborative pedagogy for academic literacy. In K. L. Weese, S. L. Fox, & S. Greene (Eds.), *Teaching academic literacy: The uses of teacher-research in developing a writing program* (pp. 21–44). Mahwah, NJ: Lawrence Erlbaum Associates.

Fulwiler, T. (1991). The quiet and insistent revolution: writing across the curriculum. In R. Bullock & J. Trimbur (Eds.), *The politics of writing instruction: Postsecondary* (pp. 179–188). Portsmouth, NH: Boynton/Cook.

Giroux, H. A., & Freire, P. (1988). Introduction. In K. Weiler (Ed.), *Women teaching for change: Gender, class & power* (pp. IX–XIV). New York: Bergin & Garvey.

Grimm, N. (1996). Rearticulating the work of the writing center. *College Composition and Communication, 47*(4), 523–548.

Gunner, J. (1993). The fate of the Wyoming resolution: A history of professional seduction. In S. I. Fontaine & S. Hunter (Eds.), *Writing ourselves into the story: Unheard voices from composition studies* (pp. 107–122). Carbondale: Southern Illinois University Press.

Haring-Smith, T. (1992). Changing students' attitudes: writing fellows programs. In S. H. McLeod & M. Soven (Eds.), *Writing across the curriculum: A guide to developing programs* (175–188). Newbury Park, CA: Sage.

Harris, M. (1995). Talking in the middle: Why writers need writing tutors. *College English 57*(1), 27–42.

Jarratt, S. (1991). Feminism and composition: The case for conflict. In P. Harkin & J. Schilb (Eds.), *Contending with words: Composition and rhetoric in a postmodern age* (pp. 105–123). New York: Modern Language Association.

Kirsch, G. E. (1999). *Ethical dilemmas in feminist research: The politics of location, interpretation, and publication.* Albany: SUNY Press.

Kirscht, J., Levine, R., & Reiff, J. (1994). Evolving paradigms: WAC and the rhetoric of inquiry. *College Composition and Communication, 45*(3), 369–380.

Lassner, P. (1987). The politics of peer tutoring. *Writing Lab Newsletter 12*(1), 4–6.

Malinowitz, H. (1998). A feminist critique of writing in the disciplines. In S. C. Jarratt & L. Worsham (Eds.), *Feminism and composition studies: In other words* (pp. 291–312). New York: Modern Language Association.

Mortensen, P. (1998). Going public. *College Composition and Communication, 50*(2), 182–205.

Petersen, C. (1998). Composition and campus diversity: Testing academic and social values. *College Composition and Communication, 50*(2), 277–291.

Ray, R. (1992). Composition from the teacher-research point of view. In G. Kirsch & P. A. Sullivan (Eds.), *Methods and methodology in composition research* (pp. 172–189). Carbondale: Southern Illinois University Press.

Reynolds, N. (1998). Interrupting our way to agency: Feminist cultural studies and composition. In S. C. Jarratt & L. Worsham (Eds.), *Feminism and composition studies: In other words* (pp. 58–73). New York: Modern Language Association.

Ritchie, J., & Boardman, K. (1999). Feminism in composition: Inclusion, metonymy, and disruption. *College Composition and Communication 50*(4), 85–106.

Rubin, D. (1993). *Gender influences: Reading student texts.* Carbondale: Southern Illinois University Press.

Sommers, N. (1982). Responding to student writing. *College Composition and Communication 33*(2), 148–156.

Soven, M. (1993). Curriculum-based peer tutoring programs: A survey. *WPA: writing Program Administration 17*, 58–74.

Sullivan, P. A. (1992). Feminism and methodology in composition studies. In G. Kirsch & P. A. Sullivan (Eds.), *Methods and methodology in composition research* (pp. 37–61). Carbondale: Southern Illinois University Press.

Author Index

Subject Index